ORDER
in the
TWILIGHT

ORDER
in the
TWILIGHT

BERNHARD WALDENFELS

Translated and with an Introduction
by David J. Parent

OHIO UNIVERSITY PRESS

ATHENS

Ohio University Press, Athens, Ohio 45701

Original edition *Ordnung in Zwilicht* © 1987 by Suhrkamp Verlag,
Frankfurt am Main.

Die Herausgabe dieses Werkes wurde aus Mitteln von Inter
Nationes, Bonn, gefördert.

01 00 99 98 97 96   5 4 3 2 1

Library of Congress Cataloging-in-Publication Data

Waldenfels, Bernhard, 1934-
    [Ordnung im Zwielicht. English]
    Order in the twilight / by Bernhard Waldenfels ; translated and
with an introduction by David J. Parent.
        p.   cm. — (Series in Continental thought ; 24)
    Includes bibliographical references and index.
    ISBN 0-8214-1168-3 (alk. paper)
    1. Order (Philosophy) I. Title. II. Series.
B105.07W2813   1996
117—dc20   96-30785
                                                           CIP

CONTENTS

Contents

ACKNOWLEDGMENTS

IN THIS AMERICAN VERSION, it seemed advisable to quote from existing translations whenever possible, and acknowledgment is made in the text together with the page number (the bibliography includes for the reader's information translations both cited and not cited). All works listed deserve recognition. However, for a few works quoted somewhat more at length or more frequently, special acknowledgment is made: to Harcourt Brace Jovanovich for quotations from Italo Calvino, *Invisible Cities;* to MIT Press, from André Leroi-Gourhan, *Gesture and Speech;* to Routledge & Kegan Paul, from Maurice Merleau-Ponty, *Phenomenology of Perception;* and to Northwestern University Press, from Maurice Merleau-Ponty, *The Visible and the Invisible.*

Thanks are also due to Bernhard Waldenfels and to Elizabeth A. Behnke for many useful suggestions. Ms. Behnke also provided the list of Waldenfels articles available in English.

FOREWORD

OUR CONTEMPORARY ERA IS SOMETIMES PORTRAYED in terms of a grand dénouement. The demise of the Cold War, in this account, has put an end to old ideological quarrels, thus ushering in a period of durable peace and stability. Governed by rational market principles and a universal rule of law, humankind is said to have finally transcended its infantile disorders and hence exited from the tumultuous course of history. Although appealing in its soothing contours, this account is clearly belied by the events of our time. Local and regional wars—pursued often with immense savagery—challenge or contest the proclaimed "new world order," while the upsurge of nationalist and fundamentalist movements makes illusory the idea of an "end of history." Looked at more closely, our era seems marked not so much by dénouement as by an intricate embroilment and contamination: the embroilment of order and disorder, of reason and nonreason, of civilization and barbarism. Politically, this tension undergirds the contest between rich nations and poor nations, between the accumulation of wealth and the "culture of poverty," or between North and South. Intellectually or philosophically, the embroilment takes the form today of a contestation between metaphysics and postmetaphysics, between modernity and postmodernity, between universalism and particularism.

By and large, modern (Western) philosophy has been averse to investigating this embroilment, that is, the twilight zone of competing elements, preferring instead to occupy the "high ground" staked out by the categories of rational knowledge, science, and progress. As it happens, however, some of the most innovative thinkers during the past hundred years have moved precisely into this terrain neglected by mainstream philosophy. Most well known among them are the names of Nietzsche, Heidegger, Merleau-Ponty, and Derrida. Although illustrious, however, these names are merely stand-ins for a larger and more complex phalanx of contemporary explorers. Both in terms of his range of inquiries and subtlety of arguments, a prominent place in the latter group must be accorded to the German philosopher Bernhard Waldenfels. Although somewhat hampered by the shortage of English-language translations, Waldenfels' work—numbering about a dozen volumes—makes an important and highly distinctive contribution to the philosophical discourse in our time. This distinctiveness is clearly evident in his native German context, a context frequently marked in the postwar period by restorative tendencies (manifest in "back to Kant," "back to Fichte" or similar formulas). In contrast to such tendencies, Waldenfels has always situated himself at the outskirts or the margins of modern "foundational" categories, seeking his intellectual abode instead in the twilight zone *"entre chien et loup,"* between reason and nonreason. Quite distinctive in his native context also is Waldenfels' determination to resume a mode of discourse nearly extinct in Germany after the war: the mode of phenomenological inquiry as inaugurated by Husserl and later continued by Alfred Schutz and Merleau-Ponty. In pursuing this mode of inquiry Waldenfels resolutely cultivated "Francophile" philosophical sympathies (not widely shared in his milieu), sympathies which led him progressively into the ambiance of French postphenomenology and poststructuralism highlighted by the names of Derrida, Levinas, and Foucault.

Yet, even when moving into the ambit of recent French thought, Waldenfels never simply joined prevailing fashions but maintained his own distinctive accents. Some of these accents deserve to be mentioned at least briefly. In an effort to escape "logocentrism" and the imperialist sway of foundational categories, French poststructuralism tends to privilege "difference" or "otherness" over the "self-same"—sometimes to the point of stylizing the status of the "other" into that of a radical exteriority or inaccessibility. At the same time, the desire to undercut teleological or dialectical models leads to a prime focus on rupture and disruption— sometimes in a manner courting destructiveness and violence. These tendencies, albeit intermittently, surface in many recent French thinkers. Thus, in the case of Derrida, the opposition between the "calculable" rule of law and the "incalculable" realm of justice encourages a conception whereby justice impinges on legal institutions only in a disruptive, possibly violent form. In his turn, Levinas has postulated a radical dichotomy between "totality" and "infinity" or between immanence and transcendence—where totality means the calculable system of mundane elements and infinity the exodus from system. In a lesser way, echoes of this outlook can be found in Foucault's confrontation of "panopticon" or carceral society, on the one hand, and local insurgency, on the other. What is chiefly troubling at this point is the return of supposedly banished ghosts. Despite the promised exit from metaphysics, the notion of the external "other" conjures up some of the hackneyed metaphysical conundrums of the past—including the antinomies between mind and matter and between consciousness and (Kantian) "thing-in-itself."

One of the exciting and promising aspects of Waldenfels' work is his ability to obviate these tendencies. Faithful to the teachings of Merleau-Ponty (and also to Husserl's exhortation "To the things themselves!"), his writings resist the lure of antinomies or unbridgeable gulfs. This is precisely the sense of his move into the margin or border zone of traditional philosophy, a zone where the boundary between inside and outside or between immanence and transcendence is in flux and where the meaning of these terms has to be continually renegotiated. The same move also has a bearing on another controverted issue in recent French thought: the status of the "subject." After initially announcing in dramatic fashion the death of the subject and even the "death of man," recent poststructuralist literature bears witness to the unexpected revival or reanimation of the subject, now almost with a vengeance. Once the "overcoming" of traditional metaphysics is seen not just as a transgression but as a leap into a total "lack" or void of categories, basic philosophical issues become as such radically indeterminate or "undecidable" (to use Derridean terminology); to become operative in the mundane domain, however, undecidability requires the intervention of human "decision"—which can only be the work of a "subject." To an extent, the Derridean scheme merely underwrites the return of the subject which has been characteristic of Levinasian philosophy from the beginning—where the "face" of the other always appears as the face of a person or subject who, in turn, functions as the source of obligation for the self. One may also recall here Foucault's fascination, late in his life, with a quasi-Stoic mode of subjectivity.

On this point again, Waldenfels' work harbors a promising initiative. Never having precipitously announced the death of the subject, his writings are free of the need to scramble for its revival. Akin to the inside-outside bifurcation, the boundary between self and other for Waldenfels can never be fixated, with the result that the meaning of self and other has to be negotiated in an open-ended, interactive process—a process in which the "subject" is simultaneously the constituted and constituting (or the passive-active) agent of transformation. This aspect brings into view another crucial feature of Waldenfels' thought: his accent on "agonal dialogue" as the medium in the border zone of self and other, order and disorder. As one should note, dialogue in his work does not mean a striving for communicative consensus (in the Habermasian sense) nor for a "fusion of horizons" (in the sense of the early Gadamer). Instead, dialogue for Waldenfels means the relation between question and answer, challenge and response—but a relation whose components can never be matched or fused in unity. Questions—while exhibiting a dominant theme—can always be interpreted in multiple (though not random) ways; in their turn, answers are not unprovoked but seek to address a given question—which, however, can be done from different angles. To put matters differently: questions or challenges stimulate but do not predetermine a response; answers in turn respond to but cannot exhaust the rich complexity or multivocity of a question or challenge. In Heideggerian terms, human existence needs to grapple with, but can only tap into some of the recessed resources or possibilities of the challenge facing it—which is ultimately the challenge or question of being.

In developing the question-response theme, Waldenfels in a sense rejoins the Levinasian argument—while simultaneously diverging from Levinas' prioritizing of the other (and also the dubious project of an ethical "first philosophy"). The need to meet a given challenge or question clearly requires intellectual integrity as well as a sense of moral responsibility on the part of the respondent—but not to the point of pliant submission or surrender. The relation between question and answer is asymmetrical for Waldenfels (as it is for Levinas), but it is not entirely devoid of a certain reciprocity; although it may be styled as a "calling" or demand, the challenge in effect "calls" the respondent into freedom, granting ample room for responsive experimentation and innovation. In accentuating this aspect, Waldenfels in a way recuperates certain ethical impulses deriving from the Nietzschean and Heideggerian strand of postmodern thought, impulses which are likely to be bypassed or at least sidelined in a one-sided "ethics of alterity." As in the case of Heidegger, ethical obligation for Waldenfels can be reduced neither to absolute principles (for example, categorical imperative) nor to the authoritative demand of an other (seen as a reverse foundation). Instead, ethics simply is part and parcel of our being-in-the-world—of our dwelling in the border zone between "being and beings" or (in Merleau-Ponty's terms) in the "chiasm" of the world characterized by open-ended, agonal dialogue and concrete "intercorporeality." Obligation in this dwelling space does indeed "happen"—but in a manner which can never be fully mapped out or codified, thus allowing room for ever new horizons of ethical sensitivity.

These comments lead me back to the more openly political issues raised at the beginning of this prefatory note. The book *Order in the Twilight* explores the difficult in-between zone between order and disorder, more specifically the zone marked by the intersection of the ordinary, the disordered, and the extra-ordinary. As one should note well, critique of "order" here does not mean a simple endorsement of chaos or anarchy. In calling into question the widely heralded idea of a "new world order," postmodern thinkers like Waldenfels do not lend support to virulent types of national or ethic chauvinism nor to simple denials of order as such (exemplified in Oklahoma City). Rule systems, as manifestations of "order," can of course be internally broken or violated— but only by testifying implicitly to the established status of rules. *Order in the Twilight* does not simply pit order versus disorder, or rule violation against rule system; instead, it pursues the more complicated path pointing beyond order and disorder in the direction of the open arena of the not-yet-fully-ordered or extra-ordinary. In the present global context, the book issues a challenge to existing hegemonic structures—not necessarily in favor of alternative power systems but in favor of a greater flexibility of structures and a more generous openness to the voices of the marginalized or dispossessed. Whatever "order" might be possible from this vantage would emerge from a general contestation, especially from the agonal dialogue between rich and poor, center and periphery, North and South. Given these implications, *Order in the Twilight* testifies amply to both the philosophical and the practical-political significance of Waldenfels' work. One can only wish the present translation the widest possible audience in the English-speaking world.

Fred Dallmayr
University of Notre Dame

INTRODUCTION TO THE AMERICAN EDITION

BERNHARD WALDENFELS' PHILOSOPHICAL THINKING moves within the phenomenological tradition of exploring the "lifeworld," begun by Edmund Husserl and expanded by Merleau-Ponty to analysis of the social "interworld" and "intercorporeality" of multiple subjects and by Michel Foucault into an exposition of dominant rationalities. Waldenfels has continued this tradition with special emphasis on the role of open discourse in the constitution of order, on "ownness" and "alienness" in reference to partial orders, and on the margins, thresholds, and boundaries of order.

In an autobiographical sketch, "In eigener Sache" [On my own Behalf], Waldenfels has described his philosophical work as belonging to an "open and adaptable form of phenomenology that could be characterized as a further development of an existential-structural phenomenology in Merleau-Ponty's sense into a responsive phenomenology, in which intentionality (intending, grasping something as something) is transformed into responsivity (responses to claims). *What* we respond to is always more than the *answer* we give under certain circumstances and within the framework of certain orders. Rationality can thus be understood as responsive rationality stemming from the creative answers themselves, which are therefore not already pregiven in things, nor can they be distributed symmetrically among various dialogue partners."

Waldenfels' contributions to philosophy have been mainly of two kinds: compendious critical surveys of French phenomenologists, and systematic elaborations of phenomenological themes. In the first genre, *Phänomenologie in Frankreich* [Phenomenology in France, 1983] traced the development of this philosophy in France by numerous German and Eastern European emigrants. Waldenfels illustrated the great variety of insights to which phenomenology is open and its readiness to amalgamate with other philosophical currents in phenomenological writings by French authors that took highly different turns, so that Jean-Paul Sartre produced a Marxist anthropology, Maurice Merleau-Ponty a structural ontology, Emmanuel Levinas a dialogical ethics, and Paul

Ricoeur a hermeneutics of symbols and texts. In *Phänomenlogie in Frankreich* Waldenfels displayed vast knowledge of the early and mainline phenomenologists, including Aron Gurwitsch and Merleau-Ponty, as well as more recent writers of the transformational phase in which structuralism, psychoanalysis, Marxism, or deconstructionism effected modifications in phenomenology—for example, Lévi-Strauss, Lacan, Althusser, Foucault, and Derrida. At this point criticism of phenomenology broadened into a sharp critique of the purported ethnocentricity, anthropocentricity, and logocentricity of Western thought. In dealing with many of these authors, Waldenfels drew valuable insights and a broad foundation for his own philosophy. Most recently, in another work in a similar genre, *Deutsch-Französische Gedankengänge* [German-French Intellectual Pathways, 1995], Waldenfels comes to terms critically with selected ideas of a wide variety of modern French thinkers and trends, not merely writing *about* them and their relationship to German philosophical activity, but engaging them in a productive dialogue and carrying their thought forward with his own ideas. A listing of some of the topics suggests the architectonic proportions of this book: Husserl's theory of the other; Fink's self-referentiality of phenomenology; Derrida on hearing oneself speak; Merleau-Ponty on expression, truth, the fragmentation of being as exemplified in modern art, and interrogative thinking; Castoriadis on the primacy of imagination; Foucault on scattered reason and order in discourses; Francis Jacques on intersubjectivity and interlocution; Lyotard on ethics in the conflict of discourses; Ricoeur on the self in the shadow of the alien and the heterogeneous; Levinas on the response of responsibility, etc.; and finally, one German thinker, Nietzsche, on the blind spot of morality.

A brief survey of Professor Waldenfels' background and thematic writings casts further light on the place of *Order in the Twilight* within his own opus. After studying philosophy, psychology, classical philology, and history at the universities of Bonn, Innsbruck, and Munich, he published his dissertation on the Platonic art of dialogue under the title *Das sokratische Fragen* [Socratic Questioning]. During further studies in Paris, under Paul Ricoeur and Merleau-Ponty, he became especially interested in phenomenology, and his next book was *Das Zwischenreich des Dialogs. Sozialphilosophische Untersuchungen in Anschluss an Edmund Husserl* [The Intermediary Realm of Dialogue: Social-Philosophical Investigations Based on Edmund Husserl, 1971], in which he moved toward an intercorporeally grounded dialogue theory in which ownness and alienness appear as co-original. Fred Dallmayr has characterized *Das Zwischenreich des Dialogs* as "a broad-gauged and rigorous scrutiny of intersubjectivity or intersubjective relations from a phenomenological vantage, matching in both depth and coverage comparable studies by Theunissen and Schutz."[1] In the 1970s Bernhard Waldenfels translated two books by Merleau-Ponty into German—*The Structure of Behavior* (1976) and *The Visible and the Invisible* (1986, together with Regula Giuliani)—and edited, with Alexandre Métraux, an anthology, *Leibhaftige Vernunft. Spuren von Merleau-Pontys Denken* [Embodied Reason: Traces of Merleau-Ponty's Thought]. He also wrote *Der Spielraum des Verhaltens* [The Scope of Behavior, 1980], proposing a non-behavioristic theory of behavior in a non-foundational, pluralistic lifeworld. This was followed by *In den Netzen der Lebenswelt* [In the Meshes of the Lifeworld, 1985] and the original of the present book, *Ordnung im Zwielicht* (1987). More recent books, *Der Stachel des Fremden* [The Goad of the Alien, 1990] and *Antwortregister* [Registers of Response, 1994], further develop themes related to the dialogical creation of order. Waldenfels has also written *Einführung in die Phänomenologie* [Introduction to Phenomenology, 1992], and he has edited a collection of excerpts from Husserl: *Arbeit an den Phänomenen. Ausgewählte Schriften* [Edmund Husserl, Work at the Phenomena. Selected Writings, 1993]. A list of articles by Bernhard Waldenfels currently available in English appears at the end of the bibliography (see p. 167).

This overview of Bernhard Waldenfels' philosophical productivity reveals a remarkably consistent concern with phenomenological themes in the mode of an "open type of phenomenology." This "dialogical openness" is for him both a theme and a methodology, manifested by a readiness to meet other thinkers on their own ground and to allow for the "otherness" of their viewpoints, without falling into an uncritical eclecticism.

For instance, over the years Professor Waldenfels has considered analytical philosophy to be an important "conversation partner," mainly as a means of "sharpening the methodological instrumentation of phenomenology"; but as a follower of Merleau-Ponty, he did not have a very high regard for the "linguistic turn"—on the one hand because "half of it seemed self-evident (that there are no pure intuitions, that all experience displays determinate meaning-structures)," on the other hand because "the other half seemed questionable (that all meaning must pass through the filter of linguistic expressions or that 'everything is language,' as Gadamer formulated it)." In contrast with the communication theory of the more recent Frankfurt School, he insisted that "the pre-predicative structures of experience must not be degraded to a preliminary stage of argumentative consensus formation" and he stressed the "multi-referentiality" and "multiple meanings" of phenomena.

His book *In den Netzen der Lebenswelt* had stressed that "the origin breaks apart": the *logos* of the old cosmologies and historical teleologies divides into a multiplicity of rationalities and irrationalities. *Order in the Twilight*, too, rejects a total order or a fundamental order in favor of a multiplicity of orders, and focuses on the boundaries and overlappings of various orders; its quest for a viable grounding at the origins of order culminates in the "open forms" modeled on the non-deterministic dialogical model of question and answer and also on literary/artistic paradigms where the normative factor ensues together with the work of art itself. These orders are contingent and "arise through processes of the selection and exclusion of possibilities" since "experience is possible only by a reduction of the *excess of possibilities.*" Yet like the phenomenological movement in general—whose analytical scrutiny tends to detect all sorts of forms, fields, figures, gestalts, relations, and distinctions—*Order in the Twilight,* despite its focus on the margins where order and disorder, rationality and irrationality, as well as the "own" and the "alien," meet without an overarching appropriation or global integration, retains an affirmative aspect: implicit in the respective recognition of ownness and alienness is a respect for objectivity, or, as Waldenfels himself would say, "something that precedes and provokes our initiatives."

The broad movement of which Waldenfels is a part, phenomenology, in its various forms, is characterized by rigorous methodology and detailed analysis of "the things themselves," as opposed to positivist reductivism. Its major advantage over some other philosophies, such as mechanism, materialism, or vitalism, is that it does not prescribe in advance what reality *can* be, but rather it is open to whatever phenomena and data may be yielded by experience. This openness has made it possible for phenomenology to blend with numerous other modern philosophical movements and to change not only the human and social sciences,[2] but even the natural sciences.

In sum, Waldenfels' thinking, with its multiple and "open" orders, is very congruent with the philosophical thinking of other prominent modern thinkers, including postmodernists and deconstructionists. Yet I believe his thinking can also contribute to attempts to move to new vantage points, such as the multiperspectivism and cultural pluralism of the "postmodern paradigm" advocated by Peter Levine,[3] the Wittgensteinian "descriptive investigations" recommended by Susan B. Brill,[4] and the receptivity of Cézanne's eyes before the mountain, so well characterized by Jean-François Lyotard.[5] Such books mark a turn toward greater flexibility of critical and philosophical approaches and more confident certainty concerning the way things are, and they seem to be heralding a new *post*-postmodern era. The advent of this new era of renewed, though critical, confidence in reason itself, and more open receptivity to all kinds of reality, including order and its norms—as well as twilight, margin, and threshold domains—has for decades been prepared by the vast current of phenomenology and related modern thought, including the works of Bernhard Waldenfels.

David J. Parent
Illinois State University, 1996

1. Fred Dallmayr, "On Bernhard Waldenfels," *Social Research* 56:3 (Autumn 1989), 684.

2. Cf. H. M. Collins, *Changing Order: Replication and Induction in Scientific Practice* (Chicago: University of Chicago Press, 1985): "The impact that phenomenology has had on sociology is to turn attention toward the possibility and actuality of different ways of seeing the world. It is the realization of these differences, and their implications for method, that has given rise to the main problems of a scientific (conceived of as positivistic) approach to social 'science'" (p. 25 n. 12).

3. Peter Levine, *Nietzsche and the Modern Crisis of the Humanities* (Albany, NY: State University of New York Press, 1995). In a well-argued polemic, Levine attempts a postmodernist move beyond deconstructivist skepticism and notions of language and conceptuality as a sort of prisonhouse.

4. Susan B. Brill, *Wittgenstein and Critical Theory: Beyond Postmodern Criticism and Toward Descriptive Investigations* (Athens, OH: Ohio University Press, 1995). Brill endorses Wittgenstein's approach for its openness to reality. Instead of imposing one same interpretive theory indiscriminately, an applicable model is tested for its usefulness and presented "'as what it is, as an object of comparison—as, so to speak, a measuring-rod; not as a preconceived idea to which reality *must* correspond'" (p. 19, citing Wittgenstein, *Philosophical Investigations,* p. 131).

5. Jean-François Lyotard, *Peregrinations: Law, Form, Event* (New York: Columbia University Press, 1988) pp. 18 ff.

PREFACE
Between Dog and Wolf

From the Philosophical Bestiary:

This too . . . can be seen from the dogs, and it is certainly very marvelous about this animal. . . . As soon as it sees a stranger, it is angry at him although he has done it no wrong; but when it sees someone it knows, it is friendly to him although he has never done anything good for it. . . . But this is certainly a magnificent quality of its nature and truly philosophical. How should what determines the tame and the wild through understanding or not understanding not be eager to learn?

Plato, *The Republic*, 376a–376b

Lupus est homo homini, non homo, quom qualis sit non novit.

Plautus, *Asinaria*

. . . that nature has made men so unsociable and even destined one to be the murderer of the other. . . . But why more proofs for intelligent men in a matter for which even dogs seem to have a feeling; they bark at whoever comes; by day at every stranger, by night however at everyone.

Hobbes, *Leviathan*, I, 13

. . . that it is necessary to give laws to men and that they must live according to laws because they otherwise would be no different than the very wildest animals.

Plato, *The Laws*, 874e

Take but degree away, untune that string,
And, hark! What discord follows . . .
Then every thing includes itself in power,
Power into will, will into appetite;
And appetite, a universal wolf,

So doubly seconded with will and power,
Must make perforce a universal prey,
And last eat up himself.

Shakespeare, *Troilus and Cressida*, I, 3

One may kill a man who declares war on one or turns out to be an enemy of one's own existence for the same reason that one kills a wolf or a lion. For such a man is not bound by the common law of reason and knows no other rules than that of brute strength and power. One can therefore deal with him as with beasts of prey—those dangerous and harmful creatures by which one will surely be destroyed as soon as one falls into their power.

Locke, *Second Treatise on Government*, III, 16

Man is an animal that, when it lives among others of its genus, needs a master. . . . But [the master] too is just as much an animal that needs a master.

Kant, *Ideas for a History with Cosmopolitan Intent*, 6th Thesis

DOG AND WOLF, DOMESTICATION AND WILDNESS are separated by a clear boundary when human beings manage to cross the threshold to culture, order, and reason once and for all. But whenever a cultural order fails to leave its origins behind, a gray twilight area extends between these two zones and order falls *entre chien et loup* [literally, "between dog and wolf"; idiomatically "in the twilight"]. Thought and being then retain characteristics of a wild way of thinking (*pensée sauvage*) and a wild being (*être sauvage*), and the recalcitrant strain foils complete domestication.

Whoever distrusts the barking of watchdogs, however, does not immediately have to begin howling with the wolves. Although in the current debates about rationality reason has fallen into the twilight, this twilight of reason could also suggest the possibility that despite new perils reason is discovering a light more suitable to its nature. This requires a rethinking that extricates itself from the tug of war of antitheses such as unity and multiplicity, continuity and discontinuity, subject and structures, lifeworld and system, or genesis and validity. Reflection on the origins, boundaries, diversity, change, and transgression of lived and thought orders should be a help to such rethinking. With the defenders of a shattered "modernism" I share the view that the great unassailable and all-encompassing orders stem from an overexuberant and forced space of rationality, which the modern "subject" pursues in vain. However, it seems to me just as doubtful that the disappearance of these orders can be remedied by minimal rationalizations plus a hermeneutic supplementary program. Grounding and explication are insufficient to fill the ensuing vacuum.

The idea of a twilight order that empowers by disempowering, includes by excluding, forms by deforming, runs like a red thread through the following investigations. This idea is tested mainly on cultural and social orders as they have developed in the Western tradition. Yet there are many indications that analogous rethinking is in progress elsewhere too, for instance, in the domain of physical, vital, and formal orders, and that even other cultures have not been spared similar problems. Such thinking in transitions will deter a person from the steep structures of the systems as well as from the detours of dialectics. Looser forms of connection, which do not approximate every "and" to a "there fore," as well as the occasional deviation to side paths without a stated destination, could ensure that the other and the semi-suitable seep in, that possibilities of cohesion are multiplied, and that the process of discovery/concealment, together with its fault lines, does not vanish too quickly behind definitions and argumentations.

Nonetheless, whoever scans about randomly in this book should not overlook the forest for the trees. The individual stages of the investigation are multiply interrelated and closely intermeshed. The whole thing begins with a heuristic prelude (Chapter 1). If the view across the *threshold of order,* searching for the unordered, is not immediately to be entangled in self-reflections, it needs cautious approaches, some samples of which are provided by the language of myths, exploratory expeditions into prehistory and paleontology, literary fictions, threshold experiences, the metaphorics of cosmogonies, and finally the quest for open places in the fabric of discourse and action. After that (in Chapter 2), a more systematic overview of order as a process of *selection* and *exclusion* is presented, diverging into different variants and stages, starting with fields of discourse and action and ending with their norms. The following two chapters (3 and 4) are organized in a more strongly aporetic fashion. First, the question of the *grounding* of order is discussed under the rubrics of totality, universality, and positivity; this then phases over into the question of a *subject's* possible achievements of order. Next (in Chapter 5) the failure of all attempts to place the positivity of variable orders on an adequate foundation draws the attention back to the genealogy of orders and the possibility of a *production* that does not merely apply standards and rules, but has a share in producing them by *deformation* and *deviation* from existing orders. The final topics of discussion (in Chapter 6) concern how the interplay of finding and inventing puts a limit to arbitrariness, although the question of what keeps order going remains unanswered as long as the *extraordinary,* whose claims strive to go beyond the existing orders, does not finally emerge from the ordinary, so that the unordered does not lie simply behind us, but rather ahead of us. Without constant transgressions, order would remain an empty shell and we could not even speak and deliberate about it. But doesn't the liberating effect depend on the transgression remaining such and not gaining a firm footing in the positive?

The interplay between light and shadow that these explorations attempt to capture can be presented only as a constant deformation of existing conceptions of order. The grounding of my own text on classical texts of Plato and Aristotle, Hobbes and Hume, Kant and Nietzsche is to be understood as an attempt to rethink by rereading. Significant and symptomatic passages of text are presented as reading signs and subjected to a process of hyper-precisioning that highlights their decisive features. My reading itself admittedly proceeds selectively and to a large extent typologically. If something is caught in the meshes of this heuristic procedure, that is good; if something escapes, where and how it escapes may be revealing. Nuances, corrections, and alternative readings are welcome as long as we do not lose sight of the matter under discussion and bury the key thoughts under the quicksand of scholarship.

Sharper focus on the object at issue is also enhanced by a general disregard of an overt and extensive critique of contemporary authors. I found it all the easier to omit this, since I have already done a great deal of that work in preparatory studies on particular areas, as can be read between the lines of this present book. Nonetheless, in order to give a view of the back of the carpet, it seemed advisable to associate secondary texts with the overall main text. An appendix called "Connecting Passages and Supporting Points" is labeled with chapter headings to show where the threads of thought are knotted together and can be spun further.

The book was conceived in Paris in the fall of 1984 and written in the spring of 1986 in Munich. That it was ready for press so quickly I owe to my colleagues who helped get it ready with typing, bibliography, indexing, and proofreading. My thanks goes to them and to Käte Meyer-Drawe as its first critical reader.

Bochum, September 1986

1

On the Threshold
between Order and Disorder

1. Preliminary Remarks

FIRST, AN ATTEMPT WILL BE MADE to give a definition of order neutral
enough not to slant our reflections one-sidedly from the outset and
broad enough not to narrow down our field of view prematurely. Order
(Lat.: *ordo;* Gr.: *cosmos, taxis*) in the general sense is *a regulated* (i.e.,
not arbitrary) *connection of one thing and another.* A distinction must
be made here between a repeatable, transferable, more or less detachable *orderly structure* of a qualitative or quantitative kind (scheme, pattern, form, eidos, formula, etc.) and the current or permanent *state of
order.* The production or emergence of such a connection, which can be
called an ordering or a self-ordering (*ordinatio*) that proceeds from an
orderer (Lat.: *ordinator,* Gr.: *cosmētōr*), differs from order in a station-
ary sense. As long as misunderstandings are avoided, "order" can also
be understood as a verb. The question of how and to what extent these
aspects are distinguishable from one another cannot be decided in advance. The question, for instance, of an order in, before, or of things
would already take us into the heart of the problem. Aside from that,
we are moving completely on the plane of classical ideas of order, which
are not restricted from the start to special or minimal claims.

Take, for example, a classical definition of the term such as Cicero's:
"*ordo*" means "the juxtaposition of things in the places suitable and
appropriate to them" (*compositio rerum aptis et accomodatis locis*)
(*On Offices,* I, 40). Similarly, we read in St. Augustine: "Order is the
distribution of like and unlike things assigning to each its own place"
(*ordo est parium disparìumque sua cuique tribuens loca dispositio*)
(*The City of God,* xix, 13). We can speak of suitable and unsuitable
only when not all arrangements are equally valid and when, rather, it
makes a difference whether something is here or there, whether it is this

way or that, whether it is done in this way or that. To establish such differences, some criterion or other is necessary—a rule (or a law, a norm) in the broadest sense, allowing for a deviation, a defect, a violation, that is, an irregularity in just such a broad sense. It can involve a preferential rule that privileges one state or process over another, a commandment or a prohibition that qualifies one behavior over another as right, and finally—this will concern us less here—an explanatory rule that posits certain events as more probable than others, or a kind of rule of the game that singles out a certain procedure over another as correct. Moreover, it does not matter, to begin with, whether a regularity is found, installed, or put into practice, or even expressly formulated and explained. On the contrary, what is presupposed in every regularity and possible irregularity is that there are *several relational components of different sorts,* even if it be merely that something is not in its place. Without a coordination of something with something else, a state or process could not be qualified as orderly compared with its opposite; it would be or not be, like Hume's simple perceptions, which are intrinsically not capable of order (*ordinabilis*). The same would apply to relational components that are completely alike; completely identical twins could not be each in its proper place, and the numbers 7 7 7 7 could not be arranged as a sequence of numbers, since any sequence would be as valid as any other. The distribution of order into determinate *types of order* (spatial, temporal, or causal orders), into *domains of order* (orders of nature, life, humankind, society, law, language, etc.), and finally— and this is particularly relevant for our inquiry—into different *styles of order* (closed, open, hierarchical, global, regional, etc.) results from differentiation of what is here generally called regularity. Pure simplicity and pure indifference would then be as much a boundary case as pure multiplicity and pure variety; both would bring us to the edge of any order.

"To the edge of order"—that is easily said. What condition do we approach when we move toward the edge of an order? What is the counterpart of order—an *irregular* connection that would still be comprehensible and whose irregularity would be removable, or a *disorderly* condition that would be intrinsically incomprehensible? To use Husserl's terms, are we dealing with countersense or nonsense? Let us take the example of language. Does what we are seeking correspond to a wrong sequence of sounds, or to a meaningless one? Of course, something that does not follow certain rules can be following other rules, e.g., those of another language or of an animal cry. There will always be some order or another; even chance distribution in space is subject to statistical rates of probability. Throw all the books of a library randomly into a room; the chance that all the authors whose name begins with A or whose birth year is 1908 will pile up in a certain corner becomes infinitesimally small, but it is calculable. But books are not interchangeable particles of gas; they invite to individual use, and an order of utilizability regulating their use cannot be derived from such a statistical numbers game. Yet the disorder that appears here is limited to a *relative* disorder. This way out remains open as long as we are asking about a *determinate* order; this order is demarcated from other orders, whether they are of equal rank, or of a higher or lower level. But what about the much-cited order as such, whether it be called cosmos, the order of creation, reason, rationality, or whatever? What is this order purely and simply delimited from? What is the guideline for the use of reason? If the question is put this way, we seem to fall into difficulties similar to those we would encounter in language if we wanted to deal with speechless or speech-alien experiences. As in the Midas legend, everything seems to be changed immediately into the gold of language, or likewise into the gold of consciousness—the type of currency makes no difference. Similarly here, the unordered would be what precedes order and is or was brought to order. One can hardly do without the assumption of something to be ordered without changing order into a pure idea or a pure possibility in which nothing would be left of a concrete orderly complex or orderly structure. Yet we must take into account the customary objection that warns us of inevitable presuppositions. When we discuss, consider, or deal with something to be arranged, we are already moving within the framework of an order behind which we cannot regress except at the cost of unconsciousness or incomprehensibility. As Kant understood his Rousseau, we can *look back* to such a prior state, but we cannot *return* to it. While looking back, we remain on solid ground; but what is the source of the uneasiness that draws us to look back? Is it the lingering anxiety of the person who has escaped, but not once and for all? In other words, is the state of disorder really *back* there? Are not ahead and back, up and down themselves already schemata with which the protectors of order arm themselves in order to drown out the "inarticulate scream" with the voice of a fortified reason?

If one definitely does not want to go back to the old convertibility of Being, the True, the Good, and the One, then one has to ask *what* is brought to order in each case and "what is present in an orderly way." That is, one must distinguish between the *disorderly* in the sense of contrariety to the rule, which falls under the binary qualification grids of an order, and a disorder this side of such an order, which for the sake of distinction we call "*unordered*." Whoever buries this distinction under the suspicion of irrationalism ends with a closed order and, for better or worse, is carrying on metaphysics in the old style, even though its foundations have been lost.

The question of how we are to speak of the mysterious *x* that is the opposite of order or that precedes it is, however, still only at its beginning. Every direct approach and every aggressive discourse runs the danger of immediately immersing the twilight of any order in an artificial light or of merely exorcizing it. This predicament compels us to use detours. Mythical interpretations, prehistoric hypotheses, paleontological finds, literary riddles, sketches from experience, cosmogonic metaphors, divergent categories of conversation and action—all these will be presented heuristically in the following pages since they lead us in various ways to the threshold where something is hinted at and delineated as to-be-ordered. Without such stealthy side-glances across the threshold, without keeping open such perspectives, the ordering mechanisms would have free rein, and after consuming the material bequeathed to them they would be kept from running in neutral only by artificial procurement of material.

2. Under Chronos and Zeus

In Plato, order and disorder are still admitted into cosmic processes in which the whole organizes and disorganizes itself. In *The Statesman* (268d–274e), which deals with the order of political rulership, Plato tells a "great story" in the way we tell it to children. Humans live in two alternating ages. One age, in which humankind steps backward and is rejuvenated, stands under the scepter of Chronos. He takes away all cares from human beings, so that everything prospers for them without effort, without war and wild antagonism, even without progeneration, for the earth takes over this task for them. In this Golden Age humans still converse with animals.

> Since Chronos's foster children enjoyed so much leisure and also the capacity to discourse rationally (*dia logōn*) not only with humans but also with the animals, if they used all this correctly for philosophy in their conversations with the animals and among themselves, inquiring of every creature whether it was in possession of any particular faculty to observe something differently from the others in order to increase insight, it is easy to conclude that the people of those times were a thousand times happier than present-day people. But if, copiously satiated with food and drink, they told such stories to one another and to the animals as are now told about them, the case can also very easily be decided, at least in my opinion.

Plato leaves open the question whether this symbiosis of closeness to nature and rational insight is more than a projection of contemporary human beings.

The age of Zeus, in which this story of the age of Chronos is told, dawns when the "helmsman of the universe" lets go of the rudder and lets the world run its own course, so that it now advances in age. Where to? The first effect of this "release" is that the corporeal, which previously was bound up within order (*cosmos*), wins back its old disorder (*ataxia*). Like the world as a whole, however, humans too are left to themselves. They discover their deficiencies compared with the animals, who now revert to their wild state.

> Then abandoned by the care of the daimon that rules and protects us, human beings now suffered greatly from the beasts, since most animals of any cruder nature went completely wild, while they themselves had become weak and unprotected; and in the early times they were completely helpless and without skills, because the food that had been readily available to them soon ran out and they did not know how to obtain food for themselves, since no kind of shortage had previously compelled them to do so.

Divine protection is now replaced by divine gifts, such as fire, the arts, agriculture, and similar things, whereby humans become self-supporting. This is necessary because "the protection of the gods was missing for humans and they now had to lead themselves and take care of themselves like the whole world (*cosmos*), which we imitate at all times. . . ."

The age of Zeus is characterized by an increase of knowledge and domination and a simultaneous breakdown of order. If the disruption reaches such a degree that there is danger that the world "will sink back completely into the unfathomable sea of dissimilarity (*apeiron ponton*)," then the god who has arranged the world as a cosmos flings the helm around so that it is restored as immortal and ageless. And what if the god leaves the world definitively to itself? If no circularity makes up for what has been lost? If order and disorder remain mixed? Does it then follow that "discursive familiarity" with nature necessarily turns into a civilized monologue from which everything wild is excluded, even the song of the Sirens, against which Socrates applies the countermagic of his discourse (*Phaidrus*, 259a–259b)?

3. Abyss and Foundation

A leap into the modern age and we discover Kant's *Reflections on the Presumed Beginning of the Human Race*, a "pleasure tour" through not altogether pleasant landscapes, for which he uses a "sacred document" as map.

First step:

He discovered in himself a faculty to choose a life-journey for himself and not be bound to a single one like the other animals. The momentary delight aroused in him by this privilege when he first became aware of it must have been followed immediately by fear and anxiety. How would he, who still did not know anything by its hidden properties and remote effects, be able to utilize this newly discovered faculty? He was standing at the edge of an abyss, as it were. For the individual objects of his desire, which had previously been assigned to him by instinct, had now opened up for him into an infinity of possible objects, and he did not know how to find his way among them. Nonetheless once he had tasted this state of freedom it was impossible for him to go back again to servitude (under the rule of instinct).

What precedes rational order is not disorder simply speaking, but a fixed order that is imposed on living creatures. Here there was still "no commandment or prohibition, and therefore still no violation." With the "fall" out of this order, a gaping abyss (Gr.: *chaos*) opens up; for one world-moment the natural order no longer applies, and the rational order does not yet apply. Humans have to cope simultaneously with a *shortage* of supporting reality and an *excess* of possibilities. With the establishment of reason, which creates its own ground, the abyss closes again. Or is it merely covered over? What becomes of the excessive possibilities? Can the "indeterminate animal" really succeed in determining itself on a higher level by the use of reason, or does there remain a thorn of possibilities that no reason can take away? Does the combination of shortage and excess become lost if the human being is defined one-sidedly as the "privative being" exposed to a distress that at first knows no commandment and in the end nothing else but commandments?
One last step:

[Man understood] that he was really the *purpose of nature* and nothing that lives on earth could compete with him in this regard. The first time he came to the sheep, he said, "*The pelt you wear was given to you by nature not for you but for me,*" and he took it from the sheep and put it on himself. He became aware of a privilege he had above all animals by his very nature and he no longer regarded them as his fellow creatures but as means and tools for him to use as he saw fit, to achieve whatever intentions he might will. . . . This step is thus related at the same time to man's *release* from nature's maternal lap, which is an honor but also very dangerous, for she drove him out of the innocent and safe conditions of childcare, like out of a garden that supplied him without effort, and sent him out into the wide world, where so many cares, toils, and unknown evils awaited him.

Domination or bondage—the release from nature's care and from service to it is replaced by domination over nature; one is the reverse of the other. What precedes the human and rational order sinks down to a means and material once the "transition" has been made "from the crudity of a merely animal creature to humanity." Nature's means have no other recourse than to assert a certain weight of their own through dangers and toils "until perfect culture again becomes nature"; but this "ultimate goal of the moral determination of the human race" applies to a second nature, which has subjugated but not fully absorbed the first. Subjugated forces remain dangerous, so that the presumed end undergoes considerable delay.

4. Branching Evolution

Following paleontological tracks imprinted beneath mythical ideas and sacred documents, we make a further leap. But what the shovel brings up is evidence neither of a mythical cycle nor of a linear progressive evolution. If we accept André Leroi-Gourhan's account under the title *Le geste et la parole* (1964; Eng.: *Gesture and Speech*, 1993), tracing the development of technology, language, and art, the fossil finds of recent decades—not only in the animal kingdom, but also in the realm of human life—speak for a "branching evolution" (*G&S*, 27), which in the strict sense is more than a mere e-volution or de-velopment of something predesigned. At certain junctures "options" emerge, leading in the animal world, for example, to a forking between walking or prehensile, aquatic or land dwelling animals, without the ones being a prior stage of the others. Thus every advance leaves possibilities open and is not heightened to a distinct progress that leaves an inferior stage behind.

Similarly in humans, the "legend of the ape man," which stems from the quest for a *missing link* within an uninterrupted *chain of being,* proves to be untenable since even the "first humans" were not semicaptive, but were already indeterminate animals.

The image of this early man in no way fits in with what two centuries of philosophical thought had accustomed us to see. Facts now show that the human is not a kind of monkey gradually improving itself; the human is not the majestic pinnacle of the paleontological edifice; from the earliest moment at which we pick up the trail, the human is something other than a monkey. At that moment, humans still have a very long way to go, but their journey will be not so much a matter of biological development as of freeing themselves from the zoological context and organizing themselves in an entirely new way, with society gradually taking the place of the phyletic stream. (*G&S*, 116)

In humans, the liberation of head, hand, and brain, which is prepared by upright locomotion, leads to a de-specialization of organs culminating in the capacity for an almost unlimited generalization.

Neither human teeth nor hand, neither human foot nor, when all is said and done, brain has attained the perfection of the mammoth's teeth, the horse's hand and foot, or the brain of certain birds—with the result that humans have remained capable of just about every possible action, can eat practically anything, can run and climb, and can use the unbelievably archaic part of their skeleton, that is, their hands, to perform operations directed by a brain superspecialized in the skill of generalizing. (*G&S,* 118)

This does more than merely make up for deficiencies, as is shown by the first evidences of an aesthetic-religious nature, which reveal two central modes of reaction: "reactions to death" and "reactions to unusual shapes" (*G&S,* 107). What physical deficiency is the cult of death supposed to remedy, since it serves not the dying but the deceased, or respectively group cohesion? If it were only a question of survival, of "biological success," then the jellyfish with its unchanging survival achievements would be absolutely equal to humans, perhaps even superior (*G&S,* 30). But achievements of hand and head, going far beyond the requirements of pure survival, wind up in the field of ambiguity and ambivalence. Despite all functionality, simple *implements* such as the hand ax or an armchair display a surplus of form and a decorative exuberance that keeps technical inventions from flowing into a perfectly mechanical formula. There always remains a certain "functional plasticity" (*G&S,* 301) and an "envelope of style," whose particularizing effects lead to the omnipresence of "aesthetics" (*G&S,* 299 ff.). "The purest art always plunges deepest; only the uppermost tip emerges from the plinth of flesh and bone without which it could not exist" (*G&S,* 273).

As for the development of *language,* prehistoric portrayals of figures show signs of a graphic expression whose multidimensional pictorialness is not yet subject to the linearity of a written language. The linearization of symbols, which increases their availability, means at the same time an impoverishment of their means of expression (*G&S,* 212). This development of language reduplicates a *triumph of technology,* whose ambivalent effect becomes more and more apparent. The externalization of the achievements of hand and head, although it unburdens the organism and controls its hyper-specialization, leads at the same time to the "regression" (*G&S,* 255) of hand and brain, for their achievements are outdone by machines and electronic brains. This ineluctable extrapolation of functions reaches into all areas of life and makes it impossible for technification to settle in the lower strata of a self-perfecting culture. The ambivalence manifested in the amalgamation of creation and destruction (*G&S,* 183) reaches back to the beginnings of culture. A domestication that was wrested from a "harmony between predatory animal and man" (*G&S,* 161) will hardly end in pure chamber music. But if the development of *homo sapiens* leaves something to be desired, there is room for "catastrophes" in the glittering sense René Thom gave back to this old word.

5. Visible and Invisible Cities

One of humankind's oldest inventions is the city, and the ramified development of urban culture can serve as a gauge for the variety and vulnerability of human order. Since ancient times, the city, serving as place of refuge and supply center and making possible social integration and public interchange, symbolized the center of the universe with a kind of "umbilical function." And down to our day it remains a "cosmic reflection of the universe" in its geographic layout and orientation. But in the last two centuries it has come under the pressure of industrialization and is undergoing a process of disintegration held back only provisionally by the network of traffic and communication. If we follow the paleontologist's long-range perspective, then the humanization and domestication of space and time, which always maintained a relationship between human territory and the "wild universe," is threatening to degenerate into a "hyper-humanization" with an excessively organized megalopolis as a vision of horror (Leroi-Gourhan, *G&S,* chap. 13).

The proliferation of imperial rule, once personified in the figure of the Emperor, is countered by Italo Calvino with the sly urban imagination of a famous explorer:

> Only in Marco Polo's accounts was Kublai Khan able to discern, through the walls and towers destined to crumble, the tracery of a pattern so subtle it could escape the termites' gnawing. (*Invisible Cities,* 5 f.)

Cities that are well known from story and by sight are undermined by the traveler by invisible twin cities, which remain allusive. That is the case with the city of Aglaura, where eccentricity is usual and the bizarre is normal.

> So if I wished to describe Aglaura to you, sticking to what I personally saw and experienced, I should have to tell you that it is a colorless city, without character, planted there at random. But this would not be true, either: at certain hours, in certain places along the street,

you see opening before you the hint of something unmistakable, rare, perhaps magnificent, you would like to say what it is, but everything previously said of Aglaura imprisons your words and obliges you to repeat rather than say. (*Invisible Cities,* 67 f.)

The author tries to capture what it means to be caught in what is seen and said, not with one model but with two, which mock each other like mirror images.

"From now on I'll describe the cities to you," the Khan had said. "In your journeys you will see if they exist."

But the cities visited by Marco Polo were always different from those thought up by the emperor.

"And yet I have constructed in my mind a model city from which all possible cities can be deduced," Kublai said. "It contains everything corresponding to the norm. Since the cities that exist diverge in varying degree from the norm, I need only foresee the exceptions to the norm and calculate the most probable combinations."

"I too have thought of a model city from which I deduce all the others," Marco answered. "It is a city made only of exceptions, exclusions, incongruities, contradictions. If such a city is the most improbable, by reducing the number of abnormal elements we increase the probability that the city really exists. So I have only to subtract exceptions from my model, and in whatever direction I proceed, I will arrive at one of the cities which, always as an exception, exist. But I cannot force my operation beyond a certain limit: I would achieve cities too probable to be real." (*Invisible Cities,* 69)

With the ironic point of excessive probability, the author lets his discoverer take care not to close the gap between what is yet to be ordered and what has been ordered. It is enough to throw sand into the gears of the work of regulation: the true is never quite probable.

6. Threshold Experiences

Rites of passage—that is what folklore calls the ceremonies accompanying death, birth, marriage, puberty, etc. In modern life these transitions have become more and more unrecognizable and un-experienced. We have become impoverished in threshold experiences. Falling asleep is perhaps the only one we have left. (But along with it, also waking up.) And finally, the ups and downs of conversation and of the sexual behavior of love also undulate across thresholds like wandering figures in a dream. . . . The threshold must be quite sharply distinguished from the boundary. The threshold (*die Schwelle*) is a zone. Change, transition, flooding are suggested by the verb *"schwellen"* [to swell, grow bigger]. . . . (Walter Benjamin, *Passagen-Werk*, I, 617f.)

There are various kinds of threshold experiences. They occur in a more or less marked and ritualized fashion where one area of life or experience makes the transition to another, such as in waking or sleeping, health or sickness, in phases of life or in decisive experiences, finally in life and death. Certain characteristics seem to persist.

(a) The threshold is not a sharp boundary line that one draws and that one can cross arbitrarily in one direction or the other; rather, it marks off a *partition zone* of a certain width that one can step onto hesitantly and on which one can pause and wait as on a doorstep. The spatially marked threshold provides the material for a rich "threshold symbolism": leaving one room and entering another, departing on a journey, returning home, parting from a companion, diving into water, and the like, resemble the set of symbols in which waking itself protrudes into the dream (Freud, *Gesammelte Werke*, Vol. II/III, 508f; *Interpretation of Dreams*, II, 504-5). In a wakeful state, moreover, coming and going are intertwined with greeting and farewell rituals, which even in the profane form of "little pieties" (Goffman 1971, 63) give the impression that it is a matter of accompanying the emergent to the light and holding back what is sinking away.

Threshold experiences are thus connected with transition experiences such as falling asleep and awakening, falling ill and recovering, growing up and aging, leaving and arriving, entering and exiting, or saying farewell or hello. They all are done in the twilight of a certain expectant state extending between the no-longer and the not-yet.

(b) Regardless of all transition experiences and transition rites there is no such thing as a "transition synthesis." Between one province of meaning and another, there is a *leap,* and hesitating at the threshold is precisely a hesitation before making the leap. Transitional rites serve to make this leap easier to interpret. We speak of a leap across a chasm insofar as there is no supporting order encompassing the two domains and insofar as no identical thing and no identical person can be found wandering back and forth according to rules that vouch for identity and continuity. Accordingly, a change of name is often associated with some rites of transition; and—to stay in the spatial foreground—Japanese do not speak of one's own or another's wife, but of an "inner" or "outer" wife. Whether such disconnected experiences can be bridged at a higher level and whether any identifying credentials exist permitting unimpeded passage in both directions can be left as open questions for the time being.

(c) In the threshold experience, what emerges beyond the threshold is not simply outside; rather, it presses more or less strongly over the threshold, enticing or frightening. The threshold is an *entry domain,* even when it develops into a barrier. And what is located this side or that side of a specific threshold can obtain access in some other way, as when a low frequency sound gradually makes the transition to feelings of vibration and a sound of excessively high frequency changes into a sensation of pain, not to mention the disguises used so masterfully in the language of dreams. The threshold experience makes itself felt in spells of drowsiness, intimations of death, longing for love, in spring-time awakening and an autumnal feeling, in homesickness and wander-lust, or in anxiety about one's profession or future. Beyond the threshold we are exposed to whatever comes flooding at us.

(d) Finally, a certain *asymmetry* pertains to the threshold experience. This side and that side of the threshold are not reversible locations that could be arbitrarily interchanged. There is always a privileged domain from which the threshold itself is crossed, and a shadowy domain from which the forbidden, alarming, and endangering streams forth. The "Boy in the Moor" is chased by ghosts until he stands at the divide and can look back from solid ground with a sigh of relief.

> With a deep sigh of relief he casts
> A timid glance back at the moor:
> Yes, in the rushes it was terrible,
> Oh, it was eerie in the heather.
> (Annette von Droste-Hülshoff)

The asymmetry between this side and that side of the threshold is also reflected in the fact that the innocent-looking left side gives us the term "sinister" and "awkward" (Ger.: *linkisch*). Threshold experiences defy all equilibrium. This asymmetry makes it possible for us, while awake, to speak about and reflect on awakeness and dream; while alive, about life and death; while wise with age, about youth and old age. This is perhaps the decisive entranceway for the illusory claim that from safe ground one can take possession of what lies beyond the threshold. How else can the dreamer respond to such an alien encroachment except by waking up? Is, then, even the interpretation of dreams in the end a Pyrrhic victory? A lulling of reason would not help us get any further here, though perhaps an alertness that jogs at one's own awakeness might do so insofar as awakeness covers over these experiences.

Even when we reserve the emphatic title of threshold experience for the transition from one domain of life or experience to another, the threshold phenomenon with its characteristic traits extends into the realm of everyday experiences, and it is by no means exalted above the thresholds of sensation that we know from the physiology of the senses and above the inhibition thresholds of which the behavioral theorists speak. "Each sensation, being strictly speaking the first, last, and only one of its kind, is a birth and a death" (Merleau-Ponty, *PhP,* 216). Would Proust's Bergotte have gone seeking so intensely for this "little patch of yellow wall" in Vermeer's scene from Delft if the senses offered merely material for an activity of the mind? Something strange can penetrate through all pores, quickening or laming, and the two reactions are often not far apart. We should learn to give new weight to stimulus and incitement (*Reiz*), for machines can also register them.

7. *Cosmogonic Metaphors and Models*

The metaphorics of ordering and self-ordering that pervade our familiar philosophical theorems and also our scientific models form a buffer zone between myth and logic. From the immense wealth of motifs I will single out only a few introduced by the question of how, in this domain where it is a matter of the origin of more comprehensive and fundamental orders, what is to be ordered and the unordered each are manifested in speech. In many cases it is a matter of designs of an orderly universe, a "cosmos"—which in the original meaning of the word designates decoration and order. Cosmogonies and cosmologies, by operating with inner-worldly models, escape the speechlessness that sets in with a direct mode of speech. One notices a certain one-sidedness that is manifested in these models.

A first list includes models of *production* that presuppose an orderer as efficient cause. The producer can appear as a *craftsperson,* such as the builder who forms matter, whether it is compact clay or the more sublime *hylē* of consciousness; the architect, who erects a founded building from building stones and whose constitutive achievements go all the way to the architectonics of reason; the machinist, who assembles individual components, fastening and unfastening them, and—unless leaving this to a separate operator and controller—starts the machine or winds it up like clockwork. In addition there are producer-figures who do not dirty their hands, such as the *surveyor,* who divides the horizon with a priestly gesture, appropriating land by dividing it into fields, terrains, and territories, signed and sealed down to the fields of a lattice box; the *general,* who like the *cosmētōr* Agamemnon (*Iliad,* I, 16) commands the army and marshals its units into a battle order (*taxis*); the *legislator,* who imposes on aimless and antagonistic forces and movements a law from which they can withdraw only at the cost of renewed chaos; finally, the *statesman,* who intervenes in what is happening with a guiding and ruling hand. The demiurge in Plato's *Timaeus,* the divine commander in Book XII of Aristotle's *Metaphysics,* the cosmic watchmaker in Leibniz's monadology, and—with an impersonal turn—reason as the lawgiver or transcendental consciousness as the constitutive center—all these are prominent examples of such model-formations. The conceptual patterns delineated in these metaphors are not decisively altered by whether production is entrusted to a god, a coalition of god and humankind, humankind alone, or an anonymous authority. By such metaphorical threads, many a modern conceptual pattern is linked back to presuppositions it officially denies.

Something similar applies to a second list presenting models of an *emergence* of order. Here the self-ordering runs more or less spontaneously without an orderer—either as *emanation* from an overflowing source, as the gradual *development* or *evolution* of something undeveloped, or as the sudden *eruption* of a new order from the slags of an old one.

Both lists are accompanied by biological models, the production metaphors by that of *generation* or *procreation* by the father, the emergence metaphors by that of *birth* from a mother's womb, generally called Mother Nature, all the way down to matter as the *mater formarum* (mother of forms) or *matrix.*

Now the question is: how does what is to be ordered or is unordered ever express itself? To begin with the less interesting evolutionary models: here order is so seamlessly anchored in things that, strictly speaking, *nothing* precedes order; order merely has to emerge and develop. What this "merely" means, however, is hard to say. If the continuous pull of evolution is broken by emergent new formations, then we have the same order in things, but multiplied; actually *nothing* needs ordering here—unless the re-formation turns out to be a transformation, but then it is more than pure emergence.

The series of production models is more instructive. In one form or another they involve formation by something else. The source of production gives this model a dualistic note so that a tiny fissure opens between order and its counterpart. This is true even when the source dwindles into an "out of nothing," for an empty slot is not sufficient to revise the model. But closer examination shows that the unordered always serves as the *negative foil* to order; it appears as amorphous, crude, confused, accidental, violent, that is, in a state that has everything to expect from order and that is not granted any objection nor any voice. Chaos appears as the hypostasized counterpart of order. One can perhaps flirt with chaos but not negotiate with it, and what is not usable counts as cosmic trash. In this context, the decisive axis of ordering is the *vertical,* whether a form is imprinted on a formless mass, or parts are combined into a whole, or accidental facts or conflicting forces are subjected to a law. This vertical axis determines the emergence metaphors in the opposite direction; something rises, makes its way up to light. Neither in the case of self-evolution nor in the case of formation by something else is a fellow player found on a horizontal plane. Since the whole and the supreme are the vanishing point of ordering, ordering really means primarily inserting and subordinating, with the consequence that order tends toward a *closed form*. This can, like Kant's system of knowledge, "grow internally (*per intus susceptionem*) but not externally (*per appositionem*), like an animal body   " (*KrV,* B 861, *CPR,* 467).

Our objection does not imply that the vertical schemata are without conjectural force and useless, but merely that such metaphorics of order, if applied exclusively, lead the existing order to deny its origin and encapsulate itself within itself: what is unordered fuses with the disorderly.

Order, understood as the regulated connection between one thing and another, does not by any means bind us to such a vertical concept of order. Indeed, there are further series of metaphors, such as those of *name-giving* and *play,* which definitely include addressees and fellow players. Even for *robots* and *machines,* since Daedalus's walking statues, the point is that something made develops its own dynamics based on staged (*inszenierten*) self-movement. And even in Plato's mythical origin of the world the *nous* (mind, spirit) does not win by coercion; rather, it uses "calm persuasion" to subordinate necessity to itself (*Timaeus,* 48a). On the other hand, name-giving too can assume features of domination, as in Hobbes's politically tinged world order (*De Homine,* chap. 9), and humankind can feel, with Plato, like a "plaything of the gods" (*Laws,* 803b) or can sink down to a figure in a cosmic game of chance.

Here we break off this exploratory patrol into the realm of metaphors, warned of excessively closed formations that seek to incorporate what is ordered into a comprehensive order so that in the end not very much manages to cross the threshold. In such cases there is need for a different beginning.

8. Open Linkage in Conversation

Changing the subject from cosmogonic metaphors and models back to the plane of human speech and action, we cannot expect the ordering conceptions that tend toward closure to disappear without further ado. On the contrary, the accustomed mirrorings between cosmology and anthropology would lead one, rather, to expect a corresponding orderly structure. A revision aiming for open forms of order should, then, take diagonal approaches to set in motion the traditional categories together with the metaphors that nourish them. If the vertically oriented metaphors of order can do absolutely without fellow players and opponents, it seems logical to resort to phenomena where fellow players and opponents are indispensable. This applies to conversation, whose mobile ordering process runs diagonally to the classical axes of order. Possibly perspectives may open up from there leading beyond mere conversation.

When details are at issue in the classical forms of order, arranging, combining, and assembling assume a central function, as our metaphorical examples illustrate—indeed, an arranging that follows determinate ideas, rules, or laws and is directed toward a goal. Sculptor, commander, legislator, and helmsman often work hand in hand; order and prescription are close neighbors. The only variable within this perspective is the kind and origin of combination. In Plato the bond (*desmos*) is woven into the cosmos as a well-proportioned relation of the parts with one another (*Timaeus,* 31c); however, with the modern fragmentation of the cosmos into individual things and individual events, this bond becomes a delicate problem. Hume settles for associative mechanisms and habits to move from atomistic perceptions to chance "conjunctions," and finally, by very problematic paths, to necessary "connections." Kant sees this mere collecting of unitary formations as the ruin of any reasonable order and removes from the senses "any combination (*conjunctio*) of the multifarious at all," assigning this function to the self-activity of the subject, the transcendental descendent of the cosmological demiurge (*KrV* B, 129 f.; *CPR,* 75). What is interesting about this "small narrative" is that the context is always regulated by a superior authority, regardless of whether unity is established or discovered. The rest is called, in Plato's cosmology, "disharmonious and disorderly movement" (*Timaeus,* 30a), in Kant "aggregate" or "rhapsody" (*KrV* B, 860, *CPR,* 466) or even "crude chaotic aggregate" (V, 186); and Hume's "sensations" are altogether too asocial to achieve association on their own: can an umbrella help it if it is standing next to a Madonna? Admittedly, Hume could also lead to other paths if he were read through the eyes of Virginia Woolf and advocated not an atomized but a splintering world of sensations that permit varying accesses in the individual case.

To thwart the collusive interplay of unity here and multiplicity there, perhaps recourse to the simple sequence of statements in a conversation would help. One statement produces the other, and the coherence becomes especially clear in the succession of question and answer. This linkage can be regarded as a specific form of cohesion mandating a more open form of regulation.

Asking a question is an interlocutory event, a remarkable kind of event. It is an event that does not come to rest in itself but aims for the answer as another event, without itself bringing that event about. Yet this does not involve a *sequence* of occurrences unreeling according to merely *empirical laws* connecting them in a kind of cause and effect, for whether one statement corresponds to the other and is a successful answer is not decided by the regularity of its actual occurrence. On the other hand, it is also not a matter of a coherence of steps of discourse following from *logical* or *axiological* laws. A logical conclusion, for instance, is not an answer to the previous propositions, even if the syllogism is spoken with divided roles. Nor is a reply, in practice, a pure following of a law. And why not? Because a question, apart from certain special cases, allows for more than one answer. And even where the answer is reduced to yes or no, the possibility still remains of evading or refusing to give an answer, in some cases while stating reasons for this. It need not go as far as an infinity of possibilities, before which Kant sees the first humans shuddering; a finite number of possibilities available for choice without one being absolutely preferable is sufficient. Whoever says "*a*" does not have to say "*b*," but that does not mean that one could say any arbitrary thing. To characterize this strange intermediate situation, which escapes the dichotomy of claim-free facts and counterfactual claims, I would like to speak of *situative* and *contextual* claims, as I have done elsewhere.

What can linkage mean in this context? One cannot speak of a given multiplicity that is brought to order by interconnection, because a statement must stand out in relief from a field of statements in order to occur as such. This standing out in relief is a process of differentiation that precedes the insertion of synthesizing and coordinating mechanisms. But at this point what matters primarily is what happens next, when the question event seeks and finds an answer as a corresponding event. The connection that is formed is what I want to focus on.

(a) The first thing noticed is that the bond does not stem from a third factor, from a superior authority that would combine a given multiplicity; the connection is formed immediately *between the members of the chain of events.* The answer is not first set into relation to something other; rather, it is itself the entrance into or continuation of the relationship. Conversation resembles the unrolling of a carpet, not the contemplation of a carpet pattern. Of course, the question can in many ways be compared with the answer, but whoever does this is not answering, or is no longer answering. Intransitive use of the verb "to link up" corresponds to this; the notion of linking up does not positively identify anything that I will connect with something else—there is only a goal of linkage, whether on the level of saying or of what is said (cf. Lat.: *sermonem nectere;* Ger.: *anknüpfen an;* or Fr.: *lier conversation or amitié avec*).

(b) Questions and answers, like speaking and listening, relate to one another *asymmetrically.* The question does not relate to the answer in the same way as the answer does to the question. In this respect, their relation is similar to that between various temporal and spatial dimensions or between father and son and not to the relationship between siblings (whose relationship, of course, is also in many ways not symmetrical). Certainly, I can understand father and son as two members of a family, two Germans, or two persons, but in doing this I lose the specific father-son relationship. One can, of course, also refer to a possible changing of conversation partners, to symmetrically distributed opportunities to speak, and the like, but these unifications do not bring about the specific relation. Insofar as I answer, I precisely do not do the same thing as the other person who listens. The relation, then, remains asymmetrical; even on the relational plane itself it does not get rounded out to a whole in which the I-Thou and the Thou-I would be abolished as relational components of a finished dialogue.

(c) Finally, a third possibility remains—namely, that the question and answer are located in a third factor that they bring about together, for instance, a theoretical insight or a common plan. But this third way of constituting a whole also never fully dissolves the event of *saying* in the result of *what is said*. A question may be answered, a request fulfilled, but the asking and the requesting are not thereby fully extinguished, for the simple reason that the question would also have allowed for other answers, and indeed perhaps still does. Every question that is not merely a prescribed one resembles a wound that never completely heals.

(d) If by cohesion one means the combining of individual components into a whole into which they are inserted or subordinated, then there is no cohesion between question and answer, but a linkage with open points of access. For the same reason interlocutory events are characterized by a *singularity* that is not that of a subsumed individual case or a particular moment, but of a constellation with series, chains, networks, that is, with pervasive and articulated relations and open points of access. This singularity has its own form of universality, which is *lateral,* not vertical. This form of universality comes about because the linkages multiply, branch out, and interweave. If the configuration of a game cannot be adequately determined by counting the individual pieces and characterizing them generally as pawn or queen, it is even less possible adequately to comprehend any open conversational situation merely by tracing back individual events to empirical regularities or subjecting them to normative regulations. The singularity of intermediate events, too, shows empirical as well as ideal traits, but their specific connection does not come into full play in this combination of factuality and ideality.

If it is true that every inquiry opens a field of junctural possibilities, that is, permits several answers and not just one, then a fissure opens up between inquiry and reply, for no answer fulfills the situative claim fully and completely, each one somehow falls short. This fissure embodies an insurmountable, strange sort of conjunction (*Und*), simultaneously separating and connecting, because a successful answer fulfills the question's intention without abolishing the need for fulfillment and linkage. This hiatus has something about it of the threshold separating different domains of experience from one another and binding them together like light and shadow. A question that would be completely answered would also cause the wellspring of conversation to dry up. We would have reached our destination with the exhaustive answer. Hence the hiatus between claim and response is also a condition for our being able to speak at all of a "between" of interlocution, interaction, intermediary world, and intermediary realm, whenever something happens between speakers and actors that can neither be mastered by the individual alone, nor controlled by a higher authority, nor integrated into a whole. Without the open form of linkage, this intermediary area could not exist.

At the same time, the multivalency of interlocutory events and the resulting hiatus between inquiry and reply is what necessitates a regulation of the connection, that is, an order that inevitably assumes a selective and exclusive character. If only one possible linkage were available or if all were open at once, we would be dealing with the extreme cases of a necessary connection or a total lack of cohesion, and there would be no alternative. The indeterminate animal has neither the one nor the other, and must therefore make determinations in order not to be completely exposed to the shifting moods of the moment. In a still very formal manner we can give a preliminary answer to our question concerning the mode of organization of interlocutory events such as question and answer. The elementary achievement of order would consist in *regulating the linkage to interlocutory events by introducing selective viewpoints*. Unordered linkages are subjected to the gridwork of the ordered and the disorderly, just as, for instance, the barriers to incest and the marriage laws steer sexual intercourse into determinate channels.

Theories dedicated to a comprehensive global order linking everything tend to make all relevant events unambiguously clear, so that decisive questions have only *one right answer* that fits like the key to a lock, or that can be compared with the one target the archer aims at: "The good is uniform, the bad variegated" (Aristotle, *Nic. Ethics,* II, 6, 1106b, 28 ff.). Of course, consensus too is uniform compared with the many minds and senses. Whoever would want to turn this sentence around and defend the bad instead of the good and dissent instead of consensus would, as much as the defender of order, take a stand this side of the threshold in an already established "either-or." In either case, the threshold would remain forgotten, along with what lies behind the threshold.

Yet the open linkage to other people's expressions is not limited to dialogue, for dialogue, in its turn, is embedded in a non-linguistic or pre-linguistic sphere of expression of bodily existence. A privileged example of social contact is the mutual look, which frequently takes the form of a *drama of the look*. Even when someone looks at me, a threshold is crossed—and not crossed. To see a look means to respond to it in some way, whether by looking back, by looking away, or by repeated and secretive looking there—a continuing game that is also explained by the fact that the other person seeing me is never where I see him or her, and the other person never sees me where I see him or her (cf. Merleau-Ponty *V&I,* 261, commentary by Lacan 1978, chap. 3). To have the other person there, I would have to fit him or her into a world. The struggle of gazes that aims at putting an end to instability by super- or sub-ordination is only the unhappy attempt to escape a claim that cannot be mastered.

The linguistic statement is thus the crystallization core for a threshold occurrence. How far it goes and whether it spreads to contact with things is a question that requires a further step of reflection.

9. Open Encounter in Action

The assumption underlying the following transition from conversation to action presupposes that in every action something cooperates, not just on the part of the person acting, who acts with or against others, but also on the part of the object of the action. If there is such a cooperating element, it can as little be fitted into a whole or subordinated to a supreme authority as can another person's statement. As it turns out, by even considering such a thing we are left in the lurch at a decisive point not only by the traditional theories of action, which are guided by a cosmic or anthropological teleology, but even more so by the newer theories, which separate goal-orientation and normative regulation. This applies particularly to theories describing and evaluating actions from the actor's perspective. The familiar distinction between questions of law and questions of fact often results in the superimposition of a clever normative logic upon a psychological infrastructure derived quite improvisatorially from traditional philosophical concepts and psychological constructs. If, however, one reaches back to a teleological theory of action in the style of Aristotle, one can expect, intentionally or unintentionally, to drift off in a cosmological direction. Yet astonishingly, whether one follows the tradition of Aristotle, Hume, or Kant, the outline of the theory of action remains surprisingly homogeneous. Disunity prevails almost only where it is a matter of weighting or delimiting the individual aspects; the overall instrumentation of goals, facts, and norms seems hardly to be contested.

The *sententia communis* on the theory of action consistently holds to the following points of view: the actor sets, finds, or pursues a goal, uses tools and materials for it, adjusts to conditions and opportunities, considers particular needs and interests, and does this within the framework of universal norms; and insofar as the action is a social one, goal-setting, work, needs, and norms acquire a relation to real or possible other persons, whether in the form of a strategic calculation that takes others into account as competitors or opponents, or in view of consensus-formation that makes others my equals in case of a conflict. Actions can, accordingly, be judged by whether they have succeeded, that is, whether they have attained their appropriate goal and have fulfilled our intentions in an economical and comparatively safe manner. Furthermore, it can be asked whether the execution and the result correspond to the relevant norms and rules, that is, whether the action was right. In this way, what is *objectively* given or achieved is separated from what is *subjectively* attained and willed, and both things differ from what should be done *transsubjectively*. In the framework of such a teleologically oriented and normatively controlled behavior, all the efficient and motivating forces we encounter in the external, internal, and social world fall under the binary grid of purposeful/counterpurposeful (suitable/unsuitable, advantageous/disadvantageous) and beneficial/harmful—and all this is subsumed under the ultimately determinative grid of normative and counternormative (right or wrong in the broadest sense). What eludes this triple matrix of technique, need, and norm is radically *indifferent,* a matter of chance, arbitrariness, or permission. Between self-preservation and the preservation of reason, need-satisfaction and norm-fulfillment, need from below and coercion from above, no room is left for any other thing to challenge us. Since everything we encounter is intercepted by foregoing orders, basically nothing happens between *one's own* action and that *of others,* for coordinated individual actions are not yet *inter*action and a subjective expression of feeling is still not mutual love, nor love play, nor a battle of the sexes. What presses across the threshold of our orders of action is still only noises, for nothing emerges that could speak with an alien or unarticulated voice. The unordered is nothing more than the unexploitable remainder of an established or emergent order. If that order opens up, it does so only upward, for downward it is sealed off, at least as long as the barriers of cultivation, civilization, and moralization hold. Otherwise, chaos and barbarity threaten.

In order to sharpen this blunted concept of action and to make room for the interplay with something other even during the course of the action, one could be almost inclined to borrow from behaviorist and system-theory doctrines of behavior, except that these schools narrow down the difference between stimulus and reaction completely in terms of the law of causality or neutralize it to a mere reduction of complexity. Even so, it is recommended that the worn-out concepts "stimulus" and "response" be revived. The terminologically pallid word "incentive" (*Reiz*) conceals a whole scale of possibilities that are manifested in terms such as *instigation, incitement, request, demand, challenge, provocation, imposition, offer, concern, infliction,* or—to show some gratitude to the transcendental philosophers—*affecting* (*Affektion*). If "affecting" is freed of the needy status of material procurement or the dubious service of incitement by a vague feeling, if the incentive is left with a bit of incitement and affecting with a bit of the affective, then the incentive regains its motive power, which of course it had in Aristotle's teleologically oriented theory of movement. Under modern conditions of a variable world-order this possibility would have to be thought through again; beginnings of this are found in the Gestalt theorists, such as Kurt Lewin and Wolfgang Köhler, when they ascribe to things themselves "demand characters" and "requirements" (*Gefordertheiten*) that are not articulated in demand statements nor derived from normative authorities of a higher order. The incentive resembles the dialogical question since, as Leibniz says, "it inclines, it does not coerce" (*inclinat, non necessitat*), or, as Kant still phrased it, the incentive affects human choice but does not determine it (*MS* B, 5). Coerced behavior, then, could no more be called an action than could an answer that was implanted. A fissure thus opens up between incitement and response. By incitement we mean an event or a condition *that instigates to a determinate behavior and directs it in a determinate direction.* The instigation may be stronger or weaker, the form more or less pronounced, the direction more or less fixed. The reaction to such a stimulus has traits of a dialogical response insofar as it links up with something else. How very much these possibilities of linkage are selected and normified by orders of action will be dealt with in more detail below. What matters here is the insight that in such orders superfluous possibilities are presupposed; without open places, orders of action would be nothing but conditioning and training.

A few examples, whose one-sidedness can be candidly admitted, are: to throw a ball, to climb stairs in the dark, to try a doorlatch, to taste a food, to swim across a river, to follow with the eyes a train that is moving away, to tune an instrument, to befriend a cat, to play in the sand, to build a bridge, to tend light signals, to lay out fishnets, to write a letter, or simply to dial a telephone number. If we analyze these and similar examples, we see that the stimuli are not mere triggering devices that set us in motion, or material we use to make something, or means that serve some other end; rather, things have a variable measure of *their own form, their own weight, their own movement, their own temporal rhythm, and their own surrounding world.* Whoever swims with or against the current, whoever has the wind in the face or at the back, is going along with a movement or resisting it; and in such going along and continuing, one's own movement and the movement of something or someone else do not stand diametrically opposed. Nor is this true of the look that follows its object, or the voice of a fugue that follows its countervoice. "The making of anything is a dialogue between the maker and the material employed" (Leroi-Gourhan, *G&S,* 306). Sand cooperates better with the shaping hand than does stone, but its form lasts only until the next high tide, whereas what is done in stone can last for centuries. One instrument is easier to tune than the other; I feel this only upon trying it out. And how does a bridge-builder notice whether a bridge fits in a landscape? "He is talking to nature and nature is replying to him. . . . Finally we reach a point at which we can cooperate with nature" (Mead 1973, 229; Eng.: 185). And my feet, which find the steps of the staircase in the dark without counting and without stumbling, would play a trick on me if I wanted to assist them with reflection and free decisions. The fisherman who is catching a fish "lures him with human cleverness and human cunning up to the deadly heat" (Goethe). And even arrangements that allow the hand little margin of error, like dialing a telephone or paging through a railway guide, can become a dealing with magic instruments transporting us to another world if we treat them with the alienating, playful skill of children and poets. If one wanted to object that these are mere bodily movements rather than actions, I would reply: all the better, for without them all that would remain are acts that smell too much of musty records (*Akten*). The bureaucratization of actions will come soon enough.

Now a provisional summary. If actions are not curtailed in dealing with things, the possibility arises of acceding to the demands and allurements of things, of venturing into interaction and risking injuries. Actions can, then, be judged not only by whether they succeeded or are right, but also by *whether we have done justice* to a thing or a task, whether we have used and developed or preserved its possibilities. This presupposes that the very goals themselves are worked out while acting and are not pregiven by subjective needs and prescribed by transsubjective norms. Since, then, in acting we always *deal with something* that comes toward us and cooperates with us in one way or another, or plays games with us, all the way to the treachery of the object, we speak with Kurt Goldstein and Merleau-Ponty of a bodily "encounter" (*Auseinandersetzung*) with something other. Humans enjoy an absolute "privilege" only when they appropriate it, but that itself is already a part of the encounter with "one's fellows."

10. Intermediary Events and Responsive Rationality

If action is understood as an encounter in which something is worked out between the actor and the thing acted upon, the impression is given that a dialogical model could be expanded beyond the intersubjective realm. It would then be easy to speak of a blurring of differences or even of neo-animism. So a few cautious explanations are in order. First, there has been almost no talk here of dialogue or dialogical behavior, because the traditional dialogue theories (including my own) run the danger of *logos* overshadowing the *dia-*, the "between." This is true, at any rate, when a more comprehensive *logos* is applied that eventually reconciles all differences and brings them into unity. These objections lead me to describe statements as *interlocutory* events and actions as *interaction* events. But why "events" and not "intentional acts or actions"? Because what happens in statements or actions must be grasped so neutrally that its "between"-character, which culminates in claim and response, can be decided on its own merits, without having an intervening conceptuality steer the look into fixed channels. The central problem, then, does not consist in the extent to which a "dialogical model" must be applied, but in whether what happens in our speech and actions displays such an intermediary character or not. What order and rationality mean depends directly on the answer to this question.

I regard as an *intermediary event* something that, when it happens, links up with something other in such a way that it is responding to the latter's incitement and claim. Insofar as this is true of every statement and every action, each one would be an interlocutory or interaction event. The order that arises from these connections and intervenes in them in a regulatory fashion is what I call *"responsive rationality."* An open kind of regulation is embodied in it, since what is ordered does not itself stem from this order. It regulates the way one deals with and gets involved with the other.

The constitutive asymmetry mentioned several times above is decisive. It runs crosswise to those orders that aim for the symmetrical assignment of the parts and their arrangement in a whole. The event with which linkage is made and the other one that does the linking first arise and exist in nothing other than the intended incitement and response itself. An idea comes to mind, a question is asked—such triggering events resemble a stone falling into the water and causing ripples. This noticeableness and questionableness contains an element of disorder (*ataxia*) that disrupts the waves of order (*taxis*). Something is noticed or becomes questionable—this challenges us in a way that is best described with impersonal verbs: one should say "it thinks," just as one says "it is lightning" (Ger.: *es blitzt*) (Lichtenberg). Hence we have questionability without a questioner, claims without a claimant, challenge without a challenger—similar to Kant's speaking of "purposefulness without purpose."

"In the last analysis, even this 'it thinks' goes too far: this 'it' already contains an *interpretation* of the process and is not part of the process itself" (Nietzsche, II, 581; *Beyond Good and Evil,* # 17). The "process itself" sounds like the "thing itself," which, however, is not accessible without interpretation. Yet the point is not to go chasing after something free of interpretation, but to so displace the interpretation grid, without which we could not speak at all, that a trace of the unordered glimmers through the orderly. One part of these interpretive grids is the pair of antonyms "to do" and "to suffer," action and passion. This pair of opposites becomes unusable, at least in the form in which action and passion mark a happening that can be seen once through the eyes of the actor who causes something, then again through the eyes of the recipient to whom something happens (cf. 4: 4, below). This one-sided in- and output leaves no room for question and answer and for the interweaving of statement and counterstatement. There are two operational centers, *between* which nothing happens. Even reciprocal action, in which two actors simultaneously affect one another, does not change this at all; and even interaction, in which different actions are coordinated, does not lead to an intermediary action. To avoid this uneven distribution and attribution of actions and passions, it is recommended to speak of events that allow for various forms of cooperation, collaboration, and, in the extreme case, also one-sided action (*Einwirkung*).

Where there is no clear attribution of actions and statements, the possibility of localizing them in certain bearers of action and speech also diminishes. Insofar as the "it" is the last successor to that kind of "subject," this would in fact still be too much. The question of who has to do with what or with whom, and who or what someone or something *is* in any given case, must be answerable in terms of the intermediary events themselves and has to be kept free of such marks of recognition as *object, subject,* or *fellow subject*. Between represented object and representing subject and co-representing co-subject, no threads of speech and action could be attached and there would be no place left for a responsive rationality, because what opposes does not play along. The orders whose indispensable work will be considered in the following pages would have all too easy a game without such fellow players and antagonists.

2
Order as Selection and Exclusion

1. Speech and Action in Context

As FAR AS POSSIBLE, the art of textual interpretation routinely regards sentences as parts of a text and treats them within the framework of a context. For they become a great deal less comprehensible if not regarded in their function as title, verse, premise, or quotation, as component of a fable, a scientific treatise, or a political speech, and left in the context where they exercise their function. A single sentence does not act here as an elementary or fundamental unit but as a textual fragment like the shards and torsos excavated by the archaeologist. And where the accidental or intentional fragment develops a special expressive power, this power depends precisely on what the fractured places suggest. That it seems to be different with everyday statements and actions is not due to their own intrinsic character but rather to the different kind of interest with which they are regarded.

First, it must be kept in mind that there "is" no such thing as independent individual sentences and individual actions or uninterpreted basic sentences and basic actions, but rather that it is by detaching them from their context and neutralizing their relations that they are processed out. Linguistic expressions occur in connection with work instructions, service agreements, medical examinations, parliamentary debates, court hearings, sermons, philosophical disputes, textbooks, love avowals, or table conversations—there is no such thing as a dialogical statement pure and simple. The same is true of moral acts such as killing or lying; they occur as negligent homicide, manslaughter while under the influence of alcohol, premeditated murder during a robbery, an organized Mafia "hit," a terrorist act, or the murder of a hostage; or as perjury, fraudulent medical malpractice, an espionage trick, a false tax statement, or a white lie. Every statement and every action thus occurs *indirectly,* refracted through the medium of intermediary sectors, forms, and authorities. Direct speech would trail off into a scream, just as a direct action would contract into a reflex, a direct item of cognition into a momentary insight; these are boundary cases that approach a purely passive occurrence, and no theory of speech and action can be derived from them.

If, nonetheless, in contexts of the theory of speech and action so much is said about individual statements, speech acts, and instrumental, strategic, and communicative actions, that is because a specific interest is dominant—namely, an interest in linguistic and logical correctness, in truth, efficiency, or rightness, i.e., in a normified regularity applicable to any cases whatsoever. Little could be said against this isolating consideration as long as it admits its methodological option, except that it runs the danger of overlooking or underestimating the determinative ordering occurrence that precedes every application of normative rules. The one-sided fixation of the look upon questions of validity tends to immerse the twilight situation of order in an artificial light that causes the origin and own constraints (*Eigenzwänge*) of order to be forgotten. To this extent the following contrasting of importance and rightness aims to shift the weights and not merely to fill the gaps left by others. The insistence on contexts does not correspond to the coziness of a "local reason"; rather, it feeds on the sparks of a "scattered reason."

2. Diachronic and Synchronic Connections

The re-articulation of speech and action into texts and contexts points in two distinguishable but not separable directions, the diachronic dimension of sequences and the synchronic dimension of fields and settings. For the diachronic aspect I suggest the following distinctions of concepts. I define "speech" (*Rede*) as an articulated, relatively coherent series of statements, which leaves open the question of with whom the discourse is carried on and to what extent it is done by linguistic means. I call a "plot" (*Intrige*) an articulated, relatively coherent series of actions, leaving open the question with whom the action is carried out, for even an individual actor consults with himself or herself. As far as "statement" and "action" are concerned, I will settle for defining them in several attempts and for various occasions. With regard to "speech," one would have to refer to text and dialogue theories and sociological analyses of conversations; in this connection, one could speak of "discourse" (*Diskurs*), but this term is already strongly occupied for other purposes. The term "plot" as a narratable story points to diverse attempts at a theory of narrativity, such as have developed mainly in the context of literary theories and historiography. In the present context we are less concerned with narrative structure than with the characterization of the sequence of action as the locus for a production and reproduction of order, in which synchrony and diachrony are closely intermeshed. I reserve the term "discourse" for a relatively self-contained domain of order encompassing speech and action. This provisional inventory of terms may suffice at this point; I will return to it later.

The synchronic dimension deals with the establishment of various forms of order. Field and setting define the space in which statements and actions solidify into preferential orders, which in turn are subject to normative regulations. This situatively developing spatiality itself has a temporal aspect, just as vice versa the temporality of the sequence in its simultaneous density takes on a spatial aspect. At this point, it is above all the concept of field that needs a detailed preliminary clarification, which takes us into a domain of investigation of a psychology inspired by physics.

3. Field of Force as Scenario

The concept of field originated, as is well known, in nineteenth-century physics and was first exploited systematically in Maxwell's theory of the electromagnetic field. Researchers inspired by Gestalt theory, such as Wolfgang Köhler and Kurt Lewin, transposed the term to the psychology of perception and to social psychology. From there it was adopted by phenomenological authors such as Husserl, Aron Gurwitsch, and Merleau-Ponty, who after cleansing it of admixtures from physics used it for a theory of consciousness, perception, and action. Bühler's two-field theory, with its duality of deictic and symbolic field, spans another bridge between action- and speech-theory and language-field research, which deals with changing word-fields. Most recently Bourdieu continues this tradition in the elaboration of a theory of the social field. This far-reaching career of a concept first restricted to a theorem in a single science should alert us: it could be, perhaps, that this concept opens a breach and indicates a more general rethinking. The attraction exerted even by the physics term probably stems from the fact that magnitudes of force are assigned to determinate points in space and thus are distributed over a field of forces. Kurt Lewin accordingly correlated human behavior with temporal and situational values, an attempted model whose limits cannot be discussed here. Decisive is that the spatiotemporal assignment of forces and processes means a turning away from the empty space-time schemata of classical physics with which philosophy since Kant too often operated. Scientific research here brings back into view something that seemed pushed back to prescientific everyday ideas but is only too familiar from ancient cosmologies—namely, that something has *its* place and accordingly also *its* time. If, however, in this connection one speaks of drawing closer to the old cosmologies' ideas of order, this must be taken with a grain of salt.

Disregarding the specific problematic of the field in physics and limiting ourselves to the field of experience as the locus of speech and action, we can define the concept of field as follows: *field is an internally articulated domain of experience, flexibly demarcated from the outside, whose boundary lines and lines of force converge on shifting locations within the domain.* Related with field are concepts such as "scene," "stage," or "setting" (G. Politzer, based on Freud), "framework" (Goffman), and "social space" (Bourdieu). Speaking of scenes or settings has the happy effect that these terms connote the entire surrounding field of what is happening, the places of the players, including in Shakespeare, for instance, storm and lightning, bright daylight and dark night, and also connoting props and backdrops, as well as the limitation of the stage setting. This artificial setting corresponds to the scene of a landscape that combines the natural and the artificial, including a "cityscape" (W. Benjamin). The essential fact about a "dramaturgical action" enacted in such places is not the self-portrayal that puts oneself on the scene, but the performance of the drama itself, which is not directly dependent on an audience (cf. Politzer 1978, 193 ff.). If the dramaturgical action, together with dramatic speech, were reduced to a drama of expression, not much would be left of the ground from which speech (*lexis*) and action (*praxis*) stem.

The form of organization of the field and fieldlike regions is set off from an empty spatiotemporal scheme, and likewise from an all-embracing spatiotemporal order assigned to things once and for all. An empty space-time scheme would offer too little, since something would never find its place in it; a universal space-time order would offer too much, because in it everything would have its place once and for all. In the first case the position from which the whole develops would be nowhere; in the second it would be everywhere. The empty scheme is an abstract construct that cannot integrate and explain the concrete field order, whereas the cosmos does not first need to be organized, because it is order itself. The field, however, resembles a cosmos that has become too small; adjustments have to be made, because too much seeks a place in it. The resulting play of forces requires attempts at ordering on an elementary level.

4. Theme and Relevance

The field would thus be a time-space in which not everything finds a place in the same way. A minimal condition for anything at all to happen in this space is that something must *stand out* and *emerge* from a background. Without such a differentiation into figure and ground there would be only a monotonous indifference; we would have no point of reference to talk about or reason to act. And we ourselves would sink into gray on gray, for where nothing is, there is also no one. Here we are dealing with a first form of selection and exclusion. One thing's occurrence means the departure or non-occurrence of the other, whereby the ground out of which something emerges itself retains something of a threshold over which one thing crosses, another not. In this way a relief is formed with a *foreground* and *background.* Echoing the language of Gestalt theory, which speaks of privileged forms of perception and movement all the way down to physiological behavior, we designate the privileged topic of discourse and object of activity as the *theme,* just as Husserl and Aron Gurwitsch do, while at the same time alluding to William James's distinction between "object" and "topic." The theme would be something that appears as *this thing.* As long as we do not from the outset presuppose an all-encompassing cosmos and usurp the position of a cosmic theorist with an overall view of everything, this thematization does not leap further ahead than other thematizations. Therefore selection, in the original sense, does not mean a choice among existing experiential realities, but rather a choice from among proffered possibilities of experience—namely, in the sense of realizing one, which at the same time makes something else impossible. The selection among existing offers can begin only once an order to which one refers back is established.

This situation, which *in a certain way* resembles that of the divine Spirit who causes a world to arise, suggests the need to modify Leibniz's formulation and ask: "Why in any given case is there this and not rather that?" When the reference to the best of all possible worlds is eliminated for lack of a universal world standard, only more modest answers can be given. A first answer is: because this is *important,* that on the other hand is *unimportant* or *less important.* In the aftermath of Dilthey, Heidegger, and Alfred Schutz, we are accustomed to speak of "significance" or "relevance."

The various terms have their particular connotations. "Significance" (*Bedeutsamkeit*) refers to the sphere of meaning (*Bedeutung*), interpretation, and sign, where something makes itself noticeable; "relevance" or "relevancy" (Lat.: *relevare*) illuminates the process of bulging forth and setting off that allows something to come into relief; finally, "importance" (*Wichtigkeit*) connotes the element of weight and weightiness. The last-mentioned term, the most everyday one of all, has the advantage of alluding to the play of forces always activated in the various modes of organization. There are further indications of this in everyday and philosophical language, for instance when St. Augustine assigns a "gravity" to the soul (*pondus animi*), when reasons are being "weighed" in the process of "pondering" (*deliberatio*), and when the attention is accompanied by tension, exertion, and release (*cf. at-tentio, in-tentio*), or when something is pushed into the background or to the margin. Orientation by a pure consciousness, a pure sense (*Sinn*), and a pure validity has led to an excessive downgrading of force, as if only blind mechanisms existed where forces rule.

Reference to importance or relevancy does not complete the task. An absolute relevancy would put us back into a universal order culminating in *the* Good, and hence it would close off the horizon of inquiry. Otherwise there remains only a relative relevancy—relative to what? Three directions of reference are open to us: (a) emergence—something sets itself off *from* a background; (b) appearance—something presents itself *to* someone; (c) concomitance—something occurs *with* something else. The question of the ground against which a theme is formed could be pursued in these three directions and the *relevancy-criteria* underlying the respective privileging would have to be examined. Insofar as it is a matter of different contexts seeking regulation we can speak of theme-formation as an ordering process.

Let us begin with the first relation. (a) Something sets itself off from a background because it is important, while on the contrary what moves back or stays back is unimportant or less important. Can there be privileging criteria for this without resorting to an absolute privileging? I can seek to compare what exists, but how can I compare what exists with something that does not exist? Gestalt theory makes a certain attempt to answer this question by its laws of form—for example, the law of meaningful detail (*Prägnanz*), which allows one to speak of "good forms" and thus to make a distinction within the sphere of the sensorily perceptible. Actually, our spontaneous perception does not realize equivalently all possibilities of what would be physiologically realizable, and something similar is true of our own movement. But apart from the fact that these regularities have remained very hypothetical to this day, the findings made in such laboratory situations merely restrict the arbitrariness of our culture- and milieu-specific forms of organization without adequately explaining them. Gestalt theory thus provides some such thing as a formal syntax of seeing and hearing that lags far behind their semantic and pragmatic contents. Wheel and apple are examples of circular or globular forms, but one can neither ride on such a form nor eat it. That there are restrictive rules here too is suggested if simple examples are called to mind. Is it conceivable that in a certain culture the ever-returning sun, cats running around, thunder, or rain get absolutely *no* attention, are given absolutely *no* name, and remain forever in the background? If we answer with a cautious "No," this refers to the phenomenon of *noticeableness,* which can be intensified all the way to *obtrusiveness.* This seems to have brought us to the second relation (b), which guides our look toward importance to someone. For is not, on the whole, this thing noticeable to one person and that thing to another?

But here the accustomed subjectivation must be avoided. Noticing something or the coming to mind of something, which makes it a theme, is, first of all, a spontaneous occurrence; it is not a positing, as the word "theme" might suggest, but rather—as Aron Gurwitsch repeatedly emphasizes—a form of *self-organization* not controlled by an ego (cf. already Kant, *KU* B, 292). If one wanted willfully and knowingly to evoke this vortex in the field of experience, producing determinate patterns, it would be necessary to have the things from which one selects on hand in advance, in order merely to sort out finished experiences rather than have new ones, and absolutely nothing would be left of the differentiation into figure and background. Plato's aporia from *Menon*—which can be summed up as follows: we cannot seek anything because we either already know what we are looking for and do not need to seek it, or we do not know it and so cannot seek it—is repeated here in the mirror-image form of *coming to mind* and *being noticeable.* Crossing the threshold or staying on it as announced in such intermediate events would, in an active interpretation, be sacrificed to a distinct this-side or beyond. But "something comes to my attention" or "something comes to my mind" signifies an occurrence that, precisely, crosses the threshold between the known and the unknown without a given "object" facing an active "subject." The question of "who?" is taken back as an indirect object "to whom." If there is here a genesis and a synthesis, then—in Husserl's words—it is a passive one.

So if activities of the "subject" are not responsible for the occurrence of something, perhaps deeper, more underlying dispositions and movements are. Following Husserl and Aron Gurwitsch once again, a specific *interest* on the part of the person experiencing, speaking, and acting corresponds to the theme; privileging in the "object sphere" has its counterpart in a privileging within the "act sphere." Experiencing persons do not, it can be pointed out, enter the world of experience as a blank page, but rather with determinate needs, drive stirrings, inclinations, and preferences that bind them bodily to the world and make them receptive to this and not to that. Yet this too would be a sufficient explanation for the occurrence of this or that only if human beings were either moving along totally in the "go-cart of instinct" or else stood completely under the "guidance of reason" (Kant, VI, 92). In the one case, nature would have made the choice by programs of heredity and learning, regulated by the pressure of survival; in the other, humans would as "super-animal" or "almost-god" (Nietzsche) have created their own world. But a seamless world that wanted to cover the abysses in either of these ways contradicts humankind's starting situation. Our peculiar combination of lack and excess forces us to make regulations that are fully covered neither by an "objective" relevancy, nor by a "subjective" relevancy. The latter is out of the question by the very fact that the allegedly selecting function of the "subject" occurs itself only in the selective form of an "interested subject." To explain selection by a "subject" would mean to explain selection by a part of itself. The first relation, which concedes a certain weight of its own to what occurs, thus cannot be absorbed by the second relation. That is exactly why something remains for the speaker or actor to link to, no matter what such a speaker or actor is dealing with.

Finally there remains the third relation (c). We will deal with it more extensively in the following pages; it too does not provide an answer to the question: "Why in any given case does this occur and not rather that?" For that with which something occurs, another thing becomes important only when that other thing itself becomes the theme. A retroaction of the accompanying thing upon what it accompanies is conceivable only when a context has already been established so that the referential relation can be reversed, as with the boy and his lyre in Plato's *Phaido*.

Our question, "Why does this occur rather than that?" finds no answer—at least not here—that would put an end to the question. If there were *no reasons* for this occurrence, the only thing left would be an allusion to a chance happening, which then recurs on a higher plane as an arbitrary positing. This answer not only contradicts experience, which shows that what we notice and what occurs to us is by no means arbitrary, but would be just as controvertible as the opposite answer, which promises a *sufficient reason*. What we encounter, here and always, are certain reasons that limit the scope of arbitrariness without closing the abyss that provokes the origin of orders.

5. Horizontal Expansion:
Thematic Field and Marginal Zones

The appearance of something in a field is connected with a further mode of organization: the respective something *points* to something else that appears *with it* and is more or less closely connected with it. This second ordering achievement is just as indispensable as the first. For something that merely sets itself off from a neutral background would be simply something, but not a determinate something. To that extent the association is equally original with the something. Something appears as the knot in the net and not as a simple and solitary element that the demiurge can make into anything whatever without reacting to something. Without the original linkage with something else, only a dissonant miscellany would remain, fleeting impressions indistinguishable from phantoms (cf. Husserl, IV, § 15). We speak of "horizontal" generalization insofar as the something that occurs points beyond itself without leaving the plane of concretion. This involves generalization by proliferation, not by subordination, and it corresponds to the *genus,* not in the logical but in the generative sense.

The Leibnizian question recurs here in a new form: "Why, in each case, is something with this and not rather with that?" The first answer is, in turn: because this is *important,* consequential, pertinent to that something while that, on the contrary, is *not.* Again a selection and exclusion occurs. The aggregate of what stands in an intrinsic, objective relation to the theme we call, with Aron Gurwitsch, the "*thematic field*"; what stands in an extrinsic, merely temporal relation to the theme would then be the "*margin.*" The thematization that brings something into the center of focus creates contexts and has a marginalization as its reverse side. The two things happen at one stroke like a double choice that is made on the two axes of language, a choice that makes one thing occur *instead* of the other (*paradigma*) and one *with* the other (*syntagma*) (Jakobson 1974a, 117 ff.). The physical measurements that use a spectrogram do not become more precise when their color scales remind one of Paul Klee's paintings, and the danger of a wound does not depend on whether a burglar is cut by smashing a windowpane or a party guest by breaking a wineglass. The change of theme immediately colors its surrounding field; what is a bothersome weed for the farmer can be a rare plant worth preserving for the botanist. One "belongs there," the other does not.

But where do we get the criteria to decide whether such contexts exist or not? If their coherence were a strict implication, in the most extreme case even a logical consequence, then something would carry along with it the comet's tail of pertinent data, and no further problem would arise. If, on the other hand, we were dealing with an initial lack of any coherence, then each thing could link up with any other random thing. The results would be only forced marriages or accidental acquaintanceships, not elective affinities, though these can be traced back all the way to the *attractio electiva* of chemical elements. If we keep away from these speculative extremes, then contexts, where they are not merely reproduced, must be posited and established. In a process of invention, a theme is struck and it detaches possibilities of execution without prescribing a determinate possibility. The theme resembles less a cornerstone than a place in the landscape from which ways to discovery and exploitation are open. The regulation of contexts, then, consists in the privileging of certain possibilities of coherence and continuation and the repression of others. In this way the multivalency and ambiguity of events is reduced.

This process of marginalization does not take place in peaceful agreement. Margins, of whatever kind, whether marginal phenomena, marginal groups, or "marginal nations" arise by something being *forced* to the edge where the light no longer reaches. This exclusion is not done without disturbance and danger. Even a "whistle from the street" can distract me from my "line of thought" and perhaps "impose itself" as a "disruptive theme" (Husserl, III, 302; *Ideas,* 344). Of course, the whistle from the street is not as such a disturbance, just as no plant as such is a weed. When something is felt to be or treated as a weed, a defense is activated; the theme is asserted against distracting forces. The disturbance need not come from banal whistles; the most beautiful musical sounds can impose themselves noisily (cf. Kant, *KU* B, 221). Thus the boundaries of the thematic fields reveal their mobility. A spotlight theory that merely has a beam of light wander back and forth without affecting the "sensory content" of what is illuminated and what is left in the shadows (Husserl, III, 230; *Ideas,* 269; critical appraisal by Gurwitsch 1966, chap. 10) lets this twilight dynamics of experience glide into irrelevancy. Marginalization does not mean a mere play of shadows. At any rate, one should beware of any one-sided imagery. The margin metaphor stems from the idea of an optical centering of the field of consciousness with a bright central zone and dark edge zones. If other metaphors are drawn upon such as that of the screen or net, this suggests possible *holes* or *gaps* in the ordering system—a system that knows not only outer boundaries, but also internal articulation of the domain of order. As Wittgenstein says: "The idea sits so to speak like eyeglasses on our nose" (*Phil. Untersuchungen,* Nr. 103)—the question is only whether one can simply take them off.

6. Vertical Elaboration: Typical and Atypical

The two primary functions of order are joined, finally, by a third one: what occurs with something else, occurs at the same time *as such a thing.* In Husserl's language, which we here apply with caution, this means that the thematic object is constituted with a determinate thematic sense, whether in the form of a material differentiation—something as a tool, natural object, symbol, etc.—or in the sense of a qualitative differentiation—something as perceived, remembered, imagined, judged, dealt with, etc. The privileged something is thus always privileged in a determinate sense. The *thematic sense* colors the thematic contexts directly, for depending on how the thematic sense is modified, we live in a world of sounds, or in a world of work or signs, or respectively in a world of perception, memory, phantasy, or practical decision. If something did not in each case occur as *such* a thing, it would not be a something that outlasts its moment, it would be an ineffable pure event.

We speak of *vertical* generalization insofar as here something grows out beyond itself, without subjecting itself to an ideal formal scheme. The gestalt in which something occurs as something still lies this side of the difference between ideality and facticity, that is, in a zone of indifference we must accept unless we want to impute givenness to products of distinction such as form and matter. The difference that appears in the "as" and makes the actual more than actual is *reiterability,* which must be thought of as a kind of permanent reembodiment, as it were, a "migration of the body" (Merleau-Ponty 1984, 69; *Prose,* 47 n.: "metemsomatics") that already impresses its stamp upon the elementary reactions of corporeal sensation and movement and conveys its specific rhythm on the incipient forms of tool use and symbolic expression (Leroi-Gourhan, *G&S,* 281 ff.). That something occurs as something means that it occurs *again:* when I speak of something, it is already there; an absolute original would be incomprehensible. The paradox of repetition now consists in something's occurring *as the same,* although this reoccurrence brings into play at least a tiny difference. Repetition is the return *as the same* of *what is not the same.* This tiny gap runs through all aspects of the "deictic field." Something appears as *this* that is simultaneously *other, here* and simultaneously *elsewhere, now* and simultaneously *another time;* and this also applies to *this person* who is simultaneously *another person* who is dealing with *this one* and *another.* The original shift in the field of experience, which allows no pure origin to come up, offers at the same time the possibility for something or someone to become involved with another without taking the detour via separate agencies that would be responsible everywhere and incessantly for each thing and person. Order arises when somewhere and sometime something or someone appears who is always only what and who it is by returning to itself without arriving there, and in this way has a future. This "sensory idea" (Merleau-Ponty *V&I,* 151, referring to Proust), based on Husserl, Schutz and Gurwitsch, we call *"type,"* an outline form such as a rubber stamp leaves behind, that is, not a free-floating eidos and not a detached concept. Gestalt theory points in the same direction when it restricts the "ideality" of materialized forms to a transposability that is not without remainder like a formula; for a formula, upon repeated use, leaves no afterimage behind, as do gestalts of color and tone. This materiality of the general corresponds to a corporeality of experience in which no mental eye or mental ear has yet detached itself from the sensory.

If we ask again in Leibniz's aftermath: "Why does something occur as such and not rather as something else?" we could answer once again: because certain traits and aspects emerge as *important,* while others do not. If we ask further about the criteria to which this privileging is subject, an old answer is available: the traits that always recur are important. This would approximate the separation into typical and atypical (cf. Schutz 1971, 108) to the difference between essential and unessential. But this answer presupposes that a true typology exists once and for all. Such an assumption fails, however, because something can appear as such *or* as something else, thereby bringing ever different typologies into play. A body of water can be used as a reservoir for drinking water, a fish pool, a bathing area, or a sewerage basin, and what must count as typical and which characteristics matter changes accordingly.

Inevitably, events are formed and the typical is separated from the atypical. One could as little respond to a concrete event or thing in which everything were equally important as the organism can react to a stimulus that is not processed according to determinate patterns. A concrete event that was not subjected to this forming would be neither repeatable nor recognizable; it could not even be named. It would rush past like an unfamiliar music or a discourse in a completely unknown language; as long as determinate structures and recurrences have not taken shape, it makes no sense for me to say that I have heard this before. It would be the same as saying I stepped into this water before. Nor can such a forming be reduced to the empirical-static occurrence of certain traits under given circumstances, that is, to what is generally expected because it usually happens. Such a methodologically leveling external view, which applies scientific relevancy criteria without reference to the speaker or actor, can serve for empirically checking out the speech and action situations; their own criteria, however, are lost in this way. The point may someday be reached that Black Forest firs, on the average, have more yellow than green needles; yet a forester would hardly think of rejecting the green needles as atypical. Typology refers to all three relations we have distinguished with regard to formation of the theme. Theme, relevancy, and typology remain closely interrelated as long as we keep the lifeworld perspectives in view.

The question of the selection criteria in typification leads us to a similar point as thematization. The choice is not made arbitrarily, nor is it guided by unchangeable selection criteria. *The type is an essence for a time.* As little as there is a disturbance pure and simple, so little is there something atypical as such. The emergence of margins through thematization corresponds to the rise of the atypical through typification. This *countercurrent* must be distinguished from the *incidental* or accidental, which finds a place within the scheme of types (x as y) such that it can be replaced by equivalent values. Thus in the usual bathing regulations it does not matter what color a bathing cap has, although of course it always has one and color as such is a category in typology. But if someone were to go into the water wearing a motorcycle helmet, the lifeguard's reaction can easily be foreseen. Yet just as a disturbance can be the condensation nucleus for a new theme, the atypical can be the nucleus for a new type. Unlike the eidos, the type is not protected, by some sort of eternal return, from any changes. This is one reason why ordering mechanisms multiply.

7. *Typology and Chronology of Speech and Action*

The formation of a field, in which something occurs with something else as such a thing, reaches into the orders of speech and action and causes them to intermesh with the structures of experience. The deictic field marks a topology and chronology of speech and action whose corporeal belonging to the field singles out determinate directions and prescribes determinate routes. The deictic gesture that singles out and highlights *this thing here* is continued in the demonstrative pronoun, for this word remains empty without reference back to a standpoint where it is pronounced. A reference to "him" or "it" on the telephone or a "today" in the body of a letter remains incomprehensible by itself. But we are not concerned here with the well-known theory of occasional or indexical expressions, but rather with the selective ordering functions that occur irreplaceably here and are continued in the acts of naming. Without such pre-linguistic work on the referent, there would be no subject of the sentence for something to be predicated of, nor any goal of action to be pondered. Neither the act of pointing nor that of naming is a mere element of a language act, because each precedes and transcends the rules of language. Thus the regulating factor of importance enters into the regulations of speech and action, and all theories that place the ordering achievements under the primacy of rightness are left with a blind spot.

Except for the cases where a field structure is merely reproduced and a ritual repeated, every speech and action presupposes a thematics in which is determined *what, when, where,* and *how, by whom, to whom,* or *with whom, under what circumstances* something is said and done and what typically can be said again and done again. When someone regards the process of thematization with the eyes of a judge after the fact, this occurrence shrinks to a preexisting state of facts, for which witnesses are summoned. But Aristotelian rhetoric already taught that the past dominates only in a particular form of discourse, namely, in court language, but not in deliberative discourse that articulates what still has to be done rather than what has already been done. The achievement of order, performed in the origination and continuation of a theme, itself precedes any normification, because it first of all defines and creates situations to which norms are applicable. If we did not speak, we could not contradict ourselves or lie; if we began no game, we could not play wrongly or unfairly. That all regulations leave some latitude for speech and activity is certainly common knowledge to every current praxis and hermeneutics, whether oriented on Aristotle or Kant, Wittgenstein or Gadamer. But the impression of matter-of-courseness is lost when we reflect on what exclusion processes are already activated in the forefield of norm-guided speech and action.

Among these, in case of conflict, are arguments that do not operate with antitheses such as true or false or right or wrong, but with statements such as: "*This is not important, this is beside the point, this has nothing to do with it, this comes too early or too late, it is not your turn.*" A pure judge of validity, whose truths neither know time pressure nor tolerate delay and are never out of place, seems to be able to accomplish little here. Examples enough, ranging from implicit to explicit and formal statements, can be found in the various thematic fields and discourses, whether it be a question of job planning, setting the daily agenda, news selection, lesson plans, examination schedules, research subsidies, economic investments, or everyday budgeting of time, food menus, or vacation plans. These selections could be removed from the conflict zone only if there existed universal orders of goods and scales of value. Something similar applies to the form of thematic contexts and the kind of exclusion: connections can be more or less loose; boundaries can be drawn more or less strictly. Think of the rules of drama such as unity of place and time, or methodological requirements for scientific treatises. How systematic must a text be? What may it allow in? How much "anarchy" can be tolerated? Or in the field of action: how much improvisation is expected of the employee, how strict are the job guidelines? What may a patient or plaintiff say without being punished by the doctor or judge by being silenced or ignored? What reading materials are allowed for children (formerly also: for women)? The reference to proven traditions is no answer to our question, because traditions themselves represent a conflicting and selective process whose selection mechanisms are covered over by canonizations, official or unofficial. A canon is a "truth" that has gained acceptance—but was it by its own power? At any rate, a task for institutional research is to detect the selective agencies and selection mechanisms that reach deep into the anonymous. Cultural leaders, school directors, art dealers, revolutionaries, captains of industry, popes, and spokespersons of every kind are often founding figures who are named after the fact, although they perhaps merely followed the most favorable wind.

It looks, then, as if whatever appears important stemmed from a dubious self-importance. This impression could be false or at least premature, for the question of how to evaluate these selections and from where they draw their possible convincing power will be asked only later when we discuss the change of orders. At this point we must stress merely the twilight of an order that begins on a pre-normative level and casts its shadows on all further order. Only the person who sees how experiences are arranged from the very beginning will distrust a normative euphoria even when it mounts to rational self-normification.

8. Importance and Rightness

The shift from the organization of fields of speech and action to the plane of the judgment and justification of acts of speech and action acquires clear contours when the criteria of both importance and rightness are tentatively counterposed. These two criteria are understood here as bundles of criteria: importance extends, as was shown, to theme, thematic field, and typology; in this global reflection, rightness shall include all forms of binary judgment, including truth as *rectitudo* (rightness). The comparison of the two criteria reveals significant differences in the kind of order-formation.

(a) The predicate "important" refers primarily to something that is the object of speech or action, and it radiates from there to all other factors of speech and action. The predicate "right" refers, on the contrary, to *behavioral* acts and their results.

(b) The predicate "important" as a rule appears as a *relative* determination: something is important in certain contexts, for someone, etc., and it can be applied without further ado comparatively: something is more important and less important. The predicate "right" as a rule occurs as an *absolute* determination; where conditions are indicated, they do not affect the character of validity itself, but the domain of application, which can be limited and admits of exceptions. Such sentences as the following are prototypical: "Whenever . . . , then . . ." or "Everyone who. . . ." The absolute mode of application is also shown by the fact that the comparative use in the strict sense is impossible: it doesn't quite make sense to say "more right than . . . , truer than. . . ." Someone who robs only $10,000 is not acting more rightly than someone who robs $20,000. A weighting of violations is different than a weighting of interests. (I add, in both cases, "as a rule," because there are theories that attempt to undermine the distinction made here, but that would take us too far afield.)

(c) Where several themes vie with one another for the attribute of importance, we speak of a *"conflict,"* whereas statements or modes of action that vie with one another for the attribute of rightness stand in *contradiction* to one another. Two conflicting claims can both be important; two contradictory statements cannot both be true. Even what we call dissent must be differentiated accordingly.

(d) What is excluded as unimportant is pushed aside, but this marginal or atypical element can become the condensation nucleus of *another* order; all that is needed is a *reordering* of the field of speech and activity. On the contrary, what is excluded as wrong bears the stain of disorder in itself; it takes a *revolution* to let what is excluded have its turn. The negative prefix does not mean the same in un-important and in-correct.

In view of these double determinations, a displacement between the two functional domains has important consequences for the status of order, which interests us.

9. Normality and Disturbed Behavioral Functions

A preliminary form of normative rightness is normality. What is involved, here too, is not the productive or reproductive organization of a field with its preferred themes, but rather the qualification or disqualification of certain modes of behavior, whose link with the content is loosened in the course of this appraisal. Normality, as here understood, presupposes a norm just as does normativity, but this norm does not approach behavior with commands and prohibitions; but rather, it is inbuilt in behavior as a standard to gauge whether it is *functioning appropriately* or not. In an elementary but not infallible way, the promotion and hindering of life are announced in pleasure and pain (cf. Kant, VI, 551). The scale of functionality extends from the boundary value of optimal performance, through the disturbed performance, to the boundary value of a *catastrophic* behavior (Goldstein 1934). What is not functional is separated off as an anomaly.

The classic example for this domain is the pair of contraries of *healthy* and *sick* or normal and pathological (Canguilhem). What is peculiar to this example is that here impairment is seen from the perspective of a patient, which carries the consideration beyond a purely statistical stocktaking of physico-chemical processes. There is no question that from a physico-chemical standpoint the metastasis of a cancer patient is something perfectly normal. But though every sickness is an anomaly, not every anomaly is a sickness (Goldstein 1934, 266; *The Organism,* 428). Body size can also be abnormal, which then is a noticeable impediment in the use of normal arrangements such as doors and beds or buying clothing. Another example would be the left-hander who is not simply the mirror-image brother of the right-handed person but rather encounters a society where writing is done from left to right, where instrumental exercises count on right-handedness, which assures the outsider of a certain surprise advantage in tennis. Normality or abnormality of the body overlap with the "prolongation of the body" in tools and machines. Deviations from the standard measurement go as far as unuseableness. Finally, even in the ordinary course of perception there are optimal and bad conditions, if we think of lighting, angle of view, or viewing distance. We also come upon the phenomena of *orthoaesthesia* (Husserl, XIII, 379) and of *orthokinesis,* which antecede the modes of behavior applied normatively to orthodoxy and orthopraxis.

The question arises here too: from where do the *criteria* come to distinguish functional or healthy from disturbed or sick behavior? Although it can be expected that our behavior in this regard also is to a certain degree released from instinctive arrangements and left to artificial regulations, it follows from this that functional disturbances and sickness, too, are not given purely by nature, but stem from processes of a selective normalization. To a certain degree, health and sickness—all the way to madness—are also products of culture. By no means does it follow that the boundary can be drawn arbitrarily, for nature would soon penalize this very painfully. A relativism would surely have to be heroic to survive the operation table. In pathology, stereotype and absolute arbitrariness appear as complementary disturbances (cf. Merleau-Ponty 1976, 49; *SB,* 44). Or to cite one of Goldstein's examples: the patient S., whose color-name amnesia is accompanied by the inability to sort balls of yarn, reaches the narrow crest where orientation variability shifts into disorientation. Foucault may intentionally apply this to shatter the order of things (1971, Foreword), but it becomes effective only in contrast to existing orders. The patient S., who struggles with the balls of yarn, and Borges, who celebrates the heterotopias of a Chinese encyclopedia, are separated by the "thin sheet of paper" that Joyce says separates the artist from madness.

Hence no removal of the difference between health and sickness is available, but surely, rather, attention to the process of differentiation and exclusion, which always runs the danger of stopping at fixed boundaries, where the dysfunctional, sick, and painful appears as absolute negativity, deficiency, and abnormality, although each form of life, including that of a patient, first must be viewed according to its own different kind of norms—and dealt with accordingly. The assessment of normality has consequences for therapy, which strives to restore order and so faces the question whether what needs to be done is merely to restore the old order or to establish a new one. The patient often stands before the choice "between greater unfreedom and greater suffering" (Goldstein 1934, 281; *Organism,* 449), whereby the lessening of suffering is paid for with a "restriction of the milieu." The overpowering of suffering, as it eliminates the disruptive and pain-causing anomalies, also removes that which goes beyond a pure preservation of life.

10. *Usual Customs and Improper Modes of Behavior*

If we now move on to normativity, we no longer are dealing with a mere disturbance of ordering functions, but with adverseness to order. By norm I understand, according to the familiar idiom, a general prescription of behavior requiring or forbidding that something be done or not done and in this way separating *orderly* from *disorderly* conduct. While normalities allow a flexible way of dealing with them and when not followed avenge themselves by the consequences, it is part of the public validity of norms that they are binding and that behavior against the norms is punished. But obligation and sanction allow for an intensification and sharpening as far as the degree of normification is concerned.

On the ground of mores, customs, or conventions, which embody what one usually says and does, *propriety* is separated from *impropriety, decency* from *indecency*. As can be seen from the classical expressions *prepon* or *decorum,* or the related expressions in our language *"tasteful"* or *"tactful,"* this qualification very easily slides over into aesthetics and applies more to the style of behavior, the paraphernalia of execution, and the splendor of presentation than to the act of behavior with the goal it strives for. The style of action must have separated itself very strongly from the requirements and goals of the action itself before one can declare that murder and torture do not belong to the right tone, and a tastefully inflicted wound no doubt falls into the domain of an aestheticizing cynicism. Generally the requirements of morals are not concerned with murder and fraud, but with the performance of commanded and permitted actions. Mores and habits therefore are generally considered good or bad, not right or wrong. This includes the entire civilized inventory of forms of greeting and address, eating and clothing etiquette, erotic rituals, language habits, styles of writing, hygienic requirements, and the like, which are familiar from old histories of mores and which we find in recent researches into the civilizing process—for instance, in Norbert Elias, Ariès, Foucault, and Bourdieu. A violation of the mores, which are spontaneously considered "good," definitely incurs sanctions, namely, those of *disapproval,* all the way to ostracism. The authority for such sanctions remains closely bound with the anonymous: it is embodied in society but variously differentiated according to milieus, strata, stations, and classes, each of which have their specific moral code and administer their determinate set of rules. To dismiss this mode of order as preliminary would mean to wait for speech, action, and feeling someday to be completely determined by performance rules and their living speakers and doers to be programmed like a computer.

This nightmare would fail, because the carrying out of performance instructions would itself have to rely on instructions; but this usual old argument known from the aporia of a regulated application of rules should not mislead one to draw the opposite conclusion that this informal and diffused form of normification is an inconsequential forefield of law and society. As little as the artist's style of writing and painting signifies an inconsequential prior form to serious ideas, so little does the everyday style of behavior signify an inconsequential prior form to serious morality. The moral of the story begins in the style itself, which in both cases is the very person as embodiment of ideas and norms. To that extent the selection mechanisms that are inevitably inbuilt in every custom strike very sensitively, cutting into the flesh. It is easier to become indignant at a judge than at "society" or a social milieu, where we depend with every fibre of our being on what we wish to be freed from, and it is easier to bribe a gatekeeper than a society, for, even if it admits a person, one can exclude oneself from it by the slightest sound or the slightest movement. "Sit down in the Louis Quatorze armchair" (Proust, II, 554; Eng.: II, 575), says Baron Charlus to his helpless guest in a tone that does not even betray snobbism, but only the self-certainty of an old nobleman who feels as much at home in fine society as a fish in water. Sometimes it is hard to say who excludes whom. Of course, a person can draw advantage from everything, and can try to convert social, cultural, and economic capital one into another (cf. Bourdieu 1983), all the way to "money that knows how to smile" (Proust, I, 639; Eng.: I, 688), but one is thereby merely changing cages. A fissure first opens up when the style and habit of behavior retain their twilight aura. The improper and offensive are not merely a lack of morals, but also a possible way out of a solidified and over-refined stylistic palace.

11. Established Norms and Wrong Behavior

With normativity in the strict sense we enter a much plowed (perhaps even leached out) field, so that I would like to limit myself to a few pertinent remarks. As soon as obligation and sanction grow beyond anonymity and are entrusted to identifiable authorities, and as soon as in addition to modes of behavior, goals and means of action are introduced, a separation between *right* and *wrong* in the strict sense results. Juridical laws are norms that must be followed because they are monitored by an external forum and their violation results in a penalty. Moral laws, moreover, are norms that must be followed by authority of an internal forum and their violation is punished by qualms of conscience and a loss of self-esteem and the respect of others. This legalization and moralization, which can be additionally supported and buttressed up by religious commandments and prohibitions, separates out *abnormalities,* which differ from the merely dysfunctional and uncustomary by their internal disqualification.

A great deal of concentration on the question of validity should not lead us to forget that a series of preliminary questions apply. A first question is: where do norms have their *seat*? If one does not want to hypostasize norms directly into an ideal world, then one must seek them in the place where they exercise their functions, that is, in speech and action, which are guided by them and either follow or do not follow them. Norms are not primarily tables of commands and prohibitions that one contemplates, but rules one observes or does not. In this sense we can speak of *functioning norms.* The question whether norms acquire validity implicitly or explicitly, informally or formally, is important in detail, but secondary with regard to the state of affairs that interests us here. The close connection between the imperative "Act in this way!" and the simple command "Act!" which does *not* draw its incentives from norms, entails that following any norm, even one that claims absolute validity, is linked with conditions that are themselves not normatively regulated. The question of the occurrence of normative validity claims is posed within the framework of fields of action and forms of life, and nowhere else, just as language rules are not suspended from their own language-sky but have their seat in determinate fields of discourse and speech situations. It makes little difference where the concept of the norm is developed, whether by a voice that promulgates its commands from Sinai or by dissuading like Socrates' *daimonion,* or, as the word "norm" itself suggests, by the standard gauge, or finally by a general regularity that also exists in nature in a different way. The linkage of the norm to action and speech has the consequence that the norm too is one of the selection and exclusion mechanisms and as superego restricts the possibilities of responsiveness, whereby a similar split opens between "should" and "can" as between *claim* and *response* on the plane of speech and action. That is so, simply because one can fulfill a promise or a request, but not a general prescription. In this the prescription resembles the unanswerable questions that we face in interlocutionary events and that outlast our answers. In this regard, every general norm first appears as a *foreign* body not assimilated by our experience. What consequences this has and whether it remains that way are questions we will deal with later.

A second question posed here is that of the possible *matter* of the normification. The answer to this question can be: whatever enters speech and action as a constitutive factor can be normified. That applies to the individual elements of any thematics of speech or action (cf. 2: 7, above). Time and place can be normified, as for instance in the case of seating orders, speakers' lists, residency permits, holidays, and examination schedules. But is an answer less true because it is given three hours after the examination? Yet that is of little help to the examinee once the bell has sounded the end of the examination period. Who can associate with whom, who is permitted to perform a surgical operation, what safety regulations have to be observed in it, etc., can be stipulated. The rules become more fixed, the more institutional actions become ceremonies ritualized down to the smallest detail. And even an innocent stroll must not lead, without further ado, through the neighbor's garden. Furthermore, anomalies, even a mere name or unfamiliar accent, can be transformed into negative designations and lead to stigmatization (Goffman). Finally, the domain of manners and rules of etiquette, though generally left to custom, can be included in normification, as in greeting and dress codes, book censorship, or marriage impediments. Conversely, normative regulations, for example in the domain of sexuality, can be weakened down to merely customary practices; or even violations, for instance in the case of kleptomania, can be relegated to sicknesses. The area of law can, as a whole, shift more strongly toward the therapeutic and the social. What keeps ordering in motion are transitions in both directions. The question of a possible general dynamics of the ordering process or the privileged trends within certain traditions cannot, of course, be answered by this typologizing consideration.

A last question concerns the *connection of the norms with one another*. The far-reaching detachment of actions from their synchronic and diachronic contexts results in the norms' profiting only in a limited way from the organization of the fields of speech and action. The old *connexio virtutum* that resulted from the binding of morality into certain forms of life cannot be replaced by normative complexes such as constitutions, law books, or tables of fundamental values; and where the point of view of universality is preponderant, the result is a combination of casuistry and abstract normativity that fails to capture the median level of typical action-contexts and specific rules. A way out might present itself in the above-mentioned recourse to milieus, professional fields, and forms of life that contain their norms entirely in the form of discourses. What is matter-of-course for a theory of language and text—namely, that there is a determinate language system and variable stylistic canon—should be appropriate for a theory of action, for actors do not speak a moral Esperanto.

12. Habit as Embodiment of Order

One-sided orientation on the validity of order leads normification to culminate in fixed norms and everything else to sink into prior and mixed forms. Measured by a rational law, however obtained, and a rational morality, customs seem to be *mere* habits and conventions, at best an arsenal of clever rules guaranteeing a happy and healthy way of life, but related only in a very limited way to obligations. One will agree with Max Weber, who writes: "Everywhere actual tradition has been the father of validity" (1976, 15), while objecting when he keeps open "fluid transitions." Unmixing actually given and internally valid norms turns the fluid transitions into purification plants. A sentence such as: "For the law has no other power to impose itself than habit (*ethos*)" (Aristotle, *Politics,* II, 8, 1269a 20f.) sounds, then, like a sentence from the Kohlberg primer; it marks a stage that precedes the neat distinction between convention and morality. Of course, conventions remain necessary even later; but such as are introduced only as mere conventions—for instance, an orthographic innovation or a tax table—are inconsequential agreements stripped of all prestige. They get their power not from habit, but from a pure positing or continuation. Demystified traditions may well remain in force when their own force is broken. A bit of functional understanding suffices to prevent anti-traditional fanaticism.

The picture changes when we desist from focusing our attention on questions of validity. Aristotle too by no means equates the good with what was handed down by the fathers (*patrion*) (Cf. *Politics,* II, 8). Like the German word "*Gewohnheit*" (habit), the Greek "*ethos*" has to do with accustoming and dwelling.

Thus where "actual practice is based on long *habituation,*" Max Weber too speaks of custom, which is more than mere usage. Once the style of behavior, the way of speaking and walking have entered one's flesh and blood, one does not change them arbitrarily like a necktie. Embodied meaning corresponds to embodied behavior. Habit as acclimatization in a domain of activity and life leads back to the organization of fields of speech and action. Just as a recurring theme outlasts the actual situation and is solidified into a familiar theme, so repeated statements and actions form into an attitude, a habit. The web of such habituations, in turn, forms specific fields of activity and professional fields that outlast specific milieus, and finally forms comprehensive ways of life and lifeworlds in which actual speaking and action are embedded. This habituation means an *incarnation* of order, an "embodiment of structures" (Bourdieu) that happens under changing conditions and can be reduced neither to mechanical processes nor to the application of rules. The acquisition of "know-how" means an ability that transcends all mere knowing. Institutions that are thought from the perspective of such embodiment are not reduced to systems of social rules, role complexes, and coordination strands, plus subjective ingredients. They are *corporations,* in the literal sense. Behind the *homo oeconomicus, politicus . . . academicus* there is no play-actor who puts on and takes off masks; the masks are cut into one's own flesh, and a branding stigmatization was and is more than a mere metaphor.

So there is no question that habituation participates decisively in the selections and exclusions of all order-formation; the learning of determinate forms of statement or action means the unlearning of other possibilities. Habituation of behavior and sedimentation of meaning denotes that even the various selection and exclusion mechanisms become ingrained. Even life, whose "business" Rousseau promises to relearn in his *Émile,* is not an endlessly streaming spring. But does habituation, then, have to do with criteria of importance or with criteria of rightness, or both together? Here we come back to the criteriological distinction by which the previous course of our reflections has been oriented. Methodologically, it can be assumed that such a distinction is not simply given, but is made on the basis of something that divides in this way. Yet the suspicion of any *unmixing* that degrades all custom to mere preliminary or residual forms of legal-moral rightness by no means forces us to go to the other extreme and speak of a fusion of reason and custom, reason and tradition, right action and a good life. The embodiment of orders that in their variability are arranged selectively and exclusively and never go so far as to integrate disorder into their binary grids opens up a intermediate field with movable boundaries. It sanctions neither the emptying of usage and custom to empty shells nor their intensification into a bulwark of morality. Such an embodiment promises, rather, changing constellations, such that even their functions and the mutual delimitation of ordering criteria are affected.

13. Competition of Faculties

Looking back at the various modes of organization, in the end we see a kind of competition of the classical faculties. The structural formation that produces and changes fields of speech and action—which we have placed under the rubric of importance—leaves room for an *economy* of forces, a play of forces, and an interchange of forces, and for a *politics* that raises questions of the dominance and imposition of points of view and standpoints, both related not only to group orders, but also to life-orders of the individual. That there can be a "civil war" in one's own soul is familiar to us, from Plato to Freud. Reference to economics and politics does not imply that the establishment and change of order can be reduced to plays of forces and power struggles; it means only that these factors inevitably affect the ordering process, precisely because orders occur selectively and exclusively.

Norm-formation, which for contrast we have brought under the comprehensive viewpoint of rightness, lands us in other faculties' area of competence. Normality is, not exclusively but prototypically, indebted to *medicine,* since here in case of a disturbance it is a matter of healing. The domain of customs and the customary forms a broad middle zone that is closely connected with specific fields of speech and action, that is, various forms of life. This middle zone is the domain of the *social sciences,* which operate synchronically and diachronically. Normativity in the strict sense finds its support in *jurisprudence,* where in case of violation punishment is the issue. A certain kind of moral philosophy (and moral theology) that focuses primarily on the checking and justification of norms stays methodologically absolutely under the spell of law, just as moralists can be called judges without enforcement power. If *philosophy* takes part in this rivalry, it should do so less one-sidedly and rather in an interdisciplinary style.

This picture may be modified and complemented in details however one wishes; even so, it is probably useful as an orientation chart. Clearly, the various forms of order do not ascend on a continuous scale or combine into an ever-increasing universal order. Above all, there is an irresolvable tension between the domain of field structures and that of norms. The first domain governs a continuous *establishment* of order in a *happening* that can be called productive or reproductive and is oriented to limited wholes such as fields of activity, everyday milieus, and lifeworlds. The second domain governs primarily the *restoration* of orders in processes with a corrective character and related primarily to individual disturbances and individual violations. Typically, the more general that norms become, the more strongly they tend toward the negative form of the prohibition. This is because the domains of life and activity cannot be commanded, but only worked on and in. If I continue to draw on medicine and law as decisive authorities in this context, it is with an important restriction. I bracket out health and legal policy and also leave out of consideration that there once was such a thing as dietetics and epitreptics, that is, doctrines concerning healthy and right living. In short, I apply a traditional outline that not only depicts but also exemplifies the state of our problem and that does not remain unaffected by the changing state of the problem. Every establishment of a normative authority has, as establishment, its economic and political implications; economics and politics do not begin and end where markets and official powers are established. But this takes us to the heart of the questions that occupy us here and will not let us go subsequently either.

We have honed down the sequence of various modes of order to the aspect of simultaneous *selections* and *exclusions,* both understood not as selection and exclusion of present realities and possibilities, but as origin of a multiply regulated context preceded by nothing but a differently regulated context. Further characterizations of the ordering process, such as securing, stabilizing, or appropriating, are consciously pushed into the background, because they begin at a later stage. What is secured, stabilized, or appropriated? In selection and exclusion there is an origination nucleus where this question is no longer posed. Besides the question of the establishment of order, many further questions of course arise, such as that of the range and duration, the kind of embodiment and security, the effects and the functions of order. Much of this goes beyond the boundaries of our theme. But one question-complex is unavoidable and crops up again and again: what is the *dynamics* that transforms all multiplicity of order into an ordering process and where does this take place? Does the movement go in one direction? And if a development to the whole, to the higher, to the more severe is excluded, from where does the movement draw its standard measure? Does not a plunge into arbitrariness and violence threaten here? We shall take up these questions by citing a much-contested point that we have intentionally left aside till now. What criteria and standards are there to distinguish good morals from bad ones, justified norms from unjustified ones? This question gives us yet another occasion to unroll the question of the justifiability of order in its full breadth, down to the zones where the contrast between importance and unimportance sets the tone. For the danger that everything unordered is converted into the disorderly increases when such exalted words as right and morality are heard.

3
Grounded or Arbitrary Order?

1. Orders of Limited Scope

ORDERS THAT ARISE through selection and exclusion produce their own boundaries. This is true of field structures that obey variable relevancy criteria and generally leave much in the background and push other things to the margin or set them aside as atypical; it applies equally to norms that disqualify irregular, abnormal, improper, and finally, wrong behavior. The boundaries that thus arise cannot be overcome on the plane of experience, speech, and action.

A *theme*, a form (*Gestalt*), a structure indeed allow themselves to be narrowed or broadened; one can choose between fine structure and coarse structure. But just as there is a close view and a far view, so there are maximal and minimal boundaries; if they are crossed, the theme blurs into emptiness or superfluity and finally disappears completely. Themes and forms persist only as long as they stand out within a surrounding field; their contours are simultaneously determinative and delimiting. The boundaries of experience can indeed be crossed by artificial means, but they are not thereby expanded in the strict sense. The macro-worlds displayed in the telescope and the micro-worlds seen in the microscope do not join continuously with the natural field of vision, but form therein artificial islands that obey their own field laws. Something similar applies to the use of computer programs; there is a leap between reading a book and utilizing computer materials because data are organized differently than a book page. To take a last example, the railroad train does not simply continue my walking stride as if I were on foot, but merely faster and farther than otherwise; rather, on the train journey I enter a travel setting with its own laws of orientation and movement. An all-comprehensive field would be like a form without contours and background or like a structure without anything structured; it would no longer be a field of experience in which the experiencing person occupies and changes standpoints.

Something similar is true of the formation of something or someone occurring in a field, which formation leads to a repeatable *type*. As a sensory idea, as materialized or embodied form, its generalness can be increased until it becomes an indefinite "something there" or "someone there" (cf. Husserl, XIX/1, 410), but the generalization of the sensory leads neither to a highest genre nor to universals. Generality can branch out in various directions, but it never comes up against a highest boundary and it never converges on a unified point, for this would require an overview that would no longer be a view at all.

For the domain of *norms,* including normalities, customs, and usages, the problem is posed somewhat differently. Here boundaries are not merely byproducts, they are drawn on purpose: the forbidden is the opposite of what is commanded and not just something else. Norms that excluded nothing would be like knives that do not cut. The question posed here is: why precisely these boundaries and not others? The question is posed all the more since norms, to begin with, are all conditioned, but not necessarily in such a way that their being followed is linked with conditions, though their existence certainly is. For like language rules and norms, norms of action too are initially bound in typically recurring contexts and in relatively closed discourses, which in their turn are variable. A norm that would prescribe what one has to do under all circumstances would have to address an actor who does not exist any more than does a field-transcending perspective and discourse-transcending speech. And a norm that determines what one may not do under any circumstances would have to declare its dependency on context and discourse in some way or other, for every voice commanding and forbidding, including that of various gods and their representatives, speaks from somewhere or other, even when it claims universal validity.

So there is no step leading directly and unmediatedly to solid ground beyond the boundaries of the fields of experience and their normative regulations. The classical attempts at a way out, which take this difficulty into account, tend to blur the boundaries. The two ways out that I have in mind can be characterized as the path of totalization, ascending to a true world, and the path of universalization, escaping to universal norms. In both cases, the way out consists in a certain reduplication, a *doubling* of the sensory world by an intelligible one, a doubling of the positively applicable norms by internally valid ones, which in each case leads to countervailing difficulties and to positivistic counterreactions. Totality, universality, and positivity are thus the three central factors around which the following reflections turn; the heightening tendency that amounts to a respective *-ism* will be the focus of our special attention.

2. *Cosmos as Total Order*

The ascent to a true world of the cosmos can be found in Plato and with certain restrictive distinctions and delimitations also in Aristotle. This is a first answer to our question about order; it has repeatedly served as a foil to the foregoing reflections and will now be discussed itself, taking into account distinctions made in the previous chapter.

The quest for a cosmos can be regarded as the attempt to develop the order of the world with the criteria of importance or vital significance, while relegating all questions of normative rightness to the background. However, this attempt requires a slight change of perspective. Importance, as the good for us, is heightened to *importance in itself,* which is the Good itself, developed in its whole amplitude and spread out with all its inner references. In modern diction, it is a matter of a substantial or material rationality that rises out of the things themselves. Because order is embodied and installed in things, norms in the strict sense— namely, as prescriptions to which behavior would be *subjected*— are out of place. Modern authors who rank such an ethics as descriptivist or intuitionist overlook the decisive point. If there is a cosmos that prescribes a universal teleology, laws are not to be enacted but discovered. The lack of dogmatic tendencies in the Attic tradition coincides with a minimization of institutional regulations and norms, such as can be found not only in everyday and political practice but also in their later interpreters. Where questions are raised about guidelines and standards, these are obtained from the measurement of things and developed further. An emphatic duty (*Sollen*) would literally have no addressee, which Kant then turns to mean that no one needs to be ordered to be happy—as if Plato and the Greeks were interested only in human happiness. The anchoring of order in things also accords with there being no creator of this order in the strict sense. The demiurge in the *Timaeus* has archetypes before his eyes like a human craftsperson and thus can be understood as the personification of order itself, and the "prime mover" does not have to concern himself about things, since in any case they strive toward him as the quintessence of reality. An order that is neither capable of nor needs any external grounding because, as the universal order, it contains all light, needs no orderer; if one did exist, he would be even more unemployed than the deistic God who gives the universe its first impetus.

Cosmos as total order means that everything fits within it as a part in the whole. It means that the lower beings subordinate themselves to the higher ones according to their respective power of being without the higher ones needing to insist on their privilege. Finally, it means that at every stage the secondary places itself at the side of the essential. Backgrounds and margins do not exist, since there is an articulated and stratified universal theme, and therefore no field with its boundaries. For the human observer's standpoint is a declining one; it dwindles the more it approaches the panorama of the divine gaze, which has its place everywhere and at all times. So the language of *everything* and *all things* is the adequate mode of expression for the universe, as the famous beginning sentences of Aristotle's treatises testify. What results in the boundary case is a form without ground, a pure blinding light to which the eye becomes accustomed only with effort (Plato, *Republic,* VII). This daylight mysticism of a form without ground finds its counterpart in the nighttime mysticism of a ground without form. The view of the cosmos shatters the framework of seeing. Is this, perhaps, the strongest indication that the boundaries of seeing only show themselves, but never let themselves be overcome? At any rate, the vision of the whole tends toward liberality in details. Even Plato foregoes the elaboration of his commonwealth in all details. Confidence in the goals toward which the individual's life, as well as that of the *oikos* and the *polis,* is ordained allows him to present the virtues only typically (*typōi*), in approximate delineations that can be filled by practical ingenuity (*Nic. Ethics,* II, 2, 1104a, 1). However, he is a hermeneutist only within limits, for what stands behind the texts of action is neither a divine voice nor pure custom, but the cosmos in which humans must seek their place, which they already have. In this cosmos everything has its natural place, not only the stone but also the *polis,* which maintains the right distance from the sea, and everything has its natural time, from the right moment to marry, and the years of study, all the way to the *acmē* as the high point of vital energy and creativity. But this universal order is generous enough to permit even chance occurrences, in which stirs a little of the refractoriness of *anankē* (necessity), which even the divine demiurge and the founder of the state had to deal with (*Laws,* 757e). This cosmology is far removed from any pedantry.

And yet, are the boundaries of selective and exclusive orders that our experiences have to deal with really deactivated or merely overruled? The answer to the question of the criteria of order cancels itself out if, whether in nature or in the human community, nothing else stands opposite order but disorder or chaos. Who but someone chaotic would ever want to defend chaos? Deniers of divine order arouse the late Plato's impatience; for the worst of them he foresees a *sōphronistērion,* a house in which they are brought to their senses and whose name Schleiermacher not inappropriately translated as "*Zuchthaus*" (prison, house of correction) (*Laws,* 908a). That it should be located in "as wild as possible a place" (*hōs agriōtatos topos*) underscores the origin of chaos: it comes from wildness, like the wolf. The cosmos presses everything disorderly back over the threshold, but thereby also shows the limits of its integrative power, which do not begin to disappear even when order is surrounded with the soft shell of everyday assent.

3. Fissures in the Universe

What classical thinkers of a physical and political cosmos use as a touchstone for order and disorder is justice, which assigns to each its own and results in a universal harmony. That is what St. Augustine's definition, which we quoted at the beginning, says in good Platonic fashion: *ordo est parium dispariumque sua cuique loca dispositio* (order is the assignment of equal and unequal things each to their places). Ordering as the distribution of locations and assignment of places has forever had to deal with the problem of prior *equality* and *inequality*. If all who claim a place at the table of nature were equal by nature, they would all have a right to equivalent places or, if these do not exist, the identical place. A stable graduated scale could thus not be expected. Now Plato and Aristotle do not have this difficulty, because these teachers of classical political thinking counted on a naturally given inequality not only in the cosmos, but also in the *polis* and between different kinds of communities. Even Aristotle, who aims for the equality of citizens in the *polis* and also foresees a rule by turns (*Politics,* II, 2), does not, of course, have in mind women, resident foreigners, and slaves. Yet it must be noted that the concept of equality is used primarily as a political term and not a formal legalistic one, so that even with the general cooperation of the citizens the actual influence on public events varies considerably both officially and unofficially, as could not be expected otherwise to this day. Under these circumstances, all considerations of order aim to a higher, namely proportional, form of *comparative equality:* order then consists in allotting to each his or her own in honors and offices, more to the capable persons, less to the incapable, so that one stands higher, the other lower, but each in his or her place. The highest form of injustice, on the contrary, would consist in "distributing a certain equality uniformly to equal and unequal people," which according to Plato happens in the rulerless form of state (*politeia anarchos*) of democracy (*Republic,* 558c; cf. also *Laws,* 757a–758a). The crux of any such distribution lies in determining the standard (*metrion*) of worthiness (*axia*) (*Nic. Ethics,* 6, 1131a 24 ff.) by which to decide who deserves more, who less. As a sober collector of political constitutions Aristotle can admit that this standard varies from constitution to constitution. And even Plato commits to "Zeus's judgment" this hard-to-fathom higher equality that humans do justice to only approximatively (*Laws,* 757b). But ultimately the answer to the question of standard is: the standard lies ready in nature, especially in human nature. Otherwise there would be orders, but not the one order, not the cosmos and no form of community that is intrinsically just.

But what if equality and inequality did not simply reside in things, what if they themselves arose under certain conditions? This suspicion crystallizes in Nietzsche to the statement: "Every concept arises through positing the unequal as equal. As certainly as no leaf ever is completely identical with another, so certainly the concept 'leaf' is formed by arbitrarily disregarding those individual differences, by forgetting what distinguishes them and now gives rise to the idea, as if in nature, besides the leaves, there were the 'leaf,' say, as an archetype according to which all leaves were woven, drawn, drafted, colored, curled, painted, but by unskillful hands so that no exemplar had turned out correctly and reliably as a true copy of the original form" (III, 313; *On Truth and Lying in the Extramoral Sense*). The Platonic resonance and counterpoint cannot be missed. The forgetting that in Plato gives the sensory world its existence here confers an apparent existence to the world of ideas. In the first instance the soul forgets what order it has seen; in the second the soul, or rather the body, forgets what order it has produced—a forgetting that is made easier by speaking of the like (*isoi*) and unlike (*anisoi*), because it looks as if equality were an attribute and not a relation. But the produced order is a dubious order, for Nietzsche's remarks suggest the idea that there is no such infallible standard enabling us to distinguish a true world from a false one. We have only a chain of metaphors, and what is transmitted to the concept from the nerve stimuli via image and sound is anything but a true copy of a true world. Yet Plato comes out with a minute victory via Hume. Hume is the author of the nerve stimulus that transmits nothing; but so much of Plato remains that without setting the dissimilar as equal, that is, without ascertaining the initial standard, without "determining" the sensory, there would be nothing to do and nothing to say. Nor do Hume's laws of association lead any further as long as the selecting viewpoints remain unclarified; for everything is similar or dissimilar to everything else in some way or other, and to that extent similarity is not given, but instituted. Without the equation of the dissimilar and without the forgetting of differences there would be *everything and thus nothing*. The "relentless memory" ascribed by Borges to his "unrestrained indigenous Zarathustra" is incapable of any Platonic idea and gives birth to an "untiring reality" whose excessive crammedness overshadows Babylon, London, and New York, and spells doom for our mnemonic hero (Borges 1970, 213 ff.).

What would emerge then would thus be—Platonically speaking—an *inescapable injustice* not given by nature but generated anew with every order. One could, however, ask whether the equation of the dissimilar and the forgetting of differences does not precede the opposite form of injustice—namely, a de-equation of monotonous similarity and a self-differentiation without which there would be nothing for us to equate. What "there is" is a happening of order preceded neither by ideas nor by individuals as simple givens. A double injustice, then? At any rate, not a seamless cosmos in which everything would find its place.

4. *Totality and Totalitarianism*

The sore point of every total order is that everything that withdraws from order assumes the character of disorder, for the alternative to a total order can be only *chaos*. If there were this total order, it would remove all shadows. Thus in St. Augustine the torments in hell do not impair the joys of heaven, because even in the fires of hell the reflection of divine justice can be discerned. Perhaps this frenzied vision stems from the convert's excessive zeal; still it points to possible consequences from which even Plato did not keep himself completely free. Nonetheless, nuances and distinctions are called for.

In the first place, one could speak of a *lived totality* that emerges when a group unquestioningly regards its own way of life as the true order. Here it is a matter of a *doxa* and a *praxis* that have solidified into an orthodoxy and an ortho-practice without abandoning the status of the "natural attitude." The status of such a closed society causes any other form of life to seem like impending chaos. Since the shielding off is not done with arguments to create a ground and basis conveying inner security, the result often is an *over-regulation* of the courses of life, resulting in a strong *isolation* from the outside. The normative regulations carry extraordinary weight and an extraordinarily wide scope, since they have fused considerably with all the forms of order that we have distinguished from normativity. Among these are strict marriage rules, dietary prescriptions, diet recipes, holiday rituals, distribution of labor, gender roles, age privileges, etc.—everything we know from the ethnologists' handbooks or even from a legal text like the second book of Moses. The preferential importance of vital interests ascribed to one's own group is not merely intensified to importance in itself, but at the same time supported normatively, as a rule, by means of religious myths and rites. In a kind of hyper-fixation of the animal level, humans mimic the closed surrounding world and instinctive certainty of the animal, although this "indigenousness" by no mean stems from nature, as cultural variants of even the most archaic societies show. This mimicry would be complete in a thoroughgoing normifying and ritualizing of life; but if this boundary value were reached, then the group's life would be immobilized and incapable of adjusting to new challenges.

The Greek cosmologies and physiologies are far removed from such a lived and hermetically closed global order. Insofar as the cosmos develops within a *logos,* and this *logos* peaks in a theory, we can speak of a *viewed totality. Doxa* is here on its way to an *epistēmē.* The totality not only stands open to everything there is of partial orders in the world, it also presents itself in an open form as long as the thinkers of the cosmos hold to the difference between order in itself and order for us, or in Aristotelian terms: between the good *simpliciter* and the good for us, and as long as divinization (*theiōsis*) remains an assimilation to God (*homoiōsis theōi*) (*Theaetetus,* 176b). For as long as this restriction is admitted, the order remains a whole to be sought that is in no one's possession. And in fact neither Plato nor Aristotle elaborated a philosophical system—not Plato, insofar as in his dialogues new questions are forever being tried; nor Aristotle, insofar as he too applies his metaphysics aporetically and, moreover, insists that various forms of knowledge have their own laws.

Even granting all this, a very central difficulty still remains. The very thought that there is this universal order, which reconciles and combines everything, suffices to push all questioning and seeking in a certain direction, downplaying differences and conflicts—and when this no longer succeeds and alternatives become uncircumventable, escaping to the great divide of order and chaos. Differences tend to glide off into the indifferent and inconsequential, to arrange themselves on a scale, or to flow into the great difference of true and false, of good and evil. This cosmic nature makes no leaps and tolerates no leaps; it is homogeneous, or it would not be what it claims to be. To deny the grandeur and dignity of this vision or its explanatory power and attractiveness would be presumptuous; yet it is also undeniable that all discoveries and inventions, in the last analysis, are coated with the varnish of immutability and that the joints and fissures are plastered over. And though the "for us" cannot be completely integrated with an "in-itself," it may happen that preferences belonging to a certain form of life flow into the order, such as in Aristotle slaves by nature, the subordination of women, and the exposure of weakly progeny, or in Plato double warfare against Greeks and barbarians, some of which things are still in vogue today. What matters is not that such collective idiosyncrasies become widespread and no time is exempted; what counts here is the way they become solidified. Yet the problem is not that nature says nothing, but that it says many things. It recommends much, excludes much else; but it gives no clear directives, so that any simple appeal to *nature* does violence to it, since it makes things clearer than they are. One reads out what one has partly read into them, and then calls it the nature of the thing. If one presumes to speak for this whole and to impose its dictates, then the universal order takes on totalitarian features; and insofar as the selective interests that pervade every form of life hide behind the concerns of the whole, the idea of the whole is exposed to the suspicion of being an ideology. The indeterminate animal that soars up to become "nearly a god," who has the whole world as its homeland, brings the whole world into order only too well.

Much is interposed between lived and viewed totality—for instance, organicist new editions of the cosmos, methodological forms of holism —and finally there is the perverted form of a *fabricated totality,* where the living boundaries are intensified to ideal boundaries and enemies are created. The vacuum left behind by a disintegrating religious or cosmological order is filled with surrogates. The prescribed order that apes the former one borrows from the unquestionedness and closedness of the *doxa,* from archaic fears and desires, but at the same time clever techniques are applied to channel them into the lanes of a new total order. Since convincing grounds for such a tribal philosophy are hard to teach, such means as propaganda, indoctrination, and drilling are used. The paradox of an artificial faith succeeds only when the machination itself appears natural. Insofar as a totality is not merely preserved or sought, but totality is elevated to a principle, we can speak of *totalitarianism,* in whose pseudo-archaism religion, science, art, politics, and education merge and are governed by functional imperatives such as: "*All for* . . ." What is of interest here are not the very scanty orderly contents, but rather the mechanisms for imposing them, and even more the needs that foster such artificial formations, such worldviews without vision.

5. *From Total Order to Fundamental Order*

A true world, in which the relative significance or importance of certain ways of behaving and forms of life is intensified and expanded to absolute importance, creates the possibility of answering the question of the rightness of our behavior based on the things themselves. The order *of* things is at the same time an order *in* things. When, as could be expected over a period of time, this exaggerated order begins to show fissures and divides into orders that to a certain extent could also be different, a threat arises precisely from what had previously been considered the only opposite of the cosmos; namely, chaos, both in cognition and in behavior. Chaos can appear in the soft form of *arbitrariness* or in the hard form of *coercion.* Whether the playful or coercive form of arbitrariness comes to the fore is a question of the political situation. What can we oppose to the impending chaos when the order of things begins to decline? Rules, which we must follow as speakers and actors, no matter what the situation may be with the "order of things" (*KrV* B, 576; *CPRb,* 260). The question of importance in itself, of the good, recedes and vanishes behind the question of the rightness of prescriptions for behavior. Ordering as cosmic *disposition* gives way to ordering in the sense of *practical imperatives.*

Drastic changes and crises on both a biographical and a historical scale can be considered from this point of view. At issue are typically recurring problematic situations, though in this case they allow for various solutions. The one sketched here is a possible one. What I have in mind, though with cautious reservations, are certain developments beginning at the dawn of the modern age with the gradual disintegration of cosmic and feudal-social orders and finding clearest expression in philosophical writers such as Hobbes or Hume. For what is only provisionally summed up under the epistemological rubric of empiricism can be seen as the striving to face the breakdown of substantial orders without immediately hiding behind an ersatz-cosmos called reason.

With the shifting of the problematic of order from the plane of importance to that of rightness, the question of the true world changes into the question of true norms. The royal road to answering this question, which begins in Königsberg, is a legal route that goes by the name of "universalization."

6. Universal Norms as Minimal Order

The look that has lost sight of the whole but continues seeking it retains only *disjecta membra,* unconnected details, a given multiplicity that is waiting for its *connection.* A being facing this abyss of possibilities and exposed to multiplicity has only one way to escape chaos. The given and the givable, as well as what is or can be done, must obey minimal conditions going exactly as far as they must to avoid chaos and make possible or guarantee *any order at all.* Just as in cognition a "negative condition of all truth," a *conditio sine qua non* appears necessary, but not sufficient (cf. *KrV* B, 84; *CPR,* 49), so in action there are negative conditions for all rightness; and, we could add, in speaking there are negative conditions for all comprehensibility. They no longer affect a comprehensive whole (*ein All*) like the positive laws of the cosmos, but only *each* thing and *each* person out of the entirety of things and persons—so far as a chaos can be avoided. The norms and laws occurring here do not explicate merely a regularity already embodied in things; rather, they owe their validity to an unmixing of experience, which separates what stems from it and what precedes it. The prototypical figure on whom this fundamental act of ordering is oriented is not the creative artist, but the lawgiver and judge—more precisely, the judge who judges by self-enacted laws. Like every legal matter, here too a distinction must be made between "the question of what is right (*quid juris*) and what the facts are (*quid facti*)" (*KrV* B, 116; *CPR,* 68). A touchstone for this is the ability of rules and norms to be universalized. Norms are grounded in reason when they can claim validity under all possible conditions and for all possible participants and affected parties. It is not a matter of details but of the basic pattern of this order, which is relatively independent of how the legislative and juridical offices are occupied, whether for instance a "subject" is reasoning with itself or a critical "discourse" is taking place.

7. *Formalization and Normative Vacuum*

Decisive for the normatively oriented idea of order is the gesture of *drawing a boundary* and excluding. Not every field to which our conceptual faculty refers is a ground on which cognition is possible, or even a *territory* where it appears as lawgiver (*KU* B, XVI). The drawing of a boundary is already implicit in the model of legislation, a model that, not without reason, accompanies the disintegration of the cosmos and first appears, as in Hobbes, in the form of a political theology. The commanding and judging God of the Old Testament overcomes the calculating and artistically creative god of the Greeks. The separation of being and what ought to be elevates the imperative to the original mood of language (*De Homine,* chap. 10). While cosmic thinking incorporates and subordinates everything that is and thus leads it out beyond itself, normative thinking restricts itself to the gesture of *subjugation:* let everything be subject to reason. The question of what happens if the subjects remain deaf to the demands of reason can be answered only by appealing to a *fact of reason;* for a "new creation" (Kant, VI, 365) is no longer the business of lawgivers and judges. Even if we go ahead and accept this cautious boundary-drawing as unproblematic, the question still arises as to what happens in the "fields" and "territories" where legislative reason does not command because it would then have to wrestle with the empirical. This can be answered as follows: just as Aristotle delineates what must be done only in broad outlines and leaves the rest to practical discretion, so Kant lays down the foundations for a moral and right action, while leaving the rest open. What person who has not succumbed to a mania for rules would not welcome such liberality? Yet this welcome proximity to practical hermeneutics glosses over important distinctions. General outlines can be extended and *filled out* seamlessly as long as one moves within a comprehensive order of cognition and action. A formal law, however, is applied to something that is not contained in it like a part within the whole (cf. Husserl, III, § 13; *Ideas,* 72 ff.). One can, with Aristotle or Wittgenstein, regard an action as an expression and part of a form of life, but it is never part of a legal order, unless someone is reduced to a legal person. If the formal legislation thus alleges only negative conditions, which are insufficient, what is the case, then, with the missing positive conditions?

We approach the question more closely when we envisage clearly what is universalized in the course of grounding and verifying and what *universalization* here means. If universalization means transformation into something universal just as totalization is an insertion into a whole, then it must be stated that action can as little be universalized as perception, speech, or feeling. Although Kant's imperative, in one of its formulations, is worded: "Act only according to those maxims by which you can at the same time will that they become a universal law," still it is I who act so, and not an I in general. Universalization accordingly begins with those elements of action that already have a general character. Kant calls them maxims, that is, "subjective principles" by which actors actually let themselves be guided (cf. *GMS* B, 52). We can thus distinguish between a *universally valid, formal basic norm* and *actually applied material norms*. The boundaries of restricted spheres of action are blurred by a doubling of norms. Are the material norms thereby converted into a universal? The answer again is: no. Formal norms offer no guide for action, as is expected of material norms. What the categorical imperative offers is nothing but "the universality of a law in general . . . to which the maxims of action should conform" (*GMS* B, 51-52). All universalizing thus consists in subjecting concrete norms to a standard that promises universal validity, because if it is disregarded, any moral-practical order would collapse. Strictly speaking, then, absolutely nothing is universalized, a *universal point of view* is merely chosen, and—like the application of the logical principle of contradiction—this makes it possible to eliminate certain norms without generating any. The model of the rational (*phronimos* or *spoudaios*), which embodies a determinate tradition, is replaced, in Kant's grounding, by a procedure of reason that rises above all traditions; but the *how* of judging action cannot replace the *what* of particular designs and fields of action. Where does this leave what is presupposed in all "universalization" and can be abolished by no "universalization"?

8. The Pressure of Universalization

Even if "universalization" first consists only in a choice of viewpoint, it exercises pressure by *subjecting* everything to that viewpoint without being sufficiently aware of the one-sidedness and origin of this viewpoint.

Indications of this can be found in the very descriptions of what is subjected to the universal standards of reason. In Kant himself and his successors, there is always talk of *subjective* maxims, *particular* interests and needs, *conditional* commands, to which are opposed objective law, rational interest, and unconditional moral law. The first series of attributes tends to be completely privative; what precedes regulation by reason is *merely* subjective, particular, and conditional. This is because human beings, after their "dismissal from the womb of nature" turn out to be sensory beings, self-centered in their feelings, needs, and inclinations, that is, in their entire sensuality, and equipped with the mental tool of an instrumental reason, which as "slave of the passions" (Hume, *Tractatus,* II, 3, 3) merely further intensifies the possibilities for self-preservation and hence the sharpness of antagonisms, and makes humans "more animalistic than any animal." This human being is an "animal that, when it lives among others of its species, *needs a master*" to counteract its "selfish animal inclinations" and to "break its will" (Kant, VI, 40). The "wild man" is "forced to give up his brutish freedom and to seek peace and security in a legal constitution" (Kant, VI, 42). Kant's "universalistic" morality thus provides an answer to problems his anthropology adopted from modern thinkers like Hobbes, Hume, and Rousseau. For Plato, too, there is a sharp turn between sensory life and rational life, but erotically fired striving lifts the rational animal from stage to stage above itself; and for Aristotle, sociality is inherent in the life of the individual and therefore does not first have to be imposed upon individuals. Here the modern age sees a break; reason intrudes into the cycle of self-preservation with its commandments and laws, and with great effort starts a process of cultivation, civilization, and moralization, which—if all goes well—gradually polishes and regulates the crude beginnings. Whatever is left behind is dross. Basically, morality means nothing more than the internalization of law, which allows one person's arbitrariness to harmonize with another's, complemented by the claim and drive that emanates from the law as such. Claims that break through the circle of self-preservation can, like the angel with the flaming sword, come only "from above," as messengers from a sphere of universal reason.

These anthropological presuppositions are anything but sacrosanct, and in the first chapter we already tried to cast doubt on them from various angles. Nor can moral and legal theory be detached from them; for any norm of action not elevated to a heaven of law but regarded in its function is determined in terms of what it normifies. The consequences of this chosen starting point are clear. What does not stem from the law itself shrinks down before the judgment chair of reason to mere "questions of fact." All the ordering processes introduced in the previous chapter are lost in this general factification.

Let us first take the fields of action with their themes, thematic fields, and the typical elaboration of these themes. They are not merely subjective, since the recurring structural arrangement and positions infringe upon the lived experience of the individuals as much as do rules; they are not merely particular, since alternatively and selectively occurring forms of order are not parts that can be fitted into a whole; they are not merely conditioned, since they themselves co-condition what we encounter. The preferential regulations seeing to it that this occurs *rather than* that, and so forth, cannot be optimized with regard to a best world. Nor can they be normified with regard to correct behavior. The criteria of importance and the criteria of rightness are located on two different planes. Thus there are significant crimes and unimportant truths. Whoever characterizes forms of organization of theoretical and practical experience as merely particular resembles a logician who classifies an empirically true statement as particular compared with a logically true one. The underdetermination of certain achievements of order is also shown in the familiar distinction between empirical and transcendental. There are absolutely no "empirical concepts" in the strict sense, for no concept comes "from experience"; it may not be prior to all experience like Kant's categories, but it is still prior to determinate experiences, and in a certain sense this applies to every sensory form of stimulus that is repeated. Not a trace of mere facts is to be found "in experience."

The case is similar when we scan the domain of material normifications, beginning with normalities, via custom and usage, all the way to normativity in the strict sense. Material norms are no more present at hand than fields of action; they emerge from normification processes that separate right from wrong or, on the level of customs, proper from improper. Since these material norms, moreover, lie on a different plane than the formal fundamental norm, it makes no sense even in this case to speak of subjective principles or of particular, conditioned norms. Negative criteria are no substitute for the *positive criteria* at work in producing material norms or, respectively, in elaborating comprehensive forms of discourse, such as science, law, or art. But where can these be obtained, from where do they derive their justification? Appeal to impending chaos may lead to reflection on principles of order in general, but it does not lead to *determinate orders*. Thus reference to the urge to communicate, which we can place at the threshold of the origin of language, cannot explain the origin of a single system of language. And the same applies wherever cultural invention is in progress. As was mentioned above, a vacuum is interposed between formal normativity and material facticity, between purely lawful and purely factual questions.

How can this vacuum be filled? A tested means consists in appealing to customs and traditions that exist, just as languages exist. But apart from the fact that this does not solve the question of the selective processes, including the ones involved in the formation of tradition, there is a danger that too much material morality will be preserved in one instance, too little in another. Kant's metaphysics of morals lets in a great deal of the existing order; for example, it leaves room for denial of active citizenship rights to women, vassals, tutors, and barbers (as opposed to wigmakers, who produce a work of their own); thus his metaphysics restores under teleological considerations what strict legality has already set aside (see Ebbinghaus 1968, chap. 7), and he repeatedly imputes the moral code of bourgeois society to the voice of nature. To prevent this, the only recourse is an exaggerated formalization no longer based on any tradition, but instead soaring, far from all friction with reality, to the empty heaven of pure tautologies.

Universalization would then do its work by undertaking, as far as possible, a *purification* of morals, eliminating whatever does not withstand the criterion of universalization, administering institutional precautions in legal support of this exclusion, and leaving the rest to the free choice of individuals and individual groups, allowing them to be happy each in their own way as long as this does not impinge upon the freedom of others, and to achieve a pragmatic consensus concerning alternatives not involving questions of principle, such as whether to drive on the right or on the left. "Universalization" would then consist in unmixing the mixture of morality and convention.

This procedure seems more unproblematic and more innocent than it is. First of all, though a mixture, it is determined one-sidedly when, like Kohlberg, one speaks of a *conventional morality* that is to be replaced by a post-conventional, *autonomous morality*. Instead of speaking of a conventional morality, one might just as well speak of a moral convention, as when violations of dietary prescriptions evoke qualms of conscience. Then it would be seen that the deconventionalization of morality has a demoralization of convention as its reverse side. Only *pure morality* is the counterpart to *mere convention* (cf. 2: 11, above).

This unmixing would be unproblematic if the sphere of material norms and customs actually were a mixture. But this is not so, for the simple reason that the combination of universal norms and lived or settled agreements does not produce one single order of life or action, and thus no act of speech or action would come about. The claims to which a discourse, an action, and even a cultural and traditional form of life respond stem neither from a universal norm nor from conventional regulations, as was shown. The admission of "cultural values" does not make the matter any better, for the satisfaction of elementary needs is thereby only expanded by a second cultural program without breaking through the cycle of self-gratification. This reinterpretation of claims into values itself belongs to determinate forms of life, making it easier for normifying morality to do its work, because then only personal claims stand against universal morality and no one else's claims assert their validity. But if claims situated and habitualized in speech and actions and fields of speech and action do indeed occur, the unmixing by universalization means that such claims are silenced. And how is this done? By the fact that, in the light of and under the pressure of universal norms, once again the unequal is posited as equal, namely, under the aegis of law, whereas cosmic thinking undertakes equalization under the aegis of a comprehensive good. Whereas cosmic thinking goes too far in reaching out for a true world by incorporating all selective orders, normative thinking, by resorting to true norms, does not go far enough, since it levels down and empties these orders, "devaluating" them like a discarded husk.

Perhaps a universality without universalization would be conceivable if the universal norms were restricted to stigmatizing such modes of behavior as run strictly counter to a response to claims. These norms would be embedded in a responsive rationality without competing with the negotiation of concrete claims. Without such a back-reference, universalization takes a similarly perilous course as totalization, because it systematically weakens the domain of concrete claims, namely, in the service of impeding chaos. Conjuring up chaos seems to be an effective way to silence all doubters. Who would want to defend murder and homicide or untruth without exposing oneself to the knife, at least of the logicians? But the difference between *saying something* and *what is said* applies here too. Dealing with norms is never identical with their content, otherwise there would be no moralists and Pharisees; and to that extent no normative discourse is right *simpliciter,* not even in the case of the grounding of norms. Strict binding force in general fosters increasing arbitrariness in particulars. Here traces are seen of a coalition between normativists and positivists, the latter being merely somewhat more cautious.

9. Positivity, Arbitrariness, and Power, or: The Principle of Insufficient Reason

If it is true that every particular order comes about by selection and exclusion, then, speaking with Nietzsche, "behind every ground, under every grounding" lurks "an abyss" (II, 751; *Beyond Good and Evil* # 289) that can be closed neither by a cosmic total order nor by a normative fundamental order. That truth, rationality, and order "exist," as Heidegger, Merleau-Ponty, and Foucault assert with different emphases, although no sufficient reason can be given for them, signifies a permanent event that attaches an element of groundless *positivity* to every order. Yet what is not necessary and fully grounded is still by no means arbitrary; what could also be *otherwise* cannot be in *just any random way.* Where sufficient reasons are lacking, there can still be conditions without which nothing is possible and good reasons in favor of something, although without a last word. Lack of necessity, then, does not at all mean that the institution and change of an order is done with complete arbitrariness, nor that the empty spaces within an order can be filled however one chooses. A great number of factors and procedures are thinkable that restrict arbitrariness and are themselves by no means arbitrary, such as the drawing of lots, which even Plato permits for political elections, though only as an emergency solution (*Laws,* 757b).

If the element of positivity is carried to an extreme, so that mere existence itself is given as ground, one does not get beyond the tautological assurance that what is, is the way it is. If we call that *"positivism,"* then we must distinguish different varieties of it. Such a positivism can rely on the *cosmos* and inherit its order, as for instance in Protagoras. When Protagoras countered the order of nature with a posited order, he was seeking a middle ground between the great all-encompassing cosmos and the great chance that disperses everything; he was seeking something like a variable and local cosmos anchored in the political constitution of a community or in the organic constitution of the individual. In that way, standards of order are indeed retained, but they are relativized. Related with this is a second variety modeled on *lawgiving* or also on lived *conventions;* normative regulations are thereby recognized, but no ultimate authority stands any longer behind the actual laws or the actual morals. In the first case one can speak of a life-order without totality, in the second of a normative order without universality. Both attempts contain elements worth considering, but they end up in difficulties, because they simply cancel what they cast doubt on. Such truncated orders remain burdened with the problems they seek to shake off.

Finally, there remains the most important and most drastic variant, which holds up to every order of nature or reason sensorily given or linguistically reproduced *facts.* This positivism follows in the wake of Hume. The cosmos has dissolved into unconnected details from which no necessity can be extracted. But the insistence on facts leads to a point of view in which order is completely lost from sight. If the regulation of the context by this or that—without which literally nothing exists—is itself made into a fact, then the facts merely double into a *lower* and a *higher* *"it is,"* and this doubling too, like the doubling of the world and of norms, misses the decisive point. It does not reach the point where ordering and what is to be ordered are combined in a genesis that opens some possibilities while closing off others. The mobility of order in general (*es gibt Ordnung*) has always already been brought to a standstill by the specific order (*es ist Ordnung*). Yet even this fact-oriented arranging means an equation of the unequal, not in the sense of classifying or subjection but in the sense of a *leveling* of difference. What primarily disappears is the difference that first lets the question of an order come up at all, the difference between a *something* (*ein Etwas*) and the selecting, heightening specification (*Als* or *Wie*) that makes possible and limits the occurrence of something (cf. 2, above). Where each and every thing is or is not simple, is or is not posited, where the question of "*rather* so and not otherwise" does not even come up, there is neither order nor disorder, but only the indifference of facts. And where all is possible, basically nothing is possible; for if the real does not congeal into a shape or structure that permits one thing and not another, nothing is ever possible until it actually is. The boundary case of an absolutely open world where everything is infinitely ambiguous thus approaches the antipodal case of a closed world where everything is fixed and clear. A world with a completely grounded order would be without shadow and allusion, just like a world whose order is absolutely arbitrary.

Finally, the problem of arbitrariness is proximate to the problem of *power*. If there were a true world that assigns each person a place, conflicts would basically already be resolved. The comprehensive order in which our cognition and action move would give us sufficient grounds to settle any quarrel by arguments. Insofar as this order is reproduced in cognition and action, the true and the good win out in the dispute—a victory that no one can personally take credit for. If there is a problem of power, then this is only insofar as unreason and disorder rule in the world. How these are to be overcome, whether by conviction, slyness, or coercion, is a second question. Conceivably, reason takes power, and power comes to reason—a marriage of reason and power that Plato celebrates in his philosopher-king and that Aristotle envisages for the open form of a government concerned with the common good.

If one begins, like Hobbes, and Kant after him, with the assumption that humankind has been dismissed from the order of nature and must first find and create a cultural order, brute force is not a mere deviation from the straight path, but rather is a stage prior to reason; it prevails in the state of nature that is no longer natural and not yet lawful. Insofar as humans never fully outgrow this state of arbitrariness, all potentates are also "carved from the same crooked wood" as their subjects (Kant, VI, 41). That kings philosophize, or philosophers become kings, "is neither to be expected, nor is it desirable" (Kant, VI, 228). The questions of power and force that occur here are generally ascribed to the actualization of reason, not to reason itself; for reason cannot enter into conflict with its own self, nor can people insofar as they let themselves be guided by reason. There is a problem of power, here too, only insofar as reason does not rule, not insofar as it does. Rebellion against a grounded order would be not only a sign of unreason, but also of unfreedom, because only the observance of a universal law of reason and morality frees the actors from dependencies on their sensory nature.

Conversely, there would also be no problem of reason and power if all order were set arbitrarily and imposed against others. The ruling ideas would then be nothing else but the ideas of the rulers, and changing a regime would change nothing about that. A problem of rationality and power arises when our speech and action respond to claims but the orders in which this happens are selective and exclusive without these selections and exclusions being covered by sufficient reasons. An element of power corresponds to the element of positivity: on all levels of order one thing opposes another as significant, typical, normal, proper, or right, without having exhaustive reasons on its side. The very attempt to close these gaps in grounding leads to an *act of coercion in the name of reason,* whether because claims, alternatives, and ambiguities are forced into a whole, or because they are devaluated and disempowered to save universal standards. The connection between validity and power cannot be set close enough. A simple question such as: "Why are you saying that?" or "Why are you doing that?" is never answered exhaustively by alluding to the truth of what is said or the rightness of what is done. There would be so much else to say and do; there are too many truths. If one were to give the Socratic questioning free rein, the Platonic cosmos would be incessantly shattered. To say something and to do something is never a mere case for the judges of speech and morals; a voice is never the pure voice of morality, a tradition is never a pure forum of reason.

Failure to recognize the problem of power that makes itself felt here exposes one all the more to it. The transformation of the unordered into the disorderly, then, takes its course on the level of importance by the choice of a determinate order, on the level of rightness by the exclusion of disorder, which has long since detached itself from early suffering. In the effort to wind back this thread of order and to rediscover the unequal in equation, the *principle of insufficient reason* is recommended as a guideline.

4
Order with or without Orderer?

1. Subject, a Question of Label

IF SOMEONE HAS A TITLE for a long enough time, the title can become so intertwined with the title-bearer that anyone who touches the one also affects the other. In the end, abolishing the monarchy and murdering the king are indistinguishable. But neither kings nor subjects are born, at most only claimants to the throne, and even they only when the succession is already legitimated. On the other hand, it is also difficult to remove all the king's clothes. A naked king would be as good as a naked truth; one would not know how to address him or to talk to him. This "someone" whom we are circling always occurs as this person or that one. When title and label, functions and offices become questionable, we end up in a process of revaluation and functional change that only reveals its semi-mythical background in simple obituaries.

In the dispute for and against the subject and about the death or return of the subject, the matter ought to be approached obliquely in order to avoid quarreling about the Emperor's beard. On the whole, the question is posed as follows: when, under what circumstances, and under what conditions does such a thing as a subject occur? For the subject "exists" no more than does an object, an electron, or a king. The process of objectivation, which generates an object, is paralleled by a *subjectivation,* which constitutes a subject (cf. Foucault 1986). Unless one wants to resort to a self-constituting original generation, which explains nothing, the subject cannot be posited as simply first; perhaps it obeys a subject-principle, but it *is* not one. The second question, which follows immediately, inquires into such an authority's functions, tasks, and achievements; just as functioning norms precede their thematization, it is the same with what we could—following Husserl—call a "functioning subject." Here an immense field of inquiry and investigation opens up. We restrict it by focusing the question of the subject down more narrowly on what this subject contributes to the variegated process of ordering.

To avoid the false alternative of "all or nothing," we would do well to cash in the big check of a subject for hard cash. The "someone" who remains modestly in the background occurs as speaker and listener, as addresser, addressee, and topic of discussion; as I, you, or as part of a we; as doer, co-adviser or victim; as a sensitive being who feels pleasure and pain; as a being who is born, begets, bears, suffers, and dies. A "subject" that could do all this would have a great deal to do; no wonder it is practically obsessed with the question of its unity. It could also perish from there being too many of it.

In the first two chapters we kept discovering traces of the "subject." The theme of the subject is already sounded in the metaphors for the production of the world, which are counterposed to the metaphors for a spontaneous origin of the world and undergo a correction in the model of linkage. Insofar as speech and action are a responsive behavior that follows a responsive rationality, we can also speak generally of a "respondent" who deals with "co-respondents." In the framework of the multiple forms of order, claims and responses are adjusted selectively and exclusively, and this intrudes directly on the experiencer, speaker, or actor, who notice and encounter something as something that occupies positions in the field of experience, who develop typical modes of behavior, and who finally in processes of normalization, civilization, and moralization become a determinate someone from whom the following of norms is expected and who is called to account for any violations. The respondent acquires the position of a responsible subject, whom judges of every kind can count on. Is even moral subjectivity just another label? I think that the king's dignity should not intimidate us so much that we elevate it to the sky. The process of moralization participates altogether in the process of subjectivization.

In the following pages, the question of the true world and true norms is first taken up from the new vantage point of the formation of the subject and carried to the point where the question of the positivity of every order acts back on the subject, namely, here too in the form of an inevitable doubling of the subject, adding a further chord to the doubling of the world and of norms. On the horizon stands the question whether what the orders leave open can be ascribed without further ado to a subject, or whether the subject, too, is so immersed in the twilight of order that such an attribution no longer is true.

2. *The Soul as Mirror of the Universe*

When limited fields of experience and ways of life expand and combine into a cosmic universal order, no room is left for an ordering subject. The human being, like every natural and living being, is preassigned a place in the world and a specific path of development. Our privilege consists solely in our being equipped with reason and insight, which make us capable of overcoming our narrow standpoint, raising questions about the laws of the universe, and directing our lives accordingly. This is true regardless of whether cosmological and political order, the good as such and the human good, theoretical and practical reason interplay, as in Plato, or whether they branch off into two domains of orientation, as in Aristotle; for the pervasive teleology remains unaffected. The situation is similar with the hierarchizing of the individual soul, which corresponds to the stratified arrangement of the cosmos. As "composite beings," humans belong physically to the sensory world and as rational beings they are related to the Ideas. As reason becomes the dominant power in the individual soul and soars to a view of the whole universe, humankind is led up beyond itself, all the way to participation in the whole, in a life deserving to be called more than human, namely, divine (cf. *Nic. Eth.*, x, 7, 1177b 26 ff.). The soul, which Plato in *Phaido* presents as related to the Ideas and which for Aristotle is "in a certain way everything," lives from this cosmic fundamental orientation, far from any merely psychological dualism. Humans are most themselves when they grow beyond themselves and are more than human. Self-preservation changes, by way of self-purification, into self-intensification, all the way to manic ecstasy, which in eroticism and poetry is elevated beyond any canon of rules.

What humans find in this way is, of course, not a superfluity of possibilities, but a well-measured reality, whose measures catch up even with mania; under the dihairetic dissecting knife eros divides into right and left, into a divine and a pathological love (*Phaidrus,* 266a). If even the divine demiurge creates according to the pattern of ideas, then humans all the more so. Despite all clever invention in individual cases, successful action and cognition, on the whole, means *reproduction* of the cosmic order in the life of the individual and the *polis*. In this sense, knowing is *remembering*. Forgetting, which precedes it, and the lack of order, which thereby becomes possible, is the price for humankind's special position. Humans do not *have* their place; rather, they must seek it by choosing their lot in life: "The guilt lies with the one who chooses; God is blameless" (*Republic,* 617e)—a guilt (*aitia*) that then also means cause. If humankind does add something to the cosmos, such as *deviation* from the right path, that is—seen in the light of the cosmos—pure privation and, in this sense, nothing. Humans can create disorder; order they find already existing. The soul is productive only as a distorting mirror. As long as *order as such* prevails, a struggle between freedom and disorder can occur, for instance, in the struggle against political tyrants, where the issue is a relative autarchy within the framework of the whole. But there can be no question of a conflict between freedom and order as such; for if anything breaks the fetters of the soul, it is the True and the Good.

3. The Subject as Epicenter

Only when the cosmos becomes fragmented, when the support of a comprehensive order of life disappears and the outlines of the whole are beginning to blur, can someone board a lifeboat, seeking refuge in oneself and reflecting on an ego that previously merely ran along, whereas now it glitters with its new self-awareness between concept and name. When the universal ground sways, it is good to reflect on something that no longer is in a certain way everything, though it does in a certain sense seem to underlie everything as a *hypokeimenon,* a *subjectum.* Perhaps this is, then, an epicenter that stems from the earthquake of the cosmos.

The shattering of a pregiven order that had seemed solid evokes the question of an orderer. As was to be expected in that early time, this question stands under theological auspices, tangibly in Descartes and Hobbes, and reaching back to the late medieval quarrel of the nominalists. A God who could also create a different mathematics, a God who steps down with Old Testament sternness into the political arena, such a God opens breaches for a human subject, but also opens door and gate to arbitrariness. How far the human being comes into play in all this as *imago dei* or God as *imago hominis* is a question that need not occupy us here; what matters is the way of thinking, whether it be phrased theologically or anthropologically, or integrated into a theological-anthropological alliance.

That one would arrogate to oneself a universal coordinating function as a "subject" is, despite centuries-long practice, anything but matter-of-course. Difficulties will not be lacking. Somewhere or sometime someone gets up, talks to oneself, and reflects on oneself; as a newcomer one still has the old slogans ringing in one's ears; the danger that an ersatz-solution is tried in order to produce the old results by scantier means is not far-fetched, and many traces of this are found. Or more modest goals are set, but then what happens with the remainder that cannot be gotten rid of?

Finally, which "subject" is supposed to make a move? There is quite a supply of Cartesian *cogitos* and it has been played in many keys, from the *cogito* (I think) to *amor, ergo sum* (I am loved, therefore I am). An underlying ambiguity is shown in all this. Everything having to do with the human being as a *sensory being* is generally ranked as subjective, whether it be sensations, feelings, perceptions, interests, or forms of ex-

pression. A rational subjectivity is distinguished from this sensory subjectivity: one concedes to the subject as a *rational being* what is no
longer merely subjective, namely, spontaneous thinking, pure will, responsible action, and the like. The defense of the subject or the subjective can thus take on either subversive or stabilizing features. A new
light is cast on the duality of sensation and reason when both are no
longer caught up in a cosmos. In the following pages I restrict myself, in
accordance with my theme, to focusing on the current state of *subjectivity* and *rationality* with the decisive question of what it can mean at
all for an orderer to order something.

4. Originator: Action and Passion

If one tries to find within oneself a center and foundation of an order
still to be explored or even created, one must first assure oneself whether
anything emanates from it or whether, for instance, a causal process
obeying other laws or even unreeling blindly and randomly is not merely
passing through it. The ongoing process must be stopped at least mo-
mentarily, otherwise there is no Archimedean point from which to in-
terfere in what is happening. There are common interlocutory events
where the door opens a small gap in this direction. To the questions:
"Who did that?" or "Who is ready to do this?" one can answer "I, I and
no other, I and nothing else," and this *I* still has no article and is not yet
a noun. It still stands in an interlocutory and interactional process,
which for its part permits no similar question. Who "did" this conversation or this story? In this form that is a senseless question and would
literally get snagged in the multiple crisscrossing lines of the fabric.
That is why in the first attempt (1: 10, above) we spoke of intermediary
events arranged into synchronically and diachronically overlapping
scenarios and sequences (2: 1–3).

For an "I" to become a noun it must step out of these relativizing
contexts and dissolve them into identifiable units. The *difference* between "I" and others, which belongs to the field of speech and action,
intensifies into a *preference*. Speaker and doer set themselves up as
originator, as author of individual statements and individual deeds,
which one ascribes to oneself—originator, that is, a cause that knows
what it is doing, that imagines a goal, and at the same time could do
something or leave it undone, and could do one thing instead of another.
We know this from Kant as "freedom in the cosmological sense," as "the
power to begin a state on one's own" (*KrV* B, 561; cf. *CPR,* 300)—or in
Hume's language, as a "liberty of spontaneity." This seems to be a very
familiar matter. That the soul is a self-moving being can be read al-

ready in Plato (*Phaidrus,* 245c), and this is transposed to the ensoulment of the cosmos. And in the more narrowly demarcated sphere of action of Aristotelian ethics, spontaneous action is distinguished from forcible occurrences; in the first case the *archē* of movement lies in the actor, in the second case it is outside of the actor, and both already in children and animals (*Nic. Ethics,* III, 1). But since the source of movement corresponds to the goal of a motive force that does not lie in the actor's power, the latter's initiative remains embedded in psychic and social contexts; actors never begin *purely from themselves.* The actor is the guide but not the originator of the movement. Only when these cosmic goals lose their drawing and orientation power and mechanically operative forces replace them does the need arise to reclaim an originatorship that keeps itself free of other influences. Although human beings, in view of their corporeal and social dependencies, can hardly regard themselves as *pure doers,* they do retain the possibility of abstracting something that presents itself as *pure act.*

Here the first great dividing line arises—namely, the distinction between *active* and *passive,* in which passion is thought of as the mere limitation and turning back of action. We have already alluded to Descartes's "passions of the soul." Active and passive are related as mirror images of one another. The very same event is passive with regard to the "subject" to whom it happens and active with regard to the "subject" who makes it happen (I, 1). The same statement is spoken by one person, heard by another; the same deed is done by one person and endured by another. Whether it be a physical or a social act, one's own action is another's passion, and vice versa. Even where active and passive are less sharply opposed, as in a pair of opposites such as spontaneity and receptivity, *self-activity* clearly has the upper hand over everything passive, which is conceived of as a limitation leading to dependencies. Yet again it is not primarily a matter of a psychological distinction affecting events within the world, but rather of an ontological distinction. Self-activity means the genuine mode of existence of a being that begins to call itself "subject" and saves from the rubble of the cosmos what can be saved, in this case a remnant of *actus purus.* For this "second mover" it is no longer true that like the first mover it "moves like something that is loved" (*Met.,* XII, 1072b, 3): modern mechanized nature obeys only coercion; it does not need eroticism, but only legislation.

5. *Possessor: The Own and the Alien*

Actors would not get beyond scintillations of the moment if their activity were not embedded in a familiar "*own world,*" in which they know and find their way, a world by which actions are incited and to which results return and shape it. This extends from one's own body to one's own ancestors and progeny, one's own children, one's own apartment, and expands all the way to available knowledge and skills; and it is rounded off in familiar circles such as one's own homeland, one's own culture, one's own history. It is the world in which the actor is at home and feels at home. And this brings us to the second great division, namely, between *one's own* and *the other's*. More precisely, we must distinguish one's own (*Eigenes*) from the familiar (*Eigenartiges*) and the other (*Fremdes*) from the alien or heterogeneous (*Fremdartiges*). The other would include unknown and unavailable *contents of experience* and *spheres of experience,* so to speak uncharted spots within one's own world, indeterminacies for which determining rules exist, and empty places that can be filled by a suitable continuation of experience. The heterogeneous, on the contrary, would be something that shatters the existing *structures of experience* and *orders of experience,* that is, something unknown in a heightened sense and for which our ordering grids are inadequate. An example of the other would be lack of knowledge within our own language; an example of the alien or heterogeneous would be an unknown foreign language. The heterogeneous can occur in various forms: at the same stage, in the guise of forms of life, cultures, and languages of similar development; at an earlier stage, such as one's own childhood and, collectively, in so-called primitive forms of life, all the way to animal prior forms; or finally, as a deviancy, as in the case of anomalies and diseases. Three central figures in which the problem of ownness and alienness is especially virulent are the child, the savage, the madman, or the fool, plus—in the shadows—the animal.

What we have sketched here in broad outlines are the shadowy sides of those selective and exclusive orders that are arranged in the structures of the lifeworld and our everyday world and precede all normative regulation. If such selections and exclusions by which certain linkage possibilities are privileged and others put at a disadvantage did not occur, chaotic multiplicity would prevent all orientation of action and planning for action. From René Spitz's investigations we know that a child that does not begin to experience otherness around the eighth month and to distinguish the known from the unknown displays elementary disturbances, often provoked by a frequent change of the primary reference persons. The dogs that Plato holds up to watchmen as models participate as domestic animals in the domestication of the world.

It becomes problematic only when, here too, we take into account precisely how the selection and exclusion takes place. As long as humans feel at home in a universe, their own sphere can expand gradually from their most immediate circles to their country and nation, all the way to the cosmos, which the cosmopolitan inhabits. The closer the observer and inhabitant draws to the whole universe, the more the shadows of alienness dwindle. In the cosmos we would have the boundary case of *ownness* without *alienness,* of a universal inclusion that makes further linkages obsolete.

But we need not repeat here that this beautiful order by no means eliminates the shadows of alienness. In any case, the state of things changes when humans find themselves in a world without center and without secure boundaries and now try to find a center within themselves. As within action pure act is distinguished, here too a *pure sphere of ownness* encompasses everything that appertains to me. The personal pronoun is continued in the possessive pronoun, and the privileging of the "I" is strengthened to a privileging of what is "mine." What is one's own (*das Eigene*) becomes the genuine (*das Eigentliche*), from which the alien and the heterogeneous are set off as deviations. The originator becomes the owner who faces everything alien and heterogeneous with the inevitable basic gesture of *appropriation,* all the way to the "courage to make use of one's own understanding."

Appropriation can take the direct road to the "I." In such *egocentricity* the alien is mastered by being grasped as a variation, doublet, or copy of what is one's own, and one has to rely on toilsome conjectural procedures such as empathy and understanding to put oneself in the other's shoes. Even Husserl, who expands one's own presence in an appresence, does not get beyond a declining scale of presence. The primary presence is occupied by one's own lived experience. What is "alien to experience" or "alien to consciousness" seems to him to be associated with the nonsensical assumption of a "hole in consciousness" (Husserl, XVII, 239 f.). The fixation on the problem of certainty belongs completely within this framework. Certainty is truth of which I know that it is such; it is an appropriatable truth that promises certitude—if not certitude of the whole, at least an anchorage.

Appropriation can also go the long route that leads through the *logos.* In such a *logocentricity* the alien is mastered by integrating one's own and the other's in a universal space of thought. If it is a matter of a formal framework, then a purification comes about: "All knowledge is called pure if it contains no admixture of anything heterogeneous" (*KrV* A, 11)—a reminiscence of Plato's catharsis in which the soul is purified of sensory admixtures and illusions, starting with pure colors, tones, and odors (*Philebus,* 51a-e), whose purity and simplicity "are not disturbed and interrupted by any heterogeneous sensation" (*KU* B, 40 f.). If the framework begins to move, then the path of reconciliation presents itself; by abolishing alienation it "removes the appearance of being burdened with anything alien" (*Phänomenologie des Geistes, Einleitung*) and leads to a unity of ownness and alienness, which—as always in transcending overlapping movements—prefers one pole: despite all inclusion of alienness, it is appropriated and not disappropriated.

The immediate owner who reaches directly for the other runs the danger of not being master in one's own house. If the "I" wanted to appropriate something other it would have to first prepare a place to receive it by appropriating the "it." The mediate owner who processes the alien indirectly, on the other hand, ends up in the coils of the superego: the logos as law, which the "I" cannot so easily master.

6. Lawgiver: Autonomy and Heteronomy

Laws are needed first of all by the actors themselves. If their freedom consisted only in their being exempted from the necessity of the laws of nature, no new center of order would arise, but only a whirlpool of irregular moods and arbitrariness. As Hume noted with mild sarcasm, the madman would be the freest person in the world, because his reactions are so incalculable (*Treatise,* II, 3, 1). Willing for something as the motive ground for action stemming from a pregiven teleology is over and done with. Thus law presents itself as the "missing link" between unrestrained desire and rational will—but which law? If the originator of an action remained subject to another's law, the proud subject would be a mere "subject" in the sense of a vassal (*Untertan*) (cf. Kant, *MS* B, 224), and would have to fear that the threatening arbitrariness of events would merely have shifted to the level of arbitrary laws. This fear would be removed if the subject's self-activity is based on a self-legislation. This leads to a third great divide—namely, between *autonomy* and *heteronomy,* again with a distinct gradient. If actors, regardless of all their own activity, remain to a certain degree dependent on another person, on a *heteron,* they must avoid being dependent on this other's *laws.* The striving for self-legislature thus means a simultaneous disempowerment of the other, in whatever form this may occur.

This brings us to the key point of our reflections on the question of the orderer, and here we run into a fundamental difficulty inherent in transcendental theories of the subject down to this day. Modifying an objection of Jean Cavaillès (1947, 65), one could argue as follows: either the lawgiving stemming from the subject takes place *without laws* and the enacted laws are arbitrary as laws, or it is something that happens *according to laws,* which means that lawgiving is not a self-legislation. In other words, either autonomy is *auto*-nomy, then it is not a legislation, or it is auto-*nomy,* then it is not self-legislation.

Very enlightening for the function of the lawgiver is a look into the sphere of politics and law, from where the nomenclature of legislation stems. The validity of positive laws becomes questionable when it remains uncertain by what authority and what procedure they were enacted, and such laws become invalid when the lawgiver replaces them with different laws. In other words, there are no positive laws without a legislator—yet the legislator is of course not a pure subject, but an authority or function, which already presupposes an order. A "first legislator" would have the same difficulties as our pure subject. Let us take as contrast other kinds of law for instance, the laws of perspective in painting, a mathematical theorem, the rules of chess, and the phonetic laws of language. What does it add to the validity of such laws and rules if one can name the "legislators" who introduced the central perspective into painting, discovered a mathematical formula, established the game of chess, or promulgated the phonetic rules? Apart from the fact that such inventions often seep away in anonymity, naming a "legislator" is strictly meaningless. Classical geometry does not gain or lose stringency by being traced back to Euclid, and the central perspective is learnable without being tagged with the great names of the Renaissance. When we read in the early Sartre: "Thus it is within the free project of the sentence that the laws of speech are organized; it is by speaking that I make grammar. Freedom is the only possible foundation of the laws of language" (1962, 653; Eng.: 493), we have not advanced beyond Descartes, whom Sartre is repeating in an existentialistic way. The free act that creates a law binding it retroactively resembles Baron Münchhausen lifting himself up by his own bootstraps. Furthermore, can mathematical laws and chess rules some day become invalid like tax laws? If the game of chess were prohibited in Iran, its rules would not be invalidated like a traffic regulation; one can continue playing according to them, whereas a deposed statesman can no longer sign bills into law. But if no authority can simply abolish those rules and laws, there can also be none that has simply enacted them. Toward laws that display an internal correctness, a lawgiving subject would be in a situation similar to that of the king in *The Little Prince* who keeps his last subject by commanding him to do what he does anyway, namely, go away. For such a subject it is entirely the same whether it is "I or he or it (the thing) that thinks" (*KrV*, B, 404; cf. *CPR*, 216); for such an orderer (*ordinateur*) would only run according to program. In the end the law itself speaks, or as Cavaillès says: "The structure speaks about itself" (1947, 24). Such a hyperbolic mode of expression amounts to a *lawgiving without a lawgiver;* proximity to the law can become fatal for the subject, as we are experiencing in the thinking of the most recent present. Or, a final possibility, does autonomy consist, then, in each person who acts according to law doing so from insight? The difference would then be like that between a calculating machine and a mathematician, but we need not repeat what the situation is with the latter's lawgiving. Self-legislature acts arbitrarily or it phases over into a lawgiving by reason, so that we would be no further than at the end of last chapter. The subject would thus not have brought us one step forward.

7. The Futile Doubling of the Subject

The subject who can merely withdraw to an epicenter remains exposed to forces and laws resistant to its attempts at centering. The three dividing lines separating action from passion, ownness from alienness, and autonomy from heteronomy run right through the subject. This thinking reed, this alienated owner, this subjected ruler constantly sees itself threatened by what it excludes and tries to possess and master, and moreover other epicenters emerge and put its uniqueness in question. A way out of this dilemma is offered when the subject undertakes a doubling and splits out of itself a truer, higher, more sublime subject. The particular subject is confronted with a *universal* one, the empirical subject with an *intelligible* one, and the mundane subject with a *transcendental* one. Thus the subject can appear both as effectuated cause and as spontaneous originator, and its act can be regarded at the same time as an "act of nature" (*KrV* B, 575; cf. *CPR*, 307) and as an act of reason in conformity with self-enacted laws. The late Husserl, who does not deny the scars of this tradition and groups together many of its difficulties, speaks of the "paradox" of a human subjectivity, which means at the same time "being a subject for the world" and "being an object in the world" (Husserl, VI, § 53; *Crisis,* 178 ff.). If subjectivity were identical with mundane humanity, then the nonsense would result that a component of the world constituted the world as a whole. "The subject part of the world swallows up, so to speak, the whole world, and this itself too." Against this nonsense of a Chronos who swallows up not only his children but himself too, Husserl posits a transcendental subjectivity that secularizes and socializes itself by mundane self-objectivation and by social self-declension and can reel back these constitutive threads by transcendental reflection. The doubling would be neutralized into a mere *self-doubling,* if the subject got to grasp itself as a self that remains intact in and despite its doubling. But this fails, as Husserl himself demonstrates, because of temporality, which introduces an otherness (*Andersheit*) into the inner sanctum of self-presence and causes a delay that can never be caught up with (cf. Derrida). Even one's own voice becomes ventriloquistic, if it comes to terms only with itself.

On the whole, the difficulty seems to consist mainly in the fact that the modern subject entertains *infinite claims* to a total or at least a fundamental order, although it has only *finite means* to realize them. The result is a squinting, an "ontological diplopia" (Merleau-Ponty, *V&I,*

166), since the subject seeks a place to stay here and everywhere, now and always, or a masquerade in which the transcendental actor constantly acquires empirical doubles—which, however, continue their duplicate existence on their own and, equipping work, life, and language with "quasi-transcendentals," promote partial autonomy strivings, reverse the role between ruler and subject, and attack the subject from behind with such machinations (Foucault 1971, chap. 9). Whether the subject settles for the *splitting off* of pure authorities or carries on the game of *mixture* or *mediation,* it does not thereby bring about a fundamental, not to mention a total order, neither in the differentiation of finite and infinite nor in their reconciliation. And if, weary of this double game, it withdraws to pure finitude, it still retains a *residuum* that also does not escape the double game anyway. The retreat to genuineness, authenticity, truthfulness is only a helpless attempt to save what can be saved within a shrunken subjectivity. Where subjectivity does not rely on an existing order it ends up in arbitrariness.

But what is especially interesting in our context are the traces—in part sunken to unrecognizability—left behind by a subject-oriented form of order, independently of whether the subject reaches an orderer or does not get beyond the position of an ordered orderer. The selections and exclusions that we have associated above with the filtering viewpoints of importance and rightness acquire a new kind of accent when the centering on a subject is added. The *reservation* that the subject establishes for itself resembles a desert rather than an oasis, for further exclusions and selections follow—and new reductions affecting the owner just as painfully as the next-door neighbors. What withdraws from ordering claims of the subjective orderer, what the subject cannot attribute to itself, appropriate, or subject to its own laws is diminished, warded off, marginalized. What is left are forms of reduction: truth as certainty, interlocution as a combination of action and passion, being oneself as ownness—all this strengthened by a lawgiving in which disposal over oneself and others is secured by a *logos.* A significant residual category is the "crude." Erudition, which is not a *creatio ex nihilo* but indeed a *creatio e rudi,* develops its laws not by an encounter with the other, but with its own preliminary designs aiming at disposal over, appropriation, and securing. The privileging of unity over multiplicity, of the self over the other, of identity over difference, of the center over the periphery is indeed found in all orders that solidify into a distinct state (*Bestand*), but this too is given a stronger emphasis by subjectivation. The familiar assumption that multiplicity is given whereas, on the contrary, the conjunction of a multiplicity "cannot be given through objects but can be originated only by the subject itself, because it is an act of its purely spontaneous activity" (*KrV* B, 130; *CPR* 75), illustrates how very specific modes of order arise from the close conjunction of subjectivity and rationality. This separation of unity and multiplicity, accompanied by a corresponding ranking of sensation and reason, of intuition and action, would be nothing more than a dubious psychology if it were not backed up by a corresponding separation of what precedes all experience and what stems from it. This is a decision "in the image of the subject" or rather "for the image of the subject"; for a subject is first formed in such methodological perspectival stances (*Blickstellungen*), that is, a subject as orderer that would miss its calling if it wanted to consider as ordered what it did not order itself. But is not a foreign language, for someone who does not know it, close to being a given multiplicity, simply because it does not follow one's own language order?

8. *Cooperation of the Body, or: The Incalculable Subject*

Doubt in the power of an ordering subject, a *cosmētor,* who would be more than a programmed *ordinateur* (Fr.: orderer / computer) should not drive us to alternatives that keep flaring up to this day: here an almighty theater director, there theater without author; here a free structurer, there self-expressive structures; in short: here an almighty subject, there almighty structures; and in between a variegated tug of war that merely changes the mixture-ratios but not the essences. We can best avoid this tug of war of appropriation and disappropriation by returning once more to the great distinctions that helped the subject to its feet.

If we consider statements and actions in the contexts where speech and action take place, action and passion prove to be fission products produced by events that in an earlier passage we called intermediary events. Nothing forces us here to alternatives like I or the other person, I or the other thing, hammer or anvil. Events that respond to one another in an intermediate field, attaching to and interlinking with one another, neither run automatically, nor are they clearly assigned to determinate guiding centers. In dealing with things done or words spoken, and with fellow speakers and fellow actors, the initiative can vary, becoming stronger or weaker. Pure passiveness, where something merely happens to somebody, is as much a boundary case as pure action, where someone is sovereignly active. Between these boundary cases, there are the "mixed actions," which Aristotle lists among the special cases of involuntary actions (*Nic. Eth.,* III, 1) but which in reality are the rule, as long as a *dosaged collaboration* is understood; it permits different variations, such as initiative, response, cooperation, letting oneself be carried away, and befalling. If one wants to continue using such words as doing and enduring, they should be totally relativized and used conceptually, as Husserl often does in his analyses of intentional stratifications and references. Actions are corporeally "inscenated" ("*inszeniert*": Husserl, IV, 98, 259), and the actors who put their actions and themselves on the scene do this in the framework of a scenery and a plot into which they are inserted by virtue of their corporeal situation.

Belonging to a sphere of "intercorporeality" (cf. Merleau-Ponty, *V&I*) also makes it impossible to cautiously demarcate ownness and alienness. A successful life, which is primarily doing and not ownership (*Nic. Ethics,* IX, 9, 1169b 29 f.), is at the same time living together, and in its commonality it forms a fabric of ownness and alienness, which the individual can appropriate only after the fact and to a certain degree. When speakers and doers are not presupposed as separate radiating centers or sources of actions but are understood in terms of interlocution and interaction, what is one's own arises through the *differentiation of ownness from alienness,* whereby the boundary lines are variable for both outcome and clarity. Broadly similar treatment in similar circumstances ("*mitgefangen, mitgehangen*") is the rule where finished results are not simply interchanged or courses of behavior simply routinely arranged and classified, but rather speech and action become productive in the quest for something that shows itself only in outlines and awaits its shaping. The more codified behavior is, the more precisely the process can be divided between sender and receiver; the more inventive it is, the less this is possible. Speech and action delve into a stratum of the nameless and anonymous, but this by no means leads to irresponsible chatter and doings in which the individual is lost, for linkage and responses set caesuras where each person is advanced. On the other hand, a responsibility still embedded in responsive behavior resists *juridization* and *moralization* emanating from the fiction that *someone or other* must be made legally responsible. If this limited interest in assurance and blame and the resulting construct are absolutized, the superstition arises that wherever speech and action occurred there must always be a determinate speaker and a determinate doer. In this way one leaps directly from the *privileging* of one's own singular action over to the *indifference* of an activity coordinating ownness and alienness, and what is lost is the *difference* between ownness and alienness, which builds up in the *interference* of different behavioral moves and permits something like a "plural without equality, without in-difference" (R. Barthes 1978, 72). The attempt at self-appropriation ends, in its turn, with a split between "I" and "me," *je* and *moi, ich* and *mich.* The countervoice does not first sound to me from the outside, it sounds in my own house as an echo that defies me or accompanies me as in the latent polyphony of some solo pieces.

The corporeal and intercorporeal belonging to a field of speech and action thus allows a cooperation that escapes from the alternative of "with or without an orderer." We hesitate in this case to speak of a "corporeal *subjectivity* and *intersubjectivity.*" For this raises the danger that the subject-function merely be shifted deeper in experience but not decisively transformed. If the body is located at the foundation of everything, boundaries between ownness and alienness are indeed opened, but only temporarily. A radical revision presupposes that the self is grasped in its innermost core as responding and cooperating. If the Gestalt-theoretical concept of *self-organization* is taken up, as Aron Gurwitsch and Merleau-Ponty do, this means that the ego, in its responsive involvement with other people and other things, is exposed to two sorts of organizational pushes—namely, to a pre-egoic *id* with its drive-forces and fields of force and to a supra-egoic *id* with its rational regulations (cf. Grathoff/Waldenfels 1983, 26). The *id* lives between *logos* and pathos; it is neither master of the ideas that come to it nor of the rules it follows. This double decentering that happens to it both as a *sensory being* and as a *rational being* does not leave intact much of the centering on a subject.

With the laws of the *rational being* we come back to the third and central divide, namely, that between autonomy and heteronomy. The variegated cooperation of the speakers and actors opens a way out of the alleged alternative that it always either *acted within order* or *created order*. What remains to be investigated in the following chapter is the possibility that someone works at order in a kind of co-creation. An orderer who could cover over the abysses of positivity is less to be expected than before. This "subject" is too *incalculable* to compete with the insufficient reasons. The twilight remains, since autonomy co-creates its *heteron,* and so the question also does not leave us: what keeps the happening of order going and preserves it from disintegration?

5

Emergent and Existing Order

1. Ordering and its Standards

THE POSITIVITY OF ORDERS, which cannot be overcome by any total or fundamental order or abolished by any ordering subject, compels us to pursue the question of criteria and standards to the place where orders are formed and solidified and where they replace and repress one another. Selective and exclusive orders prevent the genealogy of certain orders from combining into a total process in which the whole emerges and is realized little by little. If, on the other hand, we restrict ourselves to a universal framework of order, we do not get at the genealogy itself. The normative vacuum continues to exist when morality and law are satisfied with being complemented by histories of customs and traditions operating on a factual plane. So we will seek a way to inquire into the conditions of specific order-formation without succumbing to the attraction of totalization or universalization. Yet the viewpoints of totality and universality must themselves be interrogated concerning the conditions of their origin. With this historicization of standards we evoke the specters of relativism. But philosophy "instead of running away from them, will prefer to illuminate the dark corners" (Husserl, XVII, 244). In any case, the task cannot be accomplished with historico-philosophical needs and fears.

Let us refer once again to our initial definition of order. Order, as we said, is a regulated connection between one thing and another, whereby a distinction must be made between the content of order and its orderly structure. Where a regulation is expected and asserted, there is also the threat of unregulation or irregularity. To decide whether one or the other is present, certain criteria are necessary, or, as we also say, certain *measures*. By measuring, two things can be discovered: namely, whether what is to be ordered is in order and whether the orderly structure itself is in order. This results in three levels: the thing *measured* that is measured, the *measure* by which it is measured, and the *measure of the measure* by which a measure is measured, and the latter in arbitrary reiteration. The threatening regression is prevented if there is a final measuring standard for deciding in a grounded fashion the disputed questions arising at earlier stages. Such an ultimate standard is offered in the appeal to a total order: the truth is the whole—here any appeal would literally miss the mark. Another possibility would be to resort to universal basic measures, to which every positive standard must correspond. If neither the one way nor the other promises an adequate solution, we must—as far and as well as possible—seek an answer by interrogating the positive standards in their positive function without laying claim to a transcending valuation. The results will show how far we can go. But a few general questions must be cleared up in advance.

2. Standards in Experience, Cognition, and Action

The question of pertinent distinguishing criteria is not first posed on the level of propositional statements but already arises on the level of *perceptive cognitions* and *recognitions,* indeed in all cases where visual estimate and inspection do not suffice to decide experiential claims. A "measuring art of pleasures" such as is called for in Plato's *Protagoras* is relevant here. A few examples: Is the appearance on the horizon an oasis or a mere mirage? How will the mushrooms agree with us, or this wine? Does the wine come from Austrian cellars or from elsewhere? What do the red spots on the face mean, an allergy or a rising fever? Did the perpetrator wear a blue or a yellow jacket? How far is it to the next city? Apart from the last question, which does not allow the issue of the right measure to arise, these are all questions of alternatives among which a decision has to be made. The criterion (*tekmērion*) that makes it possible to solve the disputed case is therefore definitely considered to be a distinguishing mark (*kritērion*). Yet the problem arises as to who can serve as judge (*kritēs*) over this sign and pass judgment, every affected person, the expert, or the wise person—a problem discussed extensively in Plato's *Theaetetus* (cf. especially 1576, 160c, 178c). Holding to Plato once again, we can divide the art of measuring "as the one part of it setting all the arts which measure numbers, lengths, widths, depths and speeds against their opposite; as the second however all that do it against the appropriate (*metrion*), the proper (*prepon*), and the fitting (*deon*) and everything that has its seat in the middle between two outer ends" (*Statesman* 284e). Builders who try for special precision use a "ruler" (*canōn*) (*Philebus,* 56b). Of course, we can understand the experiential criteria just cited as predicate rules, but this does not mean that the organization of experience itself is no more than an implicit predication.

The obviousness of the standard pales when we change over to the plane of explicit propositions, planned actions, and productions. By what do I gauge whether a statement is true, an action right, a work artistically appropriate? The answer to this question seems to lead to a deeper-lying discrepancy between cognitive and practical standards.

A *statement of facts,* it seems, is considered true if the asserted state of affairs exists or, more simply, if it corresponds to the *facts.* This correspondence is established from case to case; there cannot be a positive criterion of truth that would have to anticipate all cases, and Kant warns us against trying "to milk the he-goat" with such irrational questions (*KrV* B, 82 ff., *CPR,* 49). The positive criterion is thus supplied by the judged state of affairs that fulfills the intention of our judgment. Hence there would remain two levels, what is measured and the measure, without the latter itself again being supported by an additional measure for judging statements. Apparently it is otherwise with the *judgment of actions.* This is not so as long as we restrict ourselves to mere success. But it does apply when the achieved state of affairs, that is, the deed, corresponds to the actor's intentions. In that case, the standard lies in the intention or the plans of the action, and this is transmitted to the entire domain of technical production, to the "technical-practical," which Kant therefore classifies in the domain of the theoretical contemplation of nature. Searle underscores this connection when he speaks of a double direction of "fitness," a "mind-to-world direction" in the case of believing and opining, and a "world-to-mind direction" in the case of wishing and intentions (1983, 7 f.). But this symmetry is disrupted when we change from the domain of the pragmatic to that of morality. Aristotle already distinguished between a theoretical and a practical truth and defined the latter not as correspondence with mere striving, but as correspondence with right striving (*orexis orthē*) (*Nic. Ethics,* VI, 2, 1139a, 30 f.). With the decline of cosmic standards, the orientation shifts to the plane of norms, and here the result is the above-mentioned doubling of norms. *Factual validity* must be distinguished from *inner validity,* "subjective recognition" from a "worthiness of recognition," for otherwise questions of law would be reduced to questions of fact. Thus in the last analysis the rightness of the act is decided by a *measure of the measure.* Something similar applies to the domain of aesthetics, since the actually prevalent taste is not, without further ado, good taste, otherwise art criticism would be null and void.

But this apparent asymmetry between cognitive and practical-moral standards is tricky and open to some objections. (a) Naked facts—it will readily be admitted—exist only for the positivist, who strips what is of all meaning. It is otherwise in cosmological thinkers like Plato and Aristotle. When Plato corrects the "man is the measure" statement by declaring God to be the measure of all things (*Laws,* 716c), what he has in mind in this passage is indeed human beings' moderate or immoderate behavior, but beyond that every being is to be measured by its idea, just as in Aristotle every being has its internal measurement in its entelechy. The *logical or ontic truth* of the human intellect that directs its cognition by things is doubled here too, namely, by an *onto-theological truth* that measures itself by the Idea, or, in the theological version, by the Divine Intellect. And for Kant's transcendental thinking, a *transcendental truth* antecedes *empirical truth*. Of the transcendental "logic of truth" he says that "no cognition can contradict it without at the same time losing all content, that is, losing all reference to an object, and therefore all truth" (*KrV* B, 87; *CPR,* 51). Transcendental logic thus provides conditions that are neither true nor false in the empirical sense, but make both possible. By demonstrating that they do this, it proves to be right. This truth-logic can be expanded, as Husserl does, by a pure doctrine of signification containing laws that contradiction and nonsense are to be avoided; formal ontology can fan out into regional ontologies; but these and similar modifications do not change the basic principle that matters here. The order of cognition arises from the interplay between *empirical-contingent experience* and *necessary conditions of knowledge* that prepare an ordering grid for experience and thereby make cognition possible. But again we run into the unsolved problem of *sufficient conditions.* If the universal order not only permits variable orders but requires them, a level of specific orders whose standards can stem neither from the empirical nor from a universal reason is inserted between the empirical sphere and universal reason. If one appeals to a totality of reason, the attempt—though also questionable—can be made to comprehend the determinate orders as stages of a rational architectonics or a rational development, enabling them to participate in its necessity. If one restricts oneself to a fundamental order, this possibility is eliminated. A vacuum opens up between universal conditions of experience and experience itself. This is blurred over when one speaks of empirical concepts and laws; these would be empirical only if they could be drawn from experience without alternatives. This hybrid empiricism thus has to be replaced by *positive ordering authorities,* such as theories, paradigms, frameworks, forms of knowledge, and discourses, which in their variability precede certain experiences, but not all. In this positivity they resemble actually prevailing norms, and the problem of a doubling of the structures of order thus arises in the cognitive as well as in the practical domain.

(b) An asymmetry between cognitive and practical-moral standards could, however, also be sought in the opposite direction. To *ontic or empirical truth,* which is derived from things, there seems to correspond no *ontic or empirical rightness,* for norms that command what should be done cannot be based on what is. But here too a certain correction is suggested. If action, like speaking, is to be understood as responsive behavior reacting to claims and dealing with unwarranted expectations, then the domain of experience also receives a determinate orientation. A challenge occurring in experience definitely has to do with what a person is supposed to do and not only with what the person does; yet whether and to what extent the person has done justice to the challenge is not measured solely by a universal norm. A claim first sinks down to a "mere claim" (*KU' II*, 114) below the commandment only when it is measured against a universal claim. But let us repeat once again, material claim and formal legality lie on disparate planes; one cannot be calculated against the other. That would be possible only if there were a positive universal that could be more or less approximated.

(c) The difference between the logic of truth and the logic of rightness therefore does not stem from experience being determinative in one case, while in the other it would be laws independent of experience; the difference lies elsewhere. Once the difference has been strictly drawn between the realm of nature and the realm of freedom, by that very fact two kinds of laws or rules must be distinguished. Taking up and modifying Searle's well-known distinction, we can say: laws of nature, both transcendental and empirical, are *constitutive rules;* laws of freedom, on the contrary, are *regulative rules.* Natural events are *subject* to valid laws; if they do not "follow" empirical laws, they are not acting contrary to rule, but the laws are false or inadequate; if they do not "follow" the transcendental laws, once again they are not acting contrary to rule, but *without rule,* and the events volatilize. In moral-practical action, however, the validity of the laws does not ensure that they will be followed; if the actors do not *follow* the rules, they are acting *contrary to rule.* An action remains an action even when it is wrong. Valid laws of nature imply that what will happen corresponds to them; valid laws of freedom do not imply this. To that extent, here the aforementioned question of what is to be ordered and of order itself bifurcates, whereas there it does not. But this too is not an exhaustive answer. Admittedly, there are regulative rules only where possibilities of choice exist, while on the contrary constitutive rules for action can be discerned that do not apply to right action, but rather to action as such. This is true, for instance, of the formation of fields of action, which is not action, any more than is the following of rules (cf. Heringer 1974, 17), but rather belongs among the conditions of acts. Only when everything not regulated by norms is pushed back into mere nature do cognitive and practical viewpoints separate so widely. The chasm diminishes when cognition of what is is compared not merely with right action, but with action as such, and one keeps in mind a *practice* (Husserl, III § 147; *Ideas,* 405 ff.) whose legality stands between a law of nature and a moral law.

Finally, cognition and action move closer together when it is not their mere claims to validity that are pondered, but attention is paid instead to what the two effectuate. Here we would do well to speak of a *cognitive* and *practical dealing with things and human beings,* in which cognizing and causing intermesh in circularity. A part of this, too, deals with knowledge, and this dealing itself is neither true nor false, but like all dealing encounters obstacles, causes expenses and efforts, permits omissions and prohibitions. Inactive cognition would be just as much a boundary case as blind activity or as a cognition promising only to be true, or an action promising only to be right. Since these are only boundary cases, rules and standards intermesh in the framework of a "discursive practice" that frees us from specters and actions fluttering around freely in space.

3. Production and Reproduction of Order

The standardness of order gives us the possibility of introducing an important distinction within the happening of order. We speak of *productive* behavior or a productive event, whether in the domain of experience, action, handiwork, or cognition, whenever along with a new product a new kind of orderly structure, a new regulation, and a new standard results, while in *reproductive* behavior the new product remains within the framework of traditional orderly structures, follows an existing regulation, and is subject to an existing standard. Of course, pure reproduction is only a boundary value; for it would exist only if the regulated context were determined down to all its details by the regulation, so that only indistinguishable copies were produced. An approximation to pure reproduction is possible, however, for instance in stereotypical behavior, in strongly ritualized speech acts or action, or in the pure triggering of technical effects that are "ready-made by an apparatus" (Blumenberg 1981, 37). That the opposite boundary case of pure production is also excluded will be discussed below. Here it suffices to state that the difference between production and reproduction must be understood as *gradual* and not disjunctive.

This distinction can be explained by referring to the familiarity of our everyday experiences and the encroachment of the unfamiliar. As a part of the normal course of experience, we are always encountering something *new* that remains within the framework of our pregiven order, filling the framework of order in different ways and increasingly testing the standards of order. The determinate indeterminacy that characterizes the structures of our experience is arranged for constant *ongoing definition* and *partial redefinition:* "This house has four stories *and* was built in the nineteenth century," or: "This house is not a home, *but* a prison." The concordance of an existing experiential order is reflected in a *social consensus* that makes normal communication possible and, despite all discrepancies and inevitable corrections and changes, promises harmony on the whole and in the long run. The typical forms we meet in experience appear as "ectypical" replicas, as re-creations, as repetitions (cf. Kant, *KU* B, 207). So we settle here for a *measuring by something other* that leaves open the question of the authoritative other, of the prototypical archetypes. Opposite this would be the possibility that some *new* kind of thing irrupts into our existing experiential order and necessitates *radical redefinitions* and *new definitions,* so that the rules and framework-conditions of our experience and our mutual communication are modified. Here we come upon a *measuring* that no longer measures by something other. Does this mean that a measuring standard is simply posited? Let us examine once again what production and reproduction really mean and in what way something is produced and reproduced.

When we set up a scale of increasing or decreasing production, it seems possible to enter all forms of order on this scale. Production could then mean many things—the redefinition of a situation, the restructuring of an established field, the introduction of new patterns of experience or action, an encroachment into normality, a change of customs, finally an implicit change in the norm-structure. This would apply not only to our traditional everyday worlds, but also to all special domains such as education, the health system, jurisprudence, the economic system, the political order, scientific research, art, and religious cult, which respectively display their specific forms of institutions, everyday routinization, and renewal. Finally, we find this alternation of production and reproduction in the individual biography as well as in the collective history of a generation, a people, a cultural community. But we really get at the productive happening only when we introduce a further important distinction.

4. Tracery and Standard, Model and Prescription

We spoke above (2: 6) of typical forms of experience, which we characterized as the way something appears repeatedly in experience. Everyday examples of this were familiar faces, hand movements, turns of phrase, melodies, aromas, stairways that have so entered our flesh and blood that we can forget them only if we forget a part of ourselves. Among them are also symbolic signs such as telephone numbers and names that are transposed into the sensory and motor system so that ultimately our body functions as "guardian" of the past (Proust, I, 6; Eng.: I, 7). In such "sensory ideas," it is as impossible to distinguish between the stock of order and its orderly structure as between lyre and harmony; the type is at the same time the prototype. The regulation manifested here is not only constitutive in the sense that without it something would not at all be what it is; beyond that, it is installed into what is regulated. Such a corporealized and materialized measure (*Mass*) can be called "*tracery*" (*Masswerk*), without being thereby restricted to geometric filling material as in the case of Gothic cathedrals. Such tracery is not *from* experience, since it itself regulates experience; nor is it *prior to* experience, because it is not an empty form filled out with corresponding materials and merely making experience possible. What is involved in this tracery is shown when we keep in mind the origination of something novel. With the production of something novel, a new measure is also produced; thus the measure arises *with* the experience that is measured by it.

The origination of order here leads us to a remarkable place of the *indifference* of the *different,* far away from all doubling. First we have an indifference of what is to be ordered and the ordering, of the regulated and the regulation, of the measured and the measure; that is, however, also: of the universal and the particular, of the ideal and the actual; for as long as the regular is not detached as a universal form, there is also nothing individual that would fall under the rule. If there were only this symbiosis of form and the formed, we would be exposed to a "tyranny of the Particular" (Proust, I, 660; Eng.: I, 710) that changes from moment to moment but never loosens its grip. The difference between measure and the measured arises through the law of the passage of time. Something appears to be *the same* insofar as it occurs one more time, over and over again, and yet is also *not the same*. With repetition, what is measured gains a certain distance from the gestalt by which it is measured and which reproduction uses as standard. Insofar as the reproduced form is identical with the produced one, it is measured by itself; insofar as it is different, by something other. The measure becomes the standard when an order reproduces itself. Rightness arises from this difference from itself.

From these embodied measures, which materialize as form or structure, we distinguish *standards* in the narrower sense, which are detachable from the measured thing and are laid by it like a rule or measuring rod. Here belong concepts, laws, formulas, and norms, which contain conditions to which certain materials must correspond without the materialization itself being presented. Thus the concept "triangle" contains no data as to whether the triangle is right-angled or not, a law of falling makes no statement as to whether the falling object is dangerous or not, and the penalty for murder during a robbery generally does not take into consideration hair color or gender. The orderly structure is here different from the orderly content. A specific standard does not precede all experience, but it does precede those experiences that are measured by it. A concept or a formula can be empty, but not a gestalt or a structure, since they are nothing but the arrangement of certain materials. This difference between measure and the measured, a difference that does not first arise through repetition and recorporealization, entails that a new standard is not simply produced together with something, like the tracery; it is *produced ad hoc,* and it is not repeated, but applied. It does not merely occur together with something else, for something that appears as something *is* always already more than what can be subsumed under a concept or a law; in this sense all standards of order are regulative, with the exception of those that contain necessary conditions (cf. 5: 2, above). However, the standard of order is not at first encountered as a new object, but in a function that can arise and persist as a function only by referring to possible contexts to be regulated. To that extent standards of order, too, are produced with regard to something that must be regulated and ordered anew.

The difference between concrete and abstract measures, between traceries and standards, can also be understood in another way. The concrete measure acts as a *model* (*Vor-bild*) or *paradigm* that one imitates and that one approximates more or less. That there also are counter-models will be disregarded here. By models we should not think only of visual images, but also of sequences of tones, hand movements, language features, patterns of action, and types of research, that is, of everything that opens new avenues. Furthermore, in this context imitating does not mean copying, but reproducing with one's own means and transportation into a new situation. One could think, for example, of learning a language by reading, listening, repeating after or together with someone—a kind of drilling that precedes all knowledge of rules. If one measures oneself by a model, that means that the "reproductions" enter a relationship of greater or lesser *participation* and allow for a perfecting. It is different with *prescriptions* (*Vor-schriften*) and *norms.* These are applied, followed or not followed, fulfilled or not fulfilled, but one cannot approximate a prescription as one does a model. The relation of participation is replaced by that of *subsumption:* something falls under a norm, to which it either corresponds or does not. While the relation to the paradigm is represented as analogous, the relation to the norm takes a digital form. A legal norm can be fulfilled or not, but it cannot be fulfilled better, any more than one can dial a number better or a sentence can be truer than the other. Thus Kant's good will cannot be intensified into a better will. An excess shatters the boundary of the prescribed. This difference penetrates into the very language: I can phrase something better, but I cannot make a statement better; the statement is either true or it is not.

With the distinction between model and prescription, we again draw closer to the alternative of cosmic and normative thinking. In the first case, the cosmos appears as a comprehensive archetype toward which one must strive; in the second case, laws govern, prescribing to nature and freedom what happens and what must be done. Orientation by an eternal model transforms all cognition into a *re*-cognition, all production into a *re*-production oriented by existing measures. The grounding of order on basic norms overleaps the problem of specific production, as long as the knower and actor are not conceded what is reserved only to artists of genius—namely, not merely to create according to rules, but rather to set the rules (Kant, *KU,* § 46), indeed without a teleological nature working in them. In this sense, speaking with Nietzsche, cognition too is a creation, and the same is true of action. Knower and actor, when they become productive, do not act simply as artists, but indeed *like* artists, with whom they coincide on this point. Insofar as phantasy does not merely reproduce an existing order, but rather produces a new one, *every model contains an element of artist-like prescription.* Between the shifting ahead *into things* of an order that was at one time produced and the restriction of a necessary order *prior to things* is interjected the possibility of a variable order *of* things, where "rationality is precisely measured by the experiences in which it is disclosed" (Merleau-Ponty, *PhP,* xix). Such an order keeps open possibilities of intensification between *perfectio* and *rectitudo.*

Now does this mean that we declare valid, true, or right orders that thus co-produce their own measure, because they arose and continue to exist in this way? One would thereby elevate a measure to being its own measure, a *mensura sui,* in which the measure and the measure of the measure coincided. Such a short-circuited solidification of position and positivity into a positivism does not merely cut off questions; in a very real sense it says nothing, but it still suggests that something is to be said. It says nothing, because the doubling of the measure into its own measure becomes a pure tautology if the doubling contains no possibility of judging the emergent measure in one way or the other. It resembles the *sic volo, sic iubeo* (that is what I want, that is what I command), which contains no argument, but only an affirmation. Such a positivism suggests that there must be a justification, and precisely here is where doubt begins. Just as ontological or transcendental truth is not itself considered true or false, but rather makes possible true or false classifications, and just as a universal basic norm is not itself considered a right or wrong maxim of behavior but is supposed to make this distinction possible, the same is true of the variable orders we are dealing with here. Conditions for true and false, right and wrong, are not true or right, but rather they are *this side of true and false, of right and wrong,* for without such a foregoing structure of order there would be nothing that could be classified as accurate or inaccurate. An example can be taken from language, which presents favorite expressions, speech habits, stylistic peculiarities, grammatical rules and norms—that is, a storehouse of forms of order that surely no one would declare to be altogether true or right. The same applies to orders of perception and action that are anchored in determinate forms of life and professional fields. To judge them as a whole, one would have to refer to a true form of life that would encompass all concrete forms of life, or else to an ultimately valid norm of life that would look down on all forms of life as a supernorm the same old dilemma that has already been discussed sufficiently.

Does it, then, follow that the variable orders of things are arbitrary? This threatening arbitrariness can be approached from various angles. We do it first by focusing on the conditions under which orders originate. This is not the only way to show that not everything is possible— but it is an important one. Even genesis has its logic.

5. Key Events and Key Experiences

To speak of production and reproduction should not be understood as if productive activity must be assigned to a determinate producer and reproducer. Except in the cases where explicit patterns are presented and norms established, it is a matter of a *happening* in which order produces or reproduces itself. The production of an order happens initially in the space of experience, namely in such a way that what happens condenses in determinate events and the reference network forms knots in determinate places. These events without a master, which cannot be fitted into an existing context but rather themselves form landscapes and trigger stories, these "primal institutions" (*Urstiftungen*) in which validity and genesis are inseparably linked, are called *"key events."* They are significant events, similar to what Mead calls the "significant other," overdetermined in what they offer in meaning potential. They must be distinguished from chance triggering events that tear me out of the accustomed paths without themselves opening up a new avenue. Key events can condense into key themes, key scenes, key things, key words, key works, key figures, in which, as it were, code and message coincide, since they give new insights to experience and make new linkages possible. The *ambivalence* of such events is based on the fact that in them *pathos* and *mathos,* attraction and repulsion, are intertwined, and any foregoing standard measure is denied. In this regard, they resemble a question or a suggestion, not a statement or a command.

Here one must think of biographical private and public events that articulate individual or collective life beneath the threshold of a repeating normal order. Among such key experiences are childhood events and authorities, family ties, childhood places, early preferences and traumas, early reading adventures; also belonging here are decisive events in life, such as love affairs, conversations, illnesses; prehistoric breakthroughs such as the discovery of fire, the beginning of livestock husbandry and of sedentary life; cultural stages such as discoveries, inventions, foundings of religions, economic crises, and refugee movements; finally, political events such as war, revolution, persecution, pogrom, or resistance movement. Such events include not only glorious events of humankind, but also destructive or at least partially destructive events such as the French Revolution; and what "can never be forgotten about it" is not only the phenomenon that for the first time a people gave itself its own constitution, but many other things besides. Kant, in his historical meditations (VI, 356 ff.), allows himself some cognitive dissonance when he allows *observers* to applaud an occurrence that they would strictly have to reject as *actors*. Picture a conversation between observers and doers, between Kant and Danton—which rules would such a conversation have to follow? Is the blame (*culpa*) ascribed to the ones, and the happy outcome (*felicitas*) to the others? What Kant here laboriously distributes to different rules would have its truth if occurrence and action were combined. What we here, right or wrong, call "key events" are such events as do not stem from the acts of those for whom they are key events. How we respond to them can be judged, but not what evokes such responses. The moralization of private and public history fails due to the fact that it comes too late. The danger of someone burning hand or mouth cannot be eliminated by mere prohibitions, and we are all burned children. If we nonetheless continue to speak of models, we must also think of dubious and deterrent models, just as there are exemplary mistakes and senseless prescriptions.

The structure of such key events may be explained by an example from childhood development. In the early history of each individual belong the ties to reference persons or authority figures, whether the biological parents or others who take their place. As Aristotle himself taught (*Physics,* I, 1), early childhood experience does not occur in such a way that the child first encounters individuals who stand out initially based on general characteristics as men, then specifically as father; rather, the father is first the quintessence of manliness, similarly to the way the mother is the quintessence of womanliness, with all cultural specifications. Only in steps of further differentiation do acquaintances separate from non-acquaintances, mothers from non-mothers, etc. This happens similarly to the way a system of colors develops in perception, or a phonetic system in language. At the beginning stands not an indeterminacy betraying a pure lack of definiteness, but an overdetermination, a condensation, a crystallization. That at this early stage we are still moving this side of the distinction between universal and particular is also shown by the fact that our children up to a certain age still attach an indefinite article to a proper name and use it as a predicate when the duplicate resembles the original in stride, facial expression, or clothing. They speak of "a Mrs. A.," just as we speak of "an early Cézanne," when we mean a peculiar type of picture. Conversely, in the taxonomies of scientific botany, proper names like *Brassica rapa,* to which the indefinite article cannot be attached and which cannot be pluralized, occur as names of species. There is *a* turnip, but not a *Brassica rapa.* Lévi-Strauss (1968, chap. 7) lists this as an example of a naming practice in which no fundamental difference is made between proper names and collective nouns, a practice that put forth variegated blossoms in the name-systems of American Indian tribes as well as in our [German] nomenclature for birds and horses, dogs and cattle.

If individualization is a mere limit that we never reach, then "determinative" established thinking has as reverse side a "reflective" wild thinking that is not prior to experience, but begins with it. It begins with the initial experiences we make when something novel breaks through and thus something occurs that does not fit into any scheme, any concept, and any law. The novel functions as *index sui,* as an image that is both archetype and copy. Only when the initial experience pales does the archetype detach itself from its original kernel and become a model, a pattern that can be manipulated in a manner that an experience never permits. Proust's "*Recherche*" [Quest] can be regarded as the attempt to rediscover such key events, starting with actual incidents that stir up resonance and awaken the lost archetype.

6. Innovation as Deformation and Deviation

The production of an order is not only counterposed to the reproduction of existing orders; as new production or innovation, it causes a new order to appear instead of the old one. So here we have no longer merely a difference *within an order,* but a difference *between one order and another.* But caution is called for in this formulation. When we place one order opposite the other, even comparing or typologizing the two, we assume the position of an external observer for whom differences are already present. We do not get at the origin of order in this way, for this consists in nothing other than the replacement of one order by another. What is juxtaposed before the comparative view is mutually displaced if we study the ordering occurrence itself. Selection and exclusion, which we have made out to be the basic element of every order, also come into force in the relation between various orders. A new order imposes itself against an old one, in whatever form this may happen. An innocence of becoming, removed from this conflict zone, would exist only if we started with a *primordial production* that were nothing but pure production. From a Gestalt-theoretical perspective, this would correspond to a first gestalt that did not have to set itself off from anything, that is, a gestalt without ground. But an order that did not set itself off from anything would not be a determinate order at all; it would be like a primeval language prior to any determinate language. The question of such a beginning contains problems that we do not wish to discuss yet, but this much is certain: the beginning we are asking about is already presupposed in the question. Even in thought, we always arrive too late to *make* a beginning.

Now the question arises, in what way a new order sets itself off from and replaces an existing one. In answering this question, we reach back to concepts with various echoes in language theory, social theory, and legal and moral theory, without our needing to go too much into detail. A first concept that presents itself is the concept of *deformation,* which points to the sphere of models or prior images (*Vor-Bilder*). Deformation, a disfigurement, relates to existing *formations,* into whose order-structure it encroaches, as opposed to the conformity of a behavior that preserves form, even if it violates it in some cases. However, not all deformations impair the existing order-structure. Think of perspectival distortions or regulated changes of form, putting on and taking off eyeglasses, language bowdlerization and errors, grimaces and similar deviations, which are not dangerous as long as they do not coalesce into a "coherent deformation" (Malraux, Merleau-Ponty). There is much that does not belong in a thematic context, that seems disturbing and burdensome or strikes one as unusual or atypical. These are, so to speak, "normal deviations" (cf. Goffman, *Stigma,* 130 ff.), noises that surround every order. A new order first stands out clearly only when a new tone enters it and develops into a new kind of sound system. By coherent deformation we understand, then, the formation of a new thematic context with a new typology, whether on a small or large scale, in a momentary or lasting form, in a special domain, or in the whole of a form of life when it develops a new life-context. The concept of deformation presents itself similarly to that of alienation (*Verfremdung*) in cases where innovation moves within the sensory domain of material significations, as in all artistic inventions.

The second concept would be the concept of *deviation.* One can deviate from a level, but mainly from a straight line, a right way, a trajectory as it is prescribed for the heavenly bodies. Thus the concept of deviation is linked with that of the *norm.* Deviations can occur in the most varied forms of order, as deviation from normal behavior, from usage and custom, from right and law, or from accepted morality. Here too we must distinguish between an occasional or repeated offense against the rule and a systematic violation of the rule aiming for a new regulation. Something similar is found in innovations in art and science; the contrast between normality and the revolutionizing of an order is a universal phenomenon. Novalis gives this a cosmic resonance when he writes: "Crooked line—victory of free nature over the rule" (*Schriften,* ed. Kluckhohn/Samuel, II, 157).

In this zone of drastic change, the key events spoken of above assume the character of *transitional events.* New models act as distorted images of existing models, new prescriptions as cancellations of old prescriptions. These transitional events are thus irregularities, *anomalies* in a broad sense. Their settlement in a transition zone gives these events a peculiar *ambivalence.* From the viewpoint of the existing order, they are violations; from the perspective of an emerging order, they appear to be advances into a new land. We know this not only from the history of changes of political regime, but also from the history of religious heresies, artistic secessions, and scientific innovations, and from changes in orders of everyday life, which in most cases occur gradually, often with unnoticeable displacements within the orderly complex. When this occurs, the emergent order and the existing order push one other mutually into the twilight. The common communication breaks down, and in extreme cases the uncertainty can go so far that the boundaries between reality and fiction, between reality and insanity, become blurred. Alfred Schutz and Foucault show this in full clarity in their interpretations of Don Quixote. If reality down to its very foundations always emerges only in determinate interpretations and views, then the new order of a "different state" (Musil) also leads to a more or less new reality (Berger 1983), but no criteria exist that would be unambiguous and indisputable enough to distinguish definitively between productive phantasy and pure phantasy. Sporadic anomalies resemble momentary perceptions in which we cannot decide with certainty whether what we have before us is a phantom or a real thing; for the latter owes its subsistence to contexts and circumstances of dependency in which it appears (Husserl, IV, § 15). We are lost without such orienting and preserving contexts. But what happens when these are being reshaped?

The ambivalence of transitional events vanishes when one starts from a total order, for here old and new order appear as parts of a given whole, or stages of an emergent one. Deviation then means either deviation from a narrower or lower order in favor of a broader and higher one—or else deviation from the right order, which is a form of disorder. The ambivalence is weakened when one refers to a fundamental order; old and new order are then merely empirical variants of a formally predelineated orderly complex. The look at the whole, like the view from on high, fails to see the proper occurrence of the change of order; but it also lacks insight into the *conflict of order* resulting from the collision of heterogeneous orders, and it cannot be settled by any universal order nor mediated by any fundamental order. Again we come up against the problem of power and violence, the context of production and destruction that cannot be removed by beautiful constructions and by good will.

What we have sketched as the conflict between old and new, existing and emergent order, also applies, other things being equal, to the *collision between existing orders* resulting when one order presents itself as, to a certain degree, the deformation of the other. The simultaneous attraction and repulsion between groups, nationalities, and cultures stems precisely from this; the unfamiliar scintillates between medicine and poison so that a strict boundary cannot be drawn. Tacitus may hold the Germanic tribes up before his Romans as a warning image of a powerful way of life, but that is possible only as long as the projected counterimage remains on the cultural canvas. Understanding between nations takes its difficult course beyond clear superiority and inferiority, beyond generation and degeneration.

7. Time Thresholds beyond Custom and Fashion

Innovation leads to a conflict between old and new. If the quarrel is to be laid aside within the temporal happening without recourse to transcendent authorities, two possibilities are available that are familiar to us as long-lasting interplay. The Good and the True can be equated with what was handed down by the ancestors, or else with what is to be achieved by coming generations. In the first case, the old is revered as *tradition;* in the second, the new is admired as *innovation;* again, in the first, custom rules; in the second, fashion does (cf. Max Weber 1976, 15) or, if that sounds too ephemeral, the modern. *Traditionalism* and *modernism,* too, are invalid means for bridging the abyss and closing the legitimation gap left behind by a positive order. Yet I do not want to repeat here the usual criticism, but rather to ask how the two time dimensions protrude into the origin and existence of order. For it does not follow from the critique of the absolutization of temporal data that time does not, in its own way, contribute to the origination of order.

Let us begin with the dimension of the past. Where a claim is made on tradition, it usually appears as foundation and forum, as authority for appeal or justification, or as a stabilizing factor, and precisely this is resisted by the opponents of traditionalism because it solidifies every right into a privilege and every judgment into a prejudice. We escape this struggle between traditionalists and anti-traditionalists when we regard tradition not primarily under the aspect of a justification or stabilization of order, but under that of a production of order. Tradition here shows itself to be something worked at, whether by deformation and change or by continuation and preservation. Even the revolutionary break, not to mention normal experimentations, pays its tribute to tradition in this way. Only conditionally, then, does the question of the weight of tradition have to do with continuity and discontinuity. But what is excluded by the heterogeneity of emergent orders is a great total tradition, which would presuppose a developing total order. Where there are orders in the plural, there are also traditions in the plural. A simple traditionalism fails by the simple fact that a determinate tradition is continued; and the selection thus brought into play is not itself pregiven, but happens now. Aside from that, the further development of an order, as well as the change from one order to another, is unthinkable without the cooperation of traditional components. The only alternative would be a *continuous creation* resulting in a sequence of unconnected moments that would permit no reliability, no contract, and no duty, and in extreme cases would lead to madness.

But this line of thinking has not yet reached its limit. Innovation does not merely work at a tradition; it draws its momentum from a beginning that has always already been made when an activity begins. In this sense, too, every personal activity retains something of an event that sinks down into anonymity. An order that on the whole cannot be ascribed to any orderer (cf. 4: 6) stems from a *primary production* that has always already happened and escapes from any reach. Not because there is an unchangeable order in things, but probably because the process of ordering has always already begun, invention takes on features of rediscovery, and all creating takes on features of re-creation; this replication (*dieses Wieder*) is the only way we draw near to our origin. The presupposed *primordial production* belongs to an anterior past (*Vorvergangenheit*) that cannot be situated on a time axis of earlier and later. It is *an early time that is not earlier, but now,* a time that does not belong to an early childhood history, but is constantly renewed when something novel breaks through *as on the first day*. Astonishment, awe, fear, alarm, horror—all these affects with which we respond to such events—point to the fact that where something novel is making a breakthrough we do not have the first word nor the initiative. This changing origin lies behind a threshold. Such pre-beginnings cannot be grounded, and yet they are not placed at our discretion, for our choice always comes too late. As we do not choose our body, our mother tongue, our original inclinations, disinclinations, and rhythms of experience, so also not tradition itself as the quintessence of a pregiven order. The pre-beginnings we are speaking of here do not lie somewhere at a far-off distance; they are inscribed in the body of the present like a birthmark.

This order, which is installed and continued with our existence, lies, then, this side of grounding and optionalness; it is not something to boast of. This order retains its weight only as long as it remains incomparable, outside any series, also outside the temporal sequence. If the past is demoted to the former, which is set off from the present, no reason can be given *why a former order should be and not far rather a later one*. The place in time as such provides no argument, and a glorification of the archaic, of the past as such, condemns itself to illusory rationalization. A tradition without traditionalism would be one we could not count on, for that is exactly from where it draws its weight.

Something similar could be said about the future. With the pre-beginning, a future is opened up that likewise reaches further than our predictions and plans. It, too, cannot be planted on the time axis as what will come sometime later; it belongs to the present as *what now has not yet happened and is still to come* and in this way it escapes our reach until death, it too being "present in absence" (Landsberg 1973, 14). The future too lies behind a threshold, affected by our choices but not stemming from them. A theory of speech and action that concentrates on questions of validity and rightness inevitably misses this happening of time, failing to recognize the weights imposed on speaking and acting as temporal events. Moral speakers and doers may lie or tell the truth, let someone live or die, yet still believe themselves in their morality to be beyond the "long, desperate, daily resistance to the fragmentary and continuous death that insinuates itself throughout the whole course of our life, detaching from us at each moment a shred of ourself, dead matter on which new cells will multiply and grow" (Proust, I, 671 f.; Eng.: I, 722). They know neither death nor rebirth, which play their game between habituation and renewal, and sometime or other their last game.

The opposite of a normativistic, functionalistic, or otherwise performed weakening of tradition is an emptying of the future. Whenever fashion is more than a spice of history, whenever it sues for and performs change as such, it winds up in a circularity in which a present system merely reproduces itself in the future. For if the *new,* which from the point of view of information theory achieves a high information value and contains little redundancy, is itself considered to be the Good that is worth striving for, one improbable unexpected event performs the function as well as another, as long as the producers control the technique of producing pleasure, whether in the framework of an economic, political, cultural, or religious system. An existing system generates noises to keep its machines from rusting, and when bread is in sufficient supply, the games must increase so that the people will stay calm. This running-in-neutral of a cultural machinery that often lauds the maxim "art is short, life is long" practically requires one to destroy the machines. For why should something function and not much rather nothing?

The archaic without archaism, a future without futurism, what could they look like? Prescriptions, however moral they may be, do not help one go any further.

8. Heterogeneous Orders and Relative Conditions for Validity

The objection of arbitrariness accompanies our reflections on the origin of order like a shrill dissonance. A few things that limit arbitrariness have already been mentioned: namely, that there are standards with relative validity, without which all speech and action would be impossible; that the production of order is not a production "out of the blue," but a production set in motion by triggering events and by key events, working at existing orders and linked back with pre-beginnings of a primordial production that cannot be caught up with and that leaves something yet to be done. Nonetheless, in the end, is not positivity explained by positivity and what is by what is, so that validity claims are lost in the actuality of speaking? Is there not the threat of a relativism—however refined—when we relegate validity questions to the domain of genealogy? Now some ideas have repeatedly been marshaled against this suspicion. But it is advisable to take up this old objection in a coherent form and once again illuminate the "dark corner."

The objection of relativism is dismissed all too easily if one suspects behind it only a presumptuous foundationalism that believes nothing right can be done and said without ultimate foundations. Two important aspects must be considered in this regard. The idea of the True and the Good, which since Plato's times has again and again put the concrete world into the shadows, performs two functions that cannot easily be done without. First, the Idea serves as an intensifying *ferment* that generates heightening and suspense; if it is sacrificed without being replaced, then egalitarianism and indifference threaten and could lead to a cultural death by freezing. Second, the Idea, together with its successors, serves as a court of appeals against pure arbitrariness, whim, and power, against everything that insists on mere facts. Here the merry deconstructionists sometimes make it far too easy for themselves when they think only of dismantling (*Abbau*), and not of rebuilding (*Umbau*).

By *relativism* I mean, as usual, the relativization of validities. The standards by which the truth of statements and the rightness of actions are judged stand under the guidance of changing circumstances and authorities. Depending on which authority one installs as decisive, relativism takes the form of psychologism, sociologism, historicism, or culturalism. As early as Protagoras, relativism has not meant a form of skepticism, for order here appears to be relative; it does not mean a form of empiricism, for general standards are by all means permitted;

nor does it mean a form of solipsism, for—at least in the practical-political arena—the standards are of a social nature (*Beschaffenheit*). In this sense it is a matter of a relativism of orders within which obligations prevail, though these are all based on mere positing. We fall into the tendency of such a relativism, so it seems, when the standards of positively existing orders are neither embedded in a total order nor secured by universally valid fundamental norms. If we choose the compromise of introducing universal standards only to eliminate this or that, we are left with a normative vacuum and, apart from that, a normative pressure arises that presses all positive orders down to the plane of the merely particular and thus systematically devaluates them.

But there are better arguments against the objection of relativism than such an emergency solution; we can scramble out of the dispute between absolutists and relativists merely by changing the plane of inquiry. This becomes clear when we examine the decisive preconditions of the old quarrel. From the vantage point of its critics, relativism consists in judging the *same* state of facts or the *same* deed from case to case or else from order to order according to contradictory criteria, so that in one case *p* is what in the other case is non-*p*. The relativists would help themselves from Plato's dovecote and take out tokens that they systematically interchange. "Fair is foul, and foul is fair." The same wine tastes bitter when it is drunk by a feverish person; it tastes sweet when drunk by a healthy person. One believes in a dream that one is flying, and upon awakening one knows that one was lying in bed. This and similar examples are familiar to us from *Theaetetus,* and indeed a lot has been made of them. Whoever asserts one thing and its opposite ends up in self-contradiction, and in the end asserts nothing. Here it is assumed that we are speaking about the same thing in the same sense. But healthy and sick people, persons awake and asleep live at the same time inside and outside the same world and cannot directly contradict one another. Now someone will reply that sickness and dream are anomalies that are understood to be different from the normal state and as modifications and deviations. But a counterargument is that anomalies are generated by normalization processes (2: 9), not arbitrarily but in such a way that what is excluded never has its full say within the exclusive and determinative sphere. Otherwise the dream would be *only* a dream, sickness *only* sickness; and that would amount to an absolutization of normality that is constantly being repeated in pairs of contraries such as adults and children, civilized people and primitives, orthodox and pagans, cultured people and barbarians. If it is accurate that all concrete orders arise through selections and exclusions, then we encounter a *heterogeneity* in the literal sense: the orders are of different origin and cannot be homogenized on the plane of positivity. From the level plane of *contradictory* (*widersprechender*) statements and recommendations we end up on the sloping plane of *conflicting* (*widerstreitender*) lines of inquiry and modes of organization, which enable one at all to say and do what may be true or false, right or wrong, and which therefore cannot themselves be subject to these criteria—unless there were simply such a thing as unconditional truth or unconditional rightness. But *of what* should this be the truth or the rightness? It is thus no longer a matter of a relativism of validity, but of a *relativity of validation conditions*, one of which is the relativity of fields of argumentation. Let us recall again the distinction between importance and rightness that affects the occurrence of sensory gestalts, language forms, conceptual fields, methods and modes of argumentation; not a single statement and not a single action is excepted from this. Insofar as not all human speech and action is drawn into an assimilation to the cosmos or to God, there results an *incomparability* of order with order, that is, an incommensurability due to lack of a common standard.

But here too caution is called for. Incomparable does not mean that different orders such as phonetic systems, kinship systems, garden layouts, methods of cure, battle techniques, and forms of greeting have nothing to do with one another. There certainly are overlappings and intersections—for instance, the Germanic-Romance doublet vocabulary of English; there are resumptions of former orders in later ones, there are related characteristics, typological commonalities, going all the way to universally demonstrable laws. But what does not exist is a comparability of different forms of life, language systems, or ways of thinking as a whole, and this is so, not because they could on comparison turn out to be completely dissimilar, which after all would merely reverse total similarity, but because they do not allow a comparison at all. Selective orders are incomparable in a radical sense: we lack a place from which we could oversee and measure them with one another, precisely because we ourselves live within an order. Every attempt at universalization and totalization starts from somewhere, and every comparison limps.

Now one could object that a total comparison may be illusory, but this does not preclude that in case of conflict, individual statements and proposed actions could be detached from their living context and tested for their validity. Does one have to be an Austrian winegrower to discern traces of poison in a wine? Does one have to live in the Middle Ages to give a plausible argument against burning witches? Does one have to be a German or even a Jew to argue against nationalistic racial laws? I would answer to this as follows: relativization of validity claims does not mean that a validity is conditioned "purely as such," but *that every claim is raised under determinate conditions,* which means in a determinate framework, under determinate cognitive, practical, and institutional preconditions, before a narrower or broader audience, which in a boundary case can be oneself, and all this at a certain time, in a certain place, and with expected consequences. It is not a matter of 2×2 suddenly possibly being 5, or a crime suddenly becoming a laudable deed by merely crossing the Pyrenees; rather, it is a matter of not anyone, anyhow, anytime, and anywhere saying to anyone "$2 \times 2 = 4$" or "Thou shalt not kill." There are no unconditioned statements and no unconditioned actions. "Of course, there are no such things," someone will reply and refer to Kant, who definitely thought the unconditionality of the moral law together with the conditionality of natural and social actions. But if one separates these two things by a chasm in order not to endanger the unconditionality of validity, one no longer has access to situations of action and orders of action. If one does not want to promote the fetishization of morality and right, then one must start from a way of *dealing with norms* that is specific in each case and not identical with their validity content, just as how to deal with mathematical laws and formulas is not deduced from the laws and formulas themselves.

Under this aspect, let us return to what we said initially about the function of an idea of the True and the Good. Is a universal norm useful as an appeals authority in cases of conflict? It is—at any rate, when someone holds a maxim that withstands no universalization, however it may be reached. Now cases of conflict in which any reasons are given at all usually have this appearance: when one side complains of human rights violations, the other speaks of medical treatment; when one side speaks of terrorist acts, the other claims the right of a people driven from its land; when one side talks of the violation of international law, the other argues for the right of a case of self-defense similar to war; when one side warns of the impending destruction of humankind, the other speaks of defending freedom; when one side alludes to depredations of nature, the other argues with economic needs and job security, etc. These are examples enough to show that what can be rejected and opposed with good reason, in most cases cannot be opposed by blaming the insufficient universalizability of maxims, quite apart from the fact that maxims never occur in isolation, but as part of a legal system, a political constitution, or a moral code. Consider the case that someone openly declares a certain group of people to be subhuman, using fallacious arguments, for instance citing the different natural talents; we do not need to be a norm-universalist to contradict this. Incidentally, in the more recent history of political resistance, skeptics, positivists, and other proponents of a modern reason, unless I am mistaken, have by no means done worse than those who set great store on massive rational grounds. Finally, the most extreme case: someone professes with cynical candor a maxim behind which nothing stands but his own will. No arguments are any help against this. One cannot convince a Callicles with reasons why he should listen to reasons. The motivating power of a universal law does not go very far; it pays for its uncondi-tionality with a clear desensitivization. Plato had it easier with the Good that everything strives for; reason, which relates to pleasure and displeasure, draws the soul gently and freely by the "golden thread" of law (*Laws,* 645a). A resensitivization could take shape if claims were not only awaited from above. Relativization, which seems like a limita-tion measured by absolute, detached claims, after all means intrinsi-cally a placing-in-relation.

9. The Art of Ordering between Finding and Inventing

"All sacred games of art," Schlegel writes, "are only remote imitations of the infinite play of the world, the eternally self-creative work of art" (*Krit. Ausg.,* II, 324), and Nietzsche (III, 495, *Nachlass*) chimes in that the world is in the end "a self-generating work of art"—even an artist would be too much. Thus the vacuum fills itself, leaving behind a min-imal fundamental order; it is filled with reminiscences of the divine demiurge, except that it is no longer a hierarchical world organized from above (1:7), but a world of increasing and weakening forces. Here too, then, we have a relativizing and a perspectivizing but without a central point that would let all perspectives be *mere* perspectives. There is no trace of relativism, nor of egalitarianism and indifference. But is the question of truth and rightness not solved here with one sweeping stroke called the "will to power," which releases us from all responsibility?

To speak of the world as a work of art, whether with or without an artist, gives the cue for a criticism that suspects aestheticism wherever the artistic goes beyond the strands of aesthetics. Artists may create a world according to rules of their own, or nature may do it in them; they may behave like a second god, as long as they do not meddle in morality and science, the guardians of what is right and true, and break through that wall "that is set between the fantasies of literature and the realities of the world" (Christa Wolf, *Kein Ort. Nirgends,* 14). A mixing of the spheres that would allow the artist to advance to an artist of life would, indeed, be aestheticism, with Nietzsche as its key witness and the early Romantics as his predecessors, not to speak of the many epigones.

The disastrous effect of this drawing of the boundaries is that artistic creativity is thereby pushed as far away from research and action as they are from it. If a cognitive and practical order lies ready-made neither in things nor prior to things, then it must be produced or in-vented. Insofar as productive imagination is at work in this, we can speak of an *artistic* moment calling for a *poetics* of cognition and ac-tion. This requires a specific technique that no longer merely marshals means for pregiven purposes, but rather participates in the modulation of fields of research and action. To that extent there is a *technical* aspect to knowing, speaking, and acting. Under the new auspices of the origination of an order, the old dimension of *technē,* the artificial, shapes itself into a new context. The "aesthetic" and the technical have been omnipresent as far back as humans can think (cf. 1: 4).

But a look into the artist's workplace as well as into that of the technical inventor teaches that production is not arbitrary; rather, the finding and inventing of order work together in changing dosages. Consider the great series of implements for flight and swimming, in which the flight of birds and the fins of fish play a central role without providing a definitive blueprint. Or consider the art of landscape gardening, which salvages an element of farming in the world of civilization. "Half work of art, half nature" (R. Arnheim), it is a threshold art par excellence that openly shapes nature in the typical stylistic variants of the French, English, and Japanese garden, catches it in a secret play of forms, or lets natural forces, such as wind and water, work for it; whether the result is more discipline or more wild growth, it would lose all charm without the interplay of intervention or forbearance. Finally, the painter, who toils with color and canvas, and the poet, who works at language, are also not dealing with a mere *materia prima,* but with preformed materials that give certain hints and open ways leading one knows not where. Where does the standard followed by the painter come from? Whenever artists are not merely copying themselves or others, the standard develops in the artistic activity itself, and a viewer or art critic will never detect it anywhere but in the clues of the work itself, which must be investigated. In what they are trying to do, artists attract their own observers and critics, and the work creates a posterity for itself (Proust I, 531 f., Eng.: I, 572). Pure invention means a setting of standards; pure finding means an acceptance of standards and also a dissolving of all standards in the paradoxical form of a "tychistic art" that lets chance work for it. These are boundary cases, which the artist's as well as the technician's creation can approximate without ever attaining. The artist is not, in this sense, an *alter deus.*

Does it means aestheticism or technicism when this way of seeing is also applied to a cognition and activity that negotiates its themes and questions in interaction with others? Why not compare concepts with a way of painting? "Is our way of painting, then arbitrary? Can we simply decide to adopt that of the Egyptians? Or does it merely have to do with pretty and ugly?" (Wittgenstein 1982, 297). Artists, it is said, cannot err and cannot do anything morally wrong, for they produce appearance as beautiful appearance, and are obligated only to themselves, whereas knowers and actors have to deal with reality and are obligated to the laws of truth and rightness. That this appearance, whether beautiful or not, strongly permeates our everyday life, private and public, may be dismissed as a disastrous boundary-crossing. At any rate, the rigorously prescribed division of labor between different validation agencies does not get at the origination of order. If there is an Archimedean point, then it is the one on which orders hinge. If one wanted to classify and prescribe this fulcrum itself as order in or above all orders, in the long run this would result in a regulated running-in-neutral. An emerging order lives on what it leaves outside.

6

The Ordinary and the Extraordinary

1. Prior to and Outside of Order

THE TWILIGHT ZONE OF ANY ORDER consists in the fact that order simultaneously makes experiences possible and prevents them, building up and demolishing, excluding as it includes, rejecting as it selects. In short, light and shadow interplay. Transition zones are formed, thresholds on which we can linger rather than leaving them behind. No total order and no fundamental order can fill the gaps that open up recurrently within a single order and between different orders, undermining the arrogated position of a centering subject. The positivity of orders placed on no secure ground repeatedly lets the threatening question arise, whether arbitrariness, power, and violence do not, then, have the last word. That they do not have the *only* word is shown by the many restrictions of arbitrariness we have often spoken of. But they would indeed have the last word if insufficient reasons and incalculable subjects were exhausted in this negativity. Are arbitrariness and power, then, the "ultimate authority"? The question of the dynamics of order is also posed in this context. If the happening of order does not culminate in a whole and move along the secure line of a fundamental norm, what is it that keeps it going? Why isn't one order "fundamentally" as good as the other?

If anything can be said in reply to these questions, then it is probably only by returning to where we began, namely, to reflections that moved on the threshold between order and disorder. If orders are not accepted as ready made and hypostasized, their selective and exclusive achievements presuppose something that comes to order and that precedes them as something to be ordered. But this unordered element prior to order, which we must distinguish from the disorder within an order, cannot be said and grasped directly, because this move always presupposes an order whose means it uses. We cannot go back prior to the orders of our speech and action; we can at most look back at them.

Therefore, at the outset we settled for a series of indirect modes of approach. We cannot get away from this indirect way, but what we can do after having examined the various forms and ways of order is take up our initial questions again and watch them emerge from order itself. This attempt aims at thematizing *what precedes order* as *what goes beyond order*. The "original" (*das "Ursprüngliche"*) in this sense would lie not behind us, but ahead of us; it would not be from formerly, but rather it would appear now, and again and again (Merleau-Ponty. *V&I,* 180, 267). This is possible only when, amid all selection-exclusion, ordering at the same time also means *transgression,* crossing beyond order. This would mean that everything that enters an order, in a certain way also moves outside it. As extraordinary, the unordered loses its purely negative tone and moves alongside the orderly and the disorderly by outbidding them. Now all depends on articulating this outside and this excess without in turn succumbing to a mere doubling of order, for that would result in a further positivity that would not advance us one step further.

2. The Shadow of the Alien

Alienness or heterogeneity (*das Fremdartige*) was described above as what is excluded from the existing structures and orders of experience (4: 5). But a disturbing, animating, and threatening effect can emanate from the alien only when what is excluded remains virulent in its exclusion and in a certain way belongs there. This is the case when the alien dwells in the midst of the familiar world and not apart from it. To understand this, we must refer the selective and exclusive achievements of order back to what is brought to order and return to the open form of relevancy and interaction (1: 8–10). The open form consists in a claim that can neither be fitted in as part of the whole nor subordinated as to a law; and precisely therefore it provokes a selective answer. Every achievement of order that responds to such a claim has the form of an *"and not rather"* (2: 4ff.). This preferential difference from which order stems is itself no longer an element of this order. The genealogy of an order leads us into it and beyond it—both in a single step.

A simultaneity of inside and outside has the result that every determination occurring in an order is present there *in broken form*. Something that occurs in experience and with which we have to deal by speaking and acting is simultaneously present and absent, itself and something else, here and elsewhere, now and at another time, connected with this thing and with another. If it were completely present and completely itself, it would fit into an existing order; if it were totally absent or something completely other, it would have nothing to do with this order. The same brokenness is found between actors and fellow actors, speakers and fellow speakers that stand to one another in a relation (*Bezug*) purchased by a simultaneous withdrawal (*Entzug*). Someone, whether a partner or myself, is always simultaneously present and absent and is simultaneously oneself and the other. The attempt to eliminate this brokenness by total presence and complete selfhood leads to fissuredness; I am all the more an other, the more I try to take possession of myself (4: 5). In the end, Narcissus's self-reflection becomes his doom: his own image entices him into the abyss. In fact, the look into a mirror can in extreme cases trigger a suicide attempt. The situation is similar with the relation to the other. "There is always another one walking beside you" (T. S. Eliot, *Wasteland,* v, 62)—there is always a third person behind and beside us, not as an observer or a mediator, but as a faraway person who excludes all exhaustive communication; and here too excessive proximity can suddenly change into aggression.

Conceptual language, which we use for better or worse, could raise the suspicion that the alien is a negation that accompanies the positivity of what is one's own: "*omnis determinatio est negatio.*" However, a shadow is not a negative, but rather something that is co-experienced and that is changed and lost with what is experienced. No synthesis is in sight.

3. The Fissure between Production and Provocation

Forms of order such as open linkage and open encounter are characterized by the fact that the claim is an *excessive claim* and the challenge an *excessive challenge,* since every response falls short of the claim that is raised. A selective and exclusive hearing and seeing at the same time fails to hear and see; every such speech also leaves something unsaid and silences something; and every such action is also a forbearance and causes something to fail, since no all-inclusive *logos* stands behind it. One could almost speak of a preestablished disharmony. A series of fissures runs through our experiencing, speaking, and acting. *Saying* does not coincide with *saying something,* nor does this coincide with *saying something true or false;* what is said falls short of what is meant; what is answered falls short of what was asked, just as what is taken falls short of what was given—"*tra un fiore colto e l'altro donato / l'inesprimibile nulla*" [between a flower picked and the other one received / the unspeakable nothing. G. Ungaretti]. Similar cracks run through action and create a distance between *doing, doing something,* and *doing something right or wrong.* These discrepancies belong to the specific nature of intermediate events, which follow one another without their confirmation being anchored in pregiven goals or guaranteed by fixed rules. Such discrepancies, however, not only provide fuel for conflicts, they are also what keeps our experiencing, speaking, and doing in operation and drives it beyond existing orders. But how does this happen?

Let us consider the fissure that is decisive for our considerations— namely, the fissure between a productive behavior, in which the orderly complex changes, and the provocation to which a productive invention responds. The art of production, which we have located between finding and inventing (5: 9), needs a further clarification. Fissure means that a context exists, but a broken, not a closed one. There is no unified ground plan behind the fissures. For the provocation—for instance, an originary question—is an event that sprouts forth orders, but itself fits into none.

Question and answer, in their *heterogeneity,* cannot be oriented teleologically toward a comprehensive goal, nor guided normatively by universal rules like two statements of fact and two suggestions for action. The connection that is established between question and answer is located prior to truth claims and consensus demands. Nor can question and answer be systematized and hierarchized like items of knowledge fitted piece by piece into the body of knowledge. The textures of insertion and subordination fail due to the fact that question and answer are not comparable elements of a quantity of statements unless I disregard their character of question and answer and consider them, for instance, as English sentences or as tactical chess moves.

Various attempts have been made to heal, mend, and bypass fissures and to deactivate the boundary between the ordinary and the extraordinary. The discrepancy can be reinterpreted into intra-ordinal differences between subject and object, subjectivity and substance, concept and thing, idea and reality, intention and fulfillment, etc. The incoherence is neutralized by an operative and ultimately valid *accommodation,* whether in the sense of a cosmic-teleological universal order, a normative fundamental order, or merely in the sense of tradition as an actually recognized order or different cultures as actually existing orders. The questionableness of being itself is eliminated in this way (cf. 3). One can, however, also try to avoid or mitigate the split by approximating pure production or pure provocation. The reduction of one pole, the pole of creation and production, leads in the extreme case to *docility* and *submissiveness;* the answerer sinks down to a tool or mouthpiece. The reduction of the other pole—namely, the pole of provocation— leads to a creation that only circles around itself, and hence to *arbitrariness* sprouting forth mere variants and modes. When it is fitted into an order, the loose bond between question and answer is tied into a loop; it is detached when only instructions or creations are left over. Either way, the *open correspondence* that characterizes the relation between question and answer, *challenge* and *response,* and keeps a door open for the extraordinary, dwindles. A question that is more than a mere phrase or routine is never completely in place, and it is not for nothing that Socrates appears as an *atopos.*

From this point of view a peculiar light is cast on the problematic of grounding and arbitrariness. If our speech and action respond to an excessive, absolutely never fulfillable claim, the insufficiency of the grounds and the incalculability of the speakers and actors does not seem to be a privation needing to be removed, but a constitutive property of responsive rationality. A fully grounded answer would not be an answer that crosses a chasm, but a conclusion that prolongs a line. The free play between question and answer retains an element of the abysmal without which question and answer would not be what they are, namely, fragile footbridges and breakable ropes. The answer is more or less motivated, but by a motive that is never compelling; what moves us happens when we follow the movement.

Now, someone could object, is not everything shifted to the justification of claims and demands? Are there not justified and unjustified claims, warranted and unwarranted challenges, by which responsive achievements of order are placed in a renewed twilight? The answer to this would be: a claim can be checked for its justification when it is a legal claim subject to universal standards. But questions, requests, or demands, whether presented verbally or not, are as such neither true nor false, neither right nor wrong. Conversely, they are not pure facts, for these could not lay a claim or even an excessive claim on me. The points of view of totality, universality, and pure positivity fail here. With every claim occurring in experience, something occurs that produces selective and exclusive formations, but is not totally used up by them. For a question is never a part of a whole, a case of a law, or a naked fact. The simple question: "Why do you say that?" causes a vortex that leads beyond all norms back to the event of saying itself. This is true also of the voice of the law. Obeying the law is something that does not itself fall under the law and its binary standards, but belongs to its genealogy. At this point, all logic and morality comes to an impasse that we cannot get beyond with arguments. Every claim retains something of the sting of an incitement that cannot be fully legitimated.

4. Between the Orders

A question or a challenge that is posed to someone is already an event that does not find a place within an existing order. To that extent we are constantly crossing beyond the existing order, since apart from boundary cases, we never behave totally reproductively (5: 3). But as long as our answers remain on the ground of an existing order, our speech and action stay within the framework of what can be said and done within determinate discourses. The order of things in which we move as a matter of course cannot be distinguished from the things themselves, and the cracks that cut across all identity remain hidden. With the matter-of-course familiarity of the ordinary, the extraordinary also remains in the background; it is there too, but not as such. For the respective order to show its boundaries, our familiar experience must be alienated; what we know must be seen with different eyes and we must get into situations where we no longer know our way. Apart from the transition between an existing and a newly emerging order, which we have discussed at length, an alienation of what is one's own arises from the confrontation with another order, with another's life, a strange milieu, a foreign language, an alien culture. We encounter the alien as something that cannot be said and done within our order, although probably in a different one. The extraordinary makes its appearance as *an order existing elsewhere*. Between discourses, cases of conflict (*différend*) assert themselves, and they cannot be resolved by the discourses in question (Lyotard 1987). If everything ended in a theoretical and practical compromise, the threat and the allurement emanating from the exotic could not be explained. Comparative studies do not produce a confrontation. So we must draw some further nuances.

The alien develops its provocative force only where it comes so close to one's own particular nature that it appears as a possible peculiarity and variant of one's own. The extraordinary is not the product of an alienation, for then an initial unity would be presupposed that permits development, but not foundational selections and alternatives. Paradoxically formulated, the extraordinary is *the outside of a certain order,* not a vague somewhere or other. This is shown at all stages where another order occurs. Take the familiar example of the foreign language. No matter how foreign a language may be, it is never totally alien, for at least language sounds differ from mere natural sounds. I see and hear somebody speaking, or even speaking to me. This means that I am dealing with forms of expression, even with traces of sound symbolism, that do not come from a totally different world. The confrontation with the event of speaking begins even before I understand what is being said. Without a "fact of signifying" (Jakobson 1972, 42) that lies at the basis of every intended meaning, one would not know how a child ever finds access to the language of adults, or indeed could even seek to do so. Of course, to understand what is said, specific, far-reaching conditions are necessary; a language is understood completely only by participating in the life of its users. Likewise, to understand the alien always requires a change in one's own form of life. But this does not preclude the alien as such from being there only as long as it is remote from what is one's own. If, then, the alien is not totally foreign to what is one's own, this does not mean primarily that the two can be compared with one another, but rather that the various orders intersect more or less and each awakens an echo in the other (5: 8). The allurement and the menace become all the greater, the closer the alien approaches. Madam Verdurin is not made uneasy by the stories happening in the elegant Faubourg Saint-Germain, but rather by intrusions and outbursts that endanger her "little clan"; and a "monstrous twin" (Leroi-Gourhan), such as the monkey, alarms and amuses us with its grimaces more than the sight of a ruminating cow or a cat's remote stare.

Such overlappings and intersections, such resonances and consonances ensure that the various orders are neither separated from one another by sharp boundaries nor seamlessly interconnected; rather, *intermediate zones, crisis-nuclei,* and *transitional domains* are formed with multiple boundary areas, which in turn are subject to specific historical conditions. A modern form of boundary situation is the quest for the "unknown" that can never be transformed into something known (Merleau-Ponty, *V&I,* 103) and that often appears as fleetingly as Baudelaire's "Lady Passing By." The sense for the lightning-like encroachment and the swiftly transitory is announced in a preference for roving, traveling, the romantic, from Baudelaire to the Surrealists and Walter Benjamin's *Passages,* where the long prepared "excessive sedentariness" (Leroi-Gourhan) awakens nomadic counterforces and the art of living seeks a place for itself in a disenchanted lifeworld (cf. Kiwitz 1986). After the disappearance of a perfect order to which one assimilates and approximates oneself, the experience of the exotic that leads beyond the existing order no longer runs via a higher regulation, but rather via a "deregulation of the senses" (Rimbaud). This experience changes rapidly into the illusory whenever *elsewhere* is positively occupied as an imaginary plenitude—"illusory" because *elsewhere* necessarily loses its attraction once it becomes a second *here.*

5. Transgression of Order

Interdiscursivity, in which the extraordinary appears as an order existing elsewhere, could not develop its provocative force if every order did not intrinsically strive beyond itself. The other's ownness must stand opposite one's own otherness, an alterity in one's own house. It is hard to imagine that a house dog or a lap dog would be fascinated by the wolf's way of life. The extraordinary as an existing other order draws its glittering brilliance from an extraordinary that suggests *an order possible elsewhere.* This elsewhere is not to be understood as a pure nowhere, as utopia, but as an atopia stemming from confrontation with a heterotopia. If *discursivity* consists in the difference that exists between what can be said and done in an order and what is said and done, and if *interdiscursivity* consists in the difference between what can be said and done in one order and what in another, then *transdiscursivity* consists in the difference between what can be said and done in an order and what cannot be said and done in it. The unsayable, invisible, inaudible, undoable, etc., is the reverse of the sayable, visible, audible, doable. This reverse side is present in the excessive claim of what must be said, seen, heard, done, and it emerges as the extraordinary when an existing order shows its limits and its gaps. "Reverse side" means that the extraordinary forms no sphere of its own and develops no life of its own; thus it behaves similarly to Saussure's sheet of paper in which the front cannot be cut without also cutting the back. The boundary zones between an existing and a new or otherwise existing order correspond to *marginal zones* and *unmapped white surfaces* within one's own order, where there is a lot of noise and a variety of *marginality* luxuriates. The ambivalence of what is excluded as irrelevant, atypical, abnormal, immoral, or contrary to norms is the driving force for a variegated movement of transgression that, for lack of a comprehensive and ultimate order, takes place as an "ascent on the spot" (Merleau-Ponty, *V&I,* 177), that is, as a departure that does not arrive elsewhere.

6. Limited Transgression: From Lack to Fulfillment

Perhaps the most sensitive point in the transgression of certain orders is the connection between the element of the negative and that of the elative, between the unordered and the extraordinary that presents itself in an excessive claim and excessive demand as *above the ordinary.* How can a negative change into a plus, *too little* ally itself with *too much?* What distinguishes pure immoderation from superabundance? This is a delicate point because a transgression that crosses boundaries without abolishing them violates those boundaries. Is a surpassing of order that is bought by a violation, then, perhaps bought at too high a price? Orientation by a universal order or by a fundamental order again offers two possibilities for defusing the transgression and removing the sting from the violations. To distinguish between these two possibilities, let us speak of one as surpassing and the other as infringement.

Starting from or moving toward a universal order, a destiny and fulfillment are predetermined for each person and can be reached in levels and stages. Striving takes its course, like the Platonic eros, between lack (*Mangel*) and abundance. There cannot be too much of *the Good,* there is only an excess of *goods,* whose use and enjoyment must be tailored toward a right measure between excess and lack; for the situation here is similar to an excess of sensory stimuli, where an excess destroys the organs of sensation (*De anima,* II, 12). Plato and Aristotle draw on Greek medicine's understanding of health as a balanced play of forces within the organism and they take to heart the old wisdom doctrines warning generally against excess, especially against the arrogance of a *hybris* seeking to rival the gods by its own power. "That of which there is no excess (*hyperbolē*) is good; but whatever is greater than it should be, is bad" (Aristotle, *Rhet.,* I, 6, 1363a 2–3). The whole is realized when every being keeps to its limits and precisely thereby participates in the whole; so too humankind, whose soul *in a certain way* is everything. The cosmos, which assigns a place to everything, embodies a measure that holds the middle between too much and too little. If there is a form of intensification and a summit of the Good, then it is precisely in the realization of this middle (*Nic. Eth.,* III, 6), which then—measured by average behavior—can attain a "superabundance" of excellence (cf. *Nic. Eth.,* VII, 1, 1145a 23 f.; *Rhet.,* 1, 9, 1367b 6 f.). But what goes beyond the right measure appears as *perissos,* as excessive, superfluous, uneven like a number that dances out of sequence. The delimited form (*peras*) keeps in check the misshapen and boundless (*apeiron*). Accordingly, where boundaries are to be crossed, it is toward a Whole and Highest, in which movement comes to rest.

When, on the contrary, a normative fundamental order is made the basis, the anticipated fulfillment of a striving is replaced by the required fulfillment of a norm, and things will not turn out right without it. As the criteria of importance and rightness separate (cf. 2: 8, above), so also do the various movements for transgressing an order. *Crossing over* the boundaries of limited fields of activity and forms of life means a gradual expansion that permits a gradation of more or less and pushes back the limits of the sayable, seeable, and doable; the violation of particular orders is caught up in an overall order. Not so with the *infringement* of norms; this does not correspond to the broadening of a range of movement, but rather to a change of direction, a deviation from the right way, like Heracles at the crossroads. The digital order of yes and no permits no analog more or less when validity claims are at stake. One can drink more or less, one can strike more or less hard; but one is a traffic offender or a murderer, or one is not. The infringement of a norm does not have to do with what cannot be said or done, but rather with what definitely can be said or done, yet should not be. When a violation is tolerated in the realm of norms, it is only with regard to norms of a higher order and more convincing norms, all the way to universal norms of reason so deserving of recognition that they permit violations only at the price of sheer unreason and radical disorder.

Naturally, a proponent of an inviolable legal and moral order does not have to stop here. Under the aegis of ineluctable imperatives, postulates can prosper that do justice to the *perfect* good of happiness and complete in the beyond what is missing in this world. Until that point is reached, a wise nature sees to it that an excess of goods and a shortage of evils do not seduce people to an Arcadian pastoral life "as good-natured as the sheep they feed" (Kant, VI, 38). This postulatory metaphysics can be replaced by a philosophy of history or evolutionary programs—or by letting end in emptiness the arch of tension that leads from deserving to be happy to heavenly bliss, from the highest to the perfect Good—but these machinations behind the stage settings of a former world-theater change little in the basic lines of thinking.

These basic lines are what convey upon excess and superfluity the index of "too much." For this thinking starts with a *lack to be removed* that corresponds to a *wholeness yet to be achieved*. Everything that exceeds merely reproductive self-preservation acquires the character of self-realization and self-intensification: the self seeks what it lacks. If the insatiable passion to have, rule, and be important is not to mount to a destructive level, at some point or other the mere incitement to pleasure must change to the *claim* of a good that is no longer a good for me or for us, but the Good in itself. This change occurs when individuals fit their striving into the whole or subordinate it to a fundamental law and hope for the fulfillment of their own striving at least as a supplement. Measured against a universal order that develops gradually, the extraordinary appears to be a handicap (*Vorgabe*); measured against a fundamental order of command and prohibition, it appears to be a defection (*Abfall*). As the transcending of finite boundaries of life, the crossing over is something temporary; as the transgression of laws and norms, it is something invalid. For the abundance of the good has nothing besides itself; the strictness of the law tolerates no exception. What lies beyond order ultimately makes no sense or else a perverted countersense.

7. Radical Transgression: Between Lack and Superabundance

Excess and superabundance appear in a different light when order moves into the twilight, and here too we have to deal with the situation of an indeterminate animal. Although it lacks a rigidly predetermined course of life, not all ways stand open to this animal, and it is caught in challenges and encounters that can be mastered only selectively—hence never completely—and that generate the surplus of an uncontrollable superabundance. Ordinary and extraordinary, lack and superabundance meet across a threshold; if the lack is definitive, so is the surplus. This means that the crossing over and transgression are *never completed without a remainder*. The phantasm of abundance arises from the expectation that one would have everything if one ever crossed the threshold and had a look behind the mirror. But not even God could do that, as Husserl says (Husserl, III, § 44; *Ideas*, 138). The *excess* is inseparably chained to the *negative;* it occurs when the boundary of an order is simultaneously set and crossed. Without back-linkage to negativity there would remain only fantasies of omnipotence, all the way to caricatures of a superman.

Traces of a hyper-ontology stemming from a negative ontology can already be found in Plato, when he pushes the experience of being beyond itself in a dual play of dying out and erotic soaring, all the way to being blinded by a light beyond being (*epekeina tēs ousias*), which triggers a cascade of hyperboles in the neo-Platonists, fed from the overflowing source of a transcendental Super-Being, whose superabundance (*hyperplēres*) creates an other (Plotinus, *Enn.*, V, 2, 2). Objections to such a surmounting and exaggeration of experience are not lacking. Is this abundance not obtained surreptitiously in the course of an exuberant experience that soars beyond the boundaries of our experience on the wings of an enthusiasm that has Plato as its father (Kant, III, 387)? All this happens, of course, only when the initiated person has been installed in the higher light, when the blinding light has been captured in an idea, and the superabundance channeled, the surplus exploited, whether in an economy of salvation, thought, or art, or in the restricted economy of pure survival. A crossing over that seeks to leave behind the threshold that joins and separates lack and superabundance leaves so much behind that excesses have to be inserted to compensate for lack. Everything *extraordinary,* in the end, becomes a stopgap within a destabilized order. "They say 'Christ' and mean 'calico'" [i.e., religious conversion is accompanied by cultural change].

Another objection is even more serious. Enthusiasm not only believes itself justified in disregarding the boundaries of experience, it also believes itself elevated above the boundaries of logic, law, and morality. Enthusiasts who overplay the boundaries of experience become lawbreakers who make themselves "outlaws" by disregarding all norms. The aesthetic, religious, or erotic phantasy may vent its enthusiasm within the bounds of pure reason, whose taciturn "yes" or "no" puts a stop to every transgression. Logic, law, and morality are correctable on their own terms, but not crossable to the other. There is a "beyond" of *this* logic, *this* law, and *this* morality, but no beyond of logic, law, and morality *in toto*.

Some replies can be made to this. First of all, the normal itself is a polemical term, and so "every preference for a possible order is accompanied, most often implicitly, by the aversion for the opposite possible order" (Canguilhem 1978, 147). In the innovative transgression of an order, construction and destruction are always combined. But if transgression were no more than a violation that chooses what runs counter to order as such and opposes the true with the false, the right with the wrong, the good with the bad, it would remain on the ground of the existing order, which by all means includes in its thought and management eventual disturbances of its state. A counter-order first enters the picture when the new revalues the existing order and withdraws from its authority, displacing its binary grids. Without such "affirmative critique" (Kiwitz 1986, 132), absolutely nothing would move. Whoever merely violates the laws of perspectival portrayal or the laws of grammar is a beginner or a fumbler, but at any rate not an innovator; it is no accident that lack of ability increases the pressure to adapt. Likewise, someone who disregards a society's laws out of mischievousness, weakness, or selfishness is still not a rebel who lifts it out of its hinges. A parking violator and a revolutionary are two different things.

But what if the order to be transgressed is an order that may claim universal validity? What counter-order can be opposed to an order that makes speech and action possible at all? Surely none. A systematic transgression of these orders would, it seems, as an *anti-logic* or *anti-morality,* have to change into pure destruction and intensify to self-destruction, since those who contradict and counteract yet are nonetheless still speakers and actors lay claim to the very laws they contest. Unless the anti-logicians and anti-moralists want to be stabbed with their own sword, silence and inaction are all they are left with, and even then the *logos* that this living creature cannot shake off, because it has reason, catches up with them. There seems to be no place even for an *alogic* and an *amorality.*

This would be the state of affairs if there were pure validity without relativizing validation conditions in which it is embodied and without a development from which it arises. It suffices to remind the reader of what was said above (3: 8, 5: 8). There can be a beyond of global orders of speech and action only if there is a this-side that assigns them their boundaries from the start. Earlier than any norm, indeed, are *excessive claims* that put our speech and action in operation, keep them going, and drive them beyond themselves, as well as *responses that fall short of the claims.* If challenge and response, provocation and production, were fully attuned to one another, there would be nothing to regulate. Thus not only do command and prohibition arise simultaneously with transgression, but from a genealogical perspective, deviation, violation, and the abnormal are prior to the normal. The temporal displacement proclaimed by this priority again marks the difference between the unordered that is to be ordered, and its division into ordinary and extraordinary. If a pre-state of order is posited in itself, then it takes on traits of retrojection. "The image of chaos is that of a denied regularity; as that of the golden age is that of a wild [*sauvage*] regularity" (Canguilhem 1977, 165, Eng.: 148). If the order that has come about is detached from its genealogy, what results is a logicism, legalism, moralism —that is, forms that in their striving for universalization are themselves particular and coercive. To remind such solidified orders of their alogical, ajuridical, and amoral origins means to transgress them without abolishing them.

A normativity not disturbed by the abnormal nor transgressed by the enormous freezes into an artificial system deprived of its driving forces. Measures encounter not only other measures that restrict them, but an excess that transgresses them. Without a "glow shining inextinguishably from the doors of the law," all that remains is a machinery of order rotating around itself and knowing only a surplus value that it itself consumes.

8. Encroachments and Eruptions of the Extraordinary

A transgression that neither ascends to a *global order* nor establishes itself as a mirror image in a *fundamental order* necessarily reaches an outside that does not stem from a relinquishment, an other, or an alienation. There is, then, an extraordinariness that is compatible with limited orders, in which inclusion and exclusion, making possible and making impossible, are one. Such a transgression also does not mean a removal of boundaries and differentiations ending in a sea of boundless undifferentiation, in pure *lack of order*. Complete indeterminacy would be merely the negative image of complete determinacy and a remnant from the dialectics of being and nothingness, which attains nothingness only by disregarding the determinacy of being, that is, thinking it without experiencing it. Total disintegration and total nihilation reside very close together.

The unsayable, invisible, inaudible, and undoable mentioned above is comprehensible only in the very saying, seeing, hearing, and doing, and has nothing to do with dumbness, blindness, deafness, and inaction. It is not a vague approximation, not an expression of an "objectless readiness to awaken," but rather a currently embodied determinate "over-and-beyond" (*Überhinaus*) that breaks at the thresholds of orders and emerges in the boundary zones between different orders, and in the marginal and empty zones of each order. Breaks that stop the ongoing life-rhythm of sleeping and waking, food procurement and sexual intercourse, and lead to many forms of boundary-crossing, belong to the oldest stock of humanity and not just to the foam and scum of a hyperbred civilization (cf. Leroi-Gourhan, *G&S,* 284). The entering or exiting of encroachments and eruptions has, like all breaks, something immediate, something powerful about it, that cannot be removed by any conceptual brackets and groups of argumentations. If it were not so, we would move on the ground and in the framework of an implicit order without its boundaries becoming visible.

The extraordinary is the reverse of the ordinary; hence encroachments and eruptions are as widespread and variegated as regularity, which presents itself differently depending on domains and types of order, modes of activation, and forms of life. The threshold experiences we started from (1: 6) would thus have to be examined again in their entire breadth. The extraordinary can be found in perception, manipulation, and feeling as well as in the riddles of thinking and the aporias of action, in painting as well as in mathematics or politics; and it will be found most intensively where a reversal is caused by unique or repeated key events in individual and collective life—such as birth, death, rebirth, or founding, inventing, revolution, renewal, or destruction (5: 5). The extraordinary knows, however, not only determinate sites for encroachment and eruption, but also determinate forms of breakthrough that can be grouped into a hyperbolic of the extraordinary, though of course not systematized. A few examples may suffice to illustrate this heterogeneous field. That we frequently refer to the language of pictures is not by chance; picture-language is not a substitute for conceptual language, but a solvent to keep it from congealing.

The forms of breakthrough of the extraordinary set themselves off from a determinate normal form of order. Often in a polemical counterposition, they constantly run the danger of being caught up in a mere counter-order or drawn into the wake of simple disorder, and they are of consequence only where they go beyond a mere reaction to the orderly.

The *unambiguousness* of a terminologically fixed order, which makes the meaning of discourse available but also immobilizes it, is countered by the introduction of *ambiguity* that preserves the "surplus" of meaning beyond what is said and of what is said beyond what is meant (Merleau-Ponty). It keeps the unsayable present as something that needs to be said and counteracts a reign of univocity by multiplying possibilities of linkage (Voloshinov 1975, 72). In multiplying equivocations, a linguistic virtuoso like Joyce appears to be practically the antipode of Husserl (Derrida 1987, 136; Eng.: 102–3). Collages and assemblages are suited to allowing the "polymorphism of wild being" (Merleau-Ponty, *V&I*, 252) to appear.

The *measuredness* of an order attuned to the middle or the mediocre contrasts with a *heightening to the extreme* that shatters our accustomed standards. Here belongs also the theory of the sublime, a neo-Platonic heritage that disturbs the circle of modern aesthetics considerably. The tremendous size and superior power of nature that exceeds our power of imagination and portrayal leads, in Kant too, to the "abyss" of an experience that brings menace, danger, and violence. But the "formlessness" of the universe, after passing through the calm of the aesthetic, is in the end caught up through the form of the moral law. What humans lack as sensory beings, they regain as rational beings, whereby, however, the power of nature changes into the "power" of the moral law that subjugates the senses (*KU* B, 110). Possibilities of making the immeasurable itself visible are found in Monet's fields of water lilies and in Barnett Newman's walls of color, which the eye no longer oversees but into which it can only immerse itself. We approach an experience of the pure ground where forms become blurred and are changed into a pictorial event.

The *concordance* of the mundane and social universe within which individuals come into play only insofar they get along with everything else and fit into the whole is shattered by a *simultaneity of the incompossible,* in which things and people rival one another, competing for my look and my attention, and yet first win back their depth and density, which they were deprived of by the presumptive overview, only in the presence that is undermined by an absence. This "shattering of Being" (cf. Merleau-Ponty, *V&I,* 265), whose splinters sparkle and injure, finds an expression in many attempts of modern art, where the classical central perspective is abandoned in favor of multiple and multivalent modes of portrayal that no longer converge on a center. Let us recall only, representative of many things, Delaunay's and Apollinaire's flimmering fragments of image and sentence, the heterogeneity thresholds in Magritte's picture riddles, the metamorphoses in M. C. Escher's picture patterns that make the impossible possible, or the grotesque as a simultaneity of ambivalent, heterogeneous, and contradictory elements (cf. Bakhtin 1968).

The *thrift* of an economic purposiveness that reduces means and risks, takes no unnecessary step, spares its energies, and has nothing happen for nothing—all the way to "nature, which does nothing in vain"—is opposed by the sense for the superfluous, festive, extravagant, combined with acts of spending, donating, wasting. The archaic custom of *potlatch,* regarded by Marcel Mauss as an early form of social exchange, has by no means become dispensable at its core, and it is heightened by Georges Bataille to the point of humanity's self-extravagance at the feast of life; it represents an abundance of ingredients whereby life, including social life, soars beyond all purposes. It includes gifts, jewelry, aroma, play, idleness, which is the "beginning of all vices," the whole assembly of *luxe, calme et volupté* (luxury, calmness, and voluptuousness) that is characterized by charm, taste, elegance, or luxuriance and not by pure accuracy. When this background of useless vital forces dwindles under the pressure of calculatory rationality, the cosmos, which once expressly included the decorative, shrinks down to a dry skeleton of order.

The *prudence* of a rulership that inevitably internalizes itself to self-mastery and produces a manageable regularity is flooded over by forms of exhilarated *ecstasy* in which humans get out of themselves and an Other speaks and acts in them and withdraws from learnable rules, as already in Plato when he counterposes to *sōphrosynē* various forms of mania, from eros, via soothsaying, to poetry.

Habituation to an old established reason is loosened by various forms of *alienation,* tomfoolery, eccentricity, all the way to the creation of the Surrealists' "syntax-free space" (Leroi-Gourhan, *G&S,* 397) that permits new possibilities of juxtaposition.

To be *caught* or *constrained* in a self-made or imposed form of life provokes departures, excursions, emigrations, that is, withdrawal movements that push forth into political, artistic, religious, or personal new land.

The *exodus* changes into an *exile* when it is coerced.

The *hierarchy* of a gradational order is fractured by *carnivalesque events* in which social roles are reversed, and in a "play without a stage," the vertical order is bent into a horizontal one—at least for a day (Bakhtin 1971, 137).

The solemn *seriousness* of the intellect that believes itself well-grounded and indispensable meets its master in *laughter,* which acts below the line of argumentation. Reason has defended itself against this attack since olden times with maxims such as: "The fool laughs, even when there is nothing to laugh about," as in the anecdote of Thales and the maid. Reason provides for an education in which there is not much to laugh at; the guardians of the city could disconcert the city if they lost all composure and spread Homeric laughter. We need lovers of wisdom, not lovers of laughter (*Republic,* 388e). Or reason tries its hand at belittling; laughter is healthy, the "vital feeling it promotes in the body" is pleasant, but certainly no big deal should be made of it: "Laughter is an affect resulting from the sudden transformation of a suspenseful expectation into nothing" (Kant, *KU* B, 225). Should laughter have anything to do with the extraordinary, it would have to be dealt with on an equal footing with reason, just as wit (Lat.: *sal*) is the salt of reason. Laughter "frees [human] consciousness, thinking and imagination for new possibilities. For that reason, a certain carnivalesque consciousness prepares the way and precedes great transformations—even in the field of the sciences" (Bakhtin 1968, 49). Something similar might be expected of a tearless reason: "There are tears of things" (Virgil). If even things have their tears, then tears are certainly more than subjective expression. Human beings break out into laughter or crying when they are overcome by something that in their ec-centric position they cannot master (Plessner, VII, 359 ff.)—and this includes not merely "their feelings." Like speech and action, laughter and crying can shake the foundations of an order.

The series of hyperboles in which the extraordinary announces itself could be continued—but all the way to arbitrariness?

9. Regression and Transgression

A transgression that retained self-mastery would cross no boundaries; it would merely displace them. Boundary-crossing, then, also always means crossing beyond oneself. This radical form of transgression cannot obtain its impetus from itself, from self-made plans and decisions, but only from a movement that has already begun (5: 7, above). To that extent *crossing beyond* a determinate level of self-awareness and self-availability at the same time means *falling short* of it. This explains why every breakthrough of the extraordinary has something childlike and barbarian about it and verges on the pathological. Chaos lurks behind it; the boundaries are blurred; in the extreme case, the loss of the world and of oneself becomes imminent.

These regressive elements of transgression are an enticement to loosen the fragile connection between the disorderly and the extraordinary and to yield to the temptation of pure regression. But the enticing *removal of boundaries* that lets itself go as *outrage and excess* contains its own failure within itself. The claim that strives beyond the existing borders would die out as soon as it were fulfilled. "If only we were our great-great-grandparents . . ." (G. Benn)—if we were, the wish would lose all meaning, its statement would no longer even be pronounceable. The extraordinary lives on the contrast with the ordinary, which it outbids. Inventions in the art of speaking and lovemaking have nothing in common with unarticulated stammering and indiscriminate copulation. Yet talk of regression can lead to misunderstandings, for even the child's babbling and wooing for love is anything but a mishmash of language and feeling. Symbiotic early stages and different forms of individuation, such as are found in archaic ways of life, should not be equated with retrogressive effects of a de-individuation; the latter is absolutely a late product, a reaction to over-individuation.

The return to a state of undifferentiation with all boundaries removed promises, together with de-individuation, also to control the negative above which transgression merely rises without abolishing it. This takes us back to the question whether the series of hyperboles can be prolonged arbitrarily.

The breakthrough to something extraordinary can fail because the transgressor breaks down under this movement. This includes the entire scale of *endured suffering,* beginning with slight injuries and ending with annihilation by *death.* At this point I would like merely to raise, and not pursue further, the question of how far suffering can be lived as a breakthrough or passageway. It can be stated, however, that an excessive shielding against the encroachment of the injurious or annihilating produces new suffering by locking up the suffering person within a se-curity zone that, along with suffering, also keeps life at a distance—an excessive mastering of suffering.

Endured suffering is heightened to *inflicted suffering* that culminates in *murder* as intentional killing. In this case, the breakdown of the suf-fering person results from a crime. Is there then, here too, a break-through of the extraordinary? Let me emphasize again that a pure option for the disorder that is a part of every order does not shatter that order. Regression here seems to open an alternative not merely by going back before the decision between good and evil, but rather by revoking this decision itself into a "hyper-individuality of life," a life that wastes and consumes itself in death, mutual self-destruction, and sexual pro-creation, so that negation and excess fuse together. "And we regard the luxury of death as well as the luxury of sexuality first as a negation of ourselves, then, in a sudden reversal, as the real truth of the movement manifested through life" (Bataille 1975, 61). Of course, such a death feast of life goes beyond political and economic wars, beyond profitable robbery, murders, and burglaries, for there the calculation of a "re-stricted economy" still prevails. The figure of the *victim* of a prodigality in which it is ultimately indifferent who sacrifices whom is tempting. If this absolute amorality were attained, we would be not only outside morality, but also outside the interplay of provocation and response that keeps all transgression going, including the transgression of a "re-stricted economy."

But if the revolutionizing of life were not to succeed to such an extent that the extraordinary itself becomes the order in a permanent festival of prodigality, what are we left with? Is it not evident that the extraor-dinary, after a period of reprieve, is itself installed within the existing order and is marketed, inherited, and medicated in the form of shocks, journeys, and exaltations of every kind? Do we not find that where sluices seemed to open wide, only too soon regulatable dams and pres-sure valves themselves serve for "total integration" (J. Ellul) into a beautiful new order? These complaints are not so new. Transgression, however, does not mean the acquisition of a "supra-ordinal status" (*status supraordinalis*), but rather a constant border traffic that resists walling in, though it is not eager to remove the boundaries.

10. Proper Name and Anonymity

The ordinary is always counterpointed by an *elsewhere* that finds no place in the order but renders it uneasy, and so this strikes back at the status of the speaker and actor. The respondents are never where the playthings of their own thinking are. "I think where I am not, therefore I am where I do not think" (Lacan, *Ecrits,* 517). This dislocation pushes the so-called subject out of the center and removes its basis. The ego is not just an *other;* looked at from the viewpoint of any current order it is also a *nobody* (Merleau-Ponty, *V&I,* 246). This removal of the self, which affects the other as well as myself, cannot be compensated for by any self-duplication. It results from a self-transgressing that participates in the various forms of transgression and keeps its own way open between self-consolidation and self-dissolution.

What should we call the speaker and actor, if not a soul in which the universe is mirrored, nor a subject in the sense of master subject governed by self-enacted law? Does not the name, which is one's own and designates what is generally not sayable, remain as a last refuge? An ineffable individuality exhibited and identified by a proper name would be a drop in the ocean of determinations and promises, something indivisible installed as the final component of any order. But if everything occurring in a field does so only by deviating and setting itself off from something other, then it is unique like the order itself, and not a mere part or element. The name to which the respondent answers when responding to a provocation carries after it a comet's tail of anonymity that brushes upon the extraordinary. The person called, who answers to the name, is the one and yet not the one. "Oh how good that no one knows . . ."—myself included.

Irresponsibility? Is it a frivolous and senseless dream to imagine that occasionally something could be said and heard, written and read, as when it is raining, without a named sender intervening? ("I read, therefore *it* writes"—I. Calvino). And what if every statement that goes beyond the normal had about it something of a message from an unknown sender?

11. On the Threshold

The ego occurring in theory may remain in the penumbra, but is this also true of the pen-wielding ego that has to take responsibility for asserting a theory? If this ego dares to state that every order stands in the twilight since it simultaneously selects and excludes, places within and outside boundaries, it would seem, as a theorist of twilight orders, itself to step out of the dim light to measure the length of the shadows in the sunlight. For if the theorist were in turn enclosed within one selective and exclusive *order among others,* how could such a theorist presume to speak about order in general? But if the theorist is not enclosed within such an order, there is at least *one order above all orders* that would be removed from the twilight, because it would have no more outside that stands or falls with it. This one order would be that of the theorist, who would thus advance to extraordinary status by salvaging the global view of metaphysics into a metatheory; and as a cave-viewer, such a theorist would outrank the cave-dwellers. Everybody for themselves, but the theorist for us all. Whether the theory is represented by a subject, a research team, or an anonymous authority is indifferent. If this position is formalized, the order of all orders becomes caught in paradoxes similar to the quantity of all quantities. Theorists, on the other hand, who speak of the boundaries of any order, of its "before" and "beyond," without doing so from a high or central place, seem, under the recoil of their own theory, to end up on the threshold [i.e., *zwischen Tür und Angel,* "in the lurch"], a place neither comfortable nor without dangers. Whether one remains consistent and submits one's own discourse to the general theory or else excludes one's own theory in the familiar ventriloquistic fashion, in either case not much is left of a theory that asserts the selective and exclusive character of any order.

Here we fall into the familiar tendency of argumentative rescue operations that count on a discrepancy between the statement and the preconditions implicit in the act of stating. What the thing does not deliver has to be brought in by the back door by methods and procedures. Just as before a court life-contexts are tailored to fit relevant states of facts, so conversational and textual contexts are reduced to stocks of sentences. Core sentences, as memorable as pictures on postage stamps, can be filtered out, allowing for critical proceedings or—with a bit of luck—a speedy trial. Exemplary sentence-corpses are: "The truth of all statements is relative; forms of life or forms of knowledge are incomparable; reason depends on something other; cognition is the exercise of power," etc. Whoever has an objection will argue, thus proving the opponents right, or else will cede the field. The self-execution of the person who refuses to argue is a standard part of this kind of procedure.

Some dilemmas can be avoided only by not getting into them in the first place. Why not turn the spear of self-referentiality around for this purpose? What speaks against the assumption that a great part of what has been said about limited fields of speech and action falls back upon the philosophical discourse that shows these boundaries? Even in philosophical discourse we are not dealing with sentences out of the clear blue sky, which are true and accurate—and nothing else. Philosophy, which is handed down like a science, consists of texts in which questions are raised and discussed, themes chosen, conceptual distinctions and comparisons made, other texts cited or not cited, other philosopher's statements commented on, chapter divisions undertaken, titles and headings decided on—and of course, assertions are made and discussed. Writing about and dealing with texts is, in turn, regulated by institutions that guide the flow of thought. Such a domain of discourse resembles variously a landscape, an artist's studio, a court, a meditation cell, and a theater stage. What we do not find are unlocated assertions that are nothing except valid or invalid. What we do find, however, are attempts to detach determinate validity claims and forms of argumentation from concrete contexts. But such a formalization, generalization, or universalization is itself a discursive process, subject to determinate conditions and producing determinate effects. It would be rather strange if philosophical discourse, too, did not have its blind spots.

A possible objection is that a discourse that did nothing else but what all other discourses do would make itself superfluous. Granted, but then the question arises how philosophical discourse differs from other discourses and relates to them. A discourse with boundaries of its own is not valid as a super-discourse presenting a total order or representing a fundamental one. But renouncing such a leading function does not compel it to settle for offering only the ancillary service of mere *meta-discourses* for actually existing discourses, since sooner or later every developed discourse is able to come up with its own meta-discourse anyway. What remains is the possibility of an *indirect discourse* that relies on other discourses, establishing itself in them and interrogating them, opening them up and analyzing them, perking them up like a salt that does not replace foods, but seasons them. Indirect discourse also means an *indirect way of speaking,* that is, speech that accompanies another, citing, varying, explaining, reproducing it, and continuing it in a broken and diagonal way. Since everything given has a challenging character, such accompanying speech also means not mere rendition, description, or unfolding of what is already there; it means, rather, a constant responding and engagement, an intervention that transgresses without abolishing. Even the repeated citation of a sentence or an author changes their specific weight, multiplying their accessibilities or leading to signs of wear. Such an indirect discourse would have its place simultaneously inside and outside the direct discourse that it accesses. So far as this indirect discourse is critical, the critique also lingers on the threshold; it would be neither merely immanent nor straightforwardly transcendent. As specifically targeted critique, it would feed on the shadows of the extraordinary that every order casts around itself.

That it is possible to preserve boundaries and holes in experience without abolishing the boundaries or closing the holes can be learned from everyday things, if only we consider also their non-everyday aspects. An example of this, in closing, takes us back to the threshold experiences with which we began. I have in mind falling asleep and sleeping, which manifest their specific nature in the way we speak about them. I cannot say, "I am falling asleep," without keeping myself awake and making a liar of myself; and I can all the less say, "I am asleep." If the sentence merely contained an undemonstrated assertion, I could improve it by indirect evidences or the testimony of others. If the sentence were grammatically incorrect, conjugation tables (*I sleep, you sleep,* etc.) would have to be erased by applying criteria for which grammar itself no longer is adequate. If the sentence were false or inaccurate, how could I then afterwards say: "I was asleep," and how could someone else say of me, "He is sleeping now"? If one wanted to undermine the accuracy of the sentence by reshaping it into "Sleeping is going on" (*es schläft*), for the reason that an ego must at all times be able to ascribe its acts and states to itself, strange conclusions would follow; waking and sleeping would split apart and there would no longer be a falling asleep and waking up that cross a threshold without bridging over the distance. So here we have a rare case before us that a statement cannot be made although it is neither uncertain, nonsensical, nor false. We have absolutely no doubt as to what we are talking about, and we can feel our way up to and circle around the experience, although it cannot be consciously lived through and expressed on the spot. The unbridgeable contrast between sleeping and waking does not make the one become the completely Other of the other.

But this boundary experience and boundary discourse is not as unique as it seems. A child who would say, "I am a child," a savage who would say, "I am a savage," an insane person who would say, "I am insane," would cease being what they say of themselves, unless they were merely repeating what others say of them. Whenever the boundary of a vital or experiential domain is crossed, there is a discourse that speaks *at* the boundary, not *about* it, and that speaks across a threshold without abolishing it. The rest is rationalization, that is, an attempt to find a place in the current order for what is to be ordered. But why should a theory be more unambiguous than reality?

APPENDIX
Connecting Passages
and Supporting Points

Between Dog and Wolf. According to Grimm's *Deutsches Wörterbuch* (1954 edition), the first half of the word "twi-light" (Ger.: *Zwie-licht*) does "not actually have the meaning 'double' at its basis, but rather the ideas of 'half, split, separated' or 'doubtful, unsteady,' such as easily derive from 'double.'" Thus 'twilight' means:

1. the weak light in the evening or morning dusk;
2. dim lighting in general; and finally,
3. "indefiniteness, unclarity" in a figurative sense.

One of the fundamental insights from Husserl's phenomenology is that indefiniteness is not a mere privation, but an ingredient of every experience (e.g., Husserl, XIX/1, 410; I, 83).

In French the twilight area wanders over to an intermediary state of spreading unrecognizability that is not without danger: *entre chien et loup* (between dog and wolf). In Greek a wolf's light (*lykophōs*), a play of shadows that is absolutely not alien to Homer's sun, spreads out (cf. Bremer 1976). In Japanese the twilight splits into a dual twilight figure: morning twilight called *Kawatare* = he (is) who? and evening twilight *Tasogare* = who (is) he?"

God or Wolf. The slogan *homo homini lupus* (man is a wolf to man), made famous but by no means invented by Hobbes, is the negative counterpart of a Greek proverb that has man be a benefactor to man: *homo homini deus* (man is a god to man). Cf. Tricaud 1969.

On 1: 1

Definitions of Order. The notion of "rule" used in the initial definition, which could also be replaced by an equally broadly conceived notion of "law" or "norm" (cf. for instance, G. H. von Wright, *Norm and Action*), is not restricted, as is customary today, to the meaning of rules or patterns of behavior or action. For although my reflections will be limited thematically mostly to sociocultural orders, a sufficiently broad framework of thinking is needed to bring into view at all the contrast between classical and modern conceptions of order. Cosmic outlooks could be dispensed with only if the Greek cosmos, for instance, were the mere product of a lack of distinction, so that a work of analytical dissection would be, if not an easy game, at any rate a successful one— all the way to reducing the Platonic seeing of Ideas to a "know-how" of action. Kant, at any rate, still needs the concept of rule, despite all breaks between theoretical and practical philosophy, even in the domain of nature.

Multiplicity of Order. As for the multiplicity of order in the diverse areas of things and life and in the pertinent disciplines, the anthology edited by Paul G. Kuntz, *The Concept of Order* (1968), to which I frequently refer, is emphatically recommended.

History and Change of the Concept of Order. Besides the long article "Ordnung" in the *Historisches Wörterbuch der Philosophie* on the Platonic origin of the concept of order, cf. Helmut Kuhn (1962, chap. 3); and on the medieval *ordo,* cf. Herman Krings (1982). The authors of the proceedings that appeared under the title *Problem der Ordnung* (Kuhn/Wiedmann 1962) seek to approach the "vanishing of order," mostly with solid ontological, transcendental, hermeneutical, or existentialist means; Hans Blumenberg has this "vanishing of order" begin in the Middle Ages and flow into a process of "assertion of the self" (cf. 1974, 158 ff.). On the more recent conception of variable orders, in which chance, probability, scales of complexity, and selection play a constitutive role, one finds more in the above-mentioned anthology by Kuntz, especially in the articles by J. K. Feibleman, P. Weiss, J. C. Greene, and C. Hartshorne, who move in the tradition of Peirce and Whitehead, which is too little heeded in Germany.

Order without Counterpart? In one of his early works St. Augustine writes:

"Say, at least, what you consider to be the opposite of order!"— "Nothing," he said, "for how can there be an opposite to a thing that encompasses and includes everything? For what were contrary to order would necessarily be located outside of order; but I see nothing that is located outside of order: consequently, one must not accept any opposite to order."—"Then . . . error is not the opposite of order? . . ." (*De ordine,* I, 6, 15)

Schelling, on the contrary, writes:

> The unregulated always lies at the ground (of everything) as if ready to break through again, and nowhere does it seem as if order and form were the original state, but rather as if an original irregularity were brought to order. This is in things the incomprehensible basis of reality, the remainder that never quite comes out. . . . (*Ausgewählte Werke,* Darmstadt, 1968, V, 303 f.).

On 1: 4

Branching Evolution. In an evolution that does not steer toward a distinct apex, the human can be grasped only in the sense of an *anthropological difference.* The free play opened up by the lack of specialization and fixation of human accouterments is filled by human beings with artifacts: technical tools, social rules, and signs responding to the "biological challenge" in specific ways. From this perspective Frank Tinland presents the rich results of a history of technology, social anthropology, and linguistics, so far as these disciplines deal with humankind's order-instituting alterity (*La différence anthropologique: Essai sur les rapports de la nature et de l'artifice,* 1977).

On 1: 7

Cosmogonic Spirit. A brilliant example from more modern times: "The mind, in short, works on the data it receives very much as a sculptor works in his block of stone. . . . Other sculptors, other statues from the same stone! Other minds, other worlds from the same monotonous and inexpressive chaos!" (W. James, *Principles of Psychology,* I, 288 f.).

Consciousness assumes the office of the demiurge by selecting and omitting—"selection of some, suppression of the rest." What emerges is not a cosmos, but one world among other possible worlds. What is the selective criterion when the material is monotonous and expressionless and no harmony of the spheres resounds in the old way? And what happens to the "rest"? Aron Gurwitsch takes a critical stance on this topic (*The Field of Consciousness* [1964], 42), pointing to the problem of first separating out and stabilizing the element that is separated out, and, in agreement with Berlin Gestalt theory, like Merleau-Ponty, he affirms an autochthonous organization of experience.

On 1: 8

Order in Conversation. The fact that order in a conversation does not derive from a governing authority but from the mutual linkage of statements leads to an "intermediary realm" that no one is the master of. I have developed this thought extensively in my *Zwischenreich des Dia-*

logs (1971, abbreviated *ZD*) based on Husserl, Merleau-Ponty, and so-called dialogue philosophy, and confirmed by Michael Theunissen's book, *Der Andere,* though with a different emphasis. Meanwhile I have come to see my earlier work as altogether too embedded within the horizon of a teleologically developing *logos,* and so I have begun to radicalize the "intermediary" discursively (see my self-revision in the essay "Dialog und Diskurse," 1986 [Eng. 1991], and On 1:10, below). On the way to this stance I learned a great deal from linguistic theories (cf. de Saussure, K. Bühler, R. Jakobson, M. Bakhtin/V. N. Voloshinov, L. S. Wygotski, H. Hörmann) as well as from analyses of interaction and conversation in the aftermath of G. H. Mead, A. Strauss, A. Schutz and H. Garfinkel; in this regard I refer to my volume of essays *Der Spielraum des Verhaltens* (abbreviated *SV,* esp. chaps. 7, 9, 10, 12).

Series and Sequences. The Stoics already assigned two different forms of order to *physis:* the structure of durative forms of being (*systēma*) and the chain of causes (*eirmos aitiōn, series causarum*); the first necessitates agreement with the whole (*homologia*), the second engagement at the right moment (*eukairia*) (cf. Forschner 1981, 209 f.). This chain of events can naturally not be equated with the "great chain of being," which like Homer's golden chain—hangs down from heaven to the earth (cf. On 3: 4, below).

A remote allusion to a shift of axis in mathematics:

> The way *mathematical* concepts were formed—as was shown in contrast to traditional logical theory—was determined by the process of *series formation.* It was not a matter of peeling off what was *common* from a multiplicity of similar impressions, but rather of discovering a principle by virtue of which *different* things diverge from one another. (E. Cassirer, *Substanzbegriff und Funktionsbegriff,* 196)

An even more remote allusion to history: in the historical school of *annals,* the history of events is countered by a serial history. *Series* here means a homogeneous, static-regular sequence of recurring facts, i.e., a regulated form of linkages. Naturally, this anonymizing long-term perspective can be applied to all courses of action and conversation. If speech- and action-events were *nothing more* than such repeatable links in a chain, then the change of order would merely have to be determined, but no longer comprehended. Change of order can be understood as change only when the regulation of linkages is more or less open. On the methodology and problematic of a serial conception of history, which also leaves its clear traces in Foucault, cf. Ricoeur, *Temps et récit,* I, 152 ff.).

Asymmetry in Conversation. That partners in a conversation do not do the same thing in a mirrorlike fashion is one of the basic insights of a philosophy of dialogue, which counterposes to the functional unity of an I-subject or the circular self-containment of a we-community the difference between "I" and "Thou" (cf. *ZD* 149–51, 306 f.). The asymmetry takes on radical form when the *logos* encompassing the dialogue itself divides into a multiplicity.

On this topic, Emmanuel Levinas: "The absence of the other is precisely his presence as belonging to the other" (*Die Zeit und der Andere*, 65). On the asymmetry between me and the other, cf. *Totalité et infini*, 24, 190 f.; Eng.: 38 f., 194 f.; *Autrement qu'être* . . . , 152, 201; Eng.: 92, 141.

Also Michail Bakhtin:

> Question and answer are not logical relations (categories); they cannot be fitted into one single (unitary and self-contained) consciousness; every answer gives rise to a new question. Question and answer presuppose mutual location outside one another. If the answer does not produce a new question out of itself, then it falls out of the dialogue and enters systematic knowledge which is by nature impersonal. Dialogue presupposes the different chronotypes of the asker and the replier (likewise, the different meaning-worlds "I" and "the other"). Question and answer are inevitably depersonified from the standpoint of a "third" consciousness and its "neutral" world. (*Die Ästhetik des Wortes*, 352)

In a dialogical author like Dostoevski, the great dialogue is conceived "as a *non-self-contained whole,* in which life is portrayed as constantly *on the threshold*" (*Probleme der Poetik Dostoevskis*, 71).

On the empirical investigation of the asymmetry of speaking and hearing see W. Deutsch and R. J. Jarvella 1984. On asymmetry in the pragmatic consensus: "*a* knows that *b* believes that *S p*," "*b knows* . . ."—an assumption on both sides that does not enter into an objective consensus—cf. Jacques 1986, 344 ff.

Saying and the Said. On the event of saying (*dire*) and unsaying (*dédire*) that in its diachrony is never absorbed into what is said (*dit*), cf. Levinas, *Autrement qu'être* . . . , 6 f., 58 ff., and chap. 5; Eng.: 7, 45 ff., 134 f. This distinction strikes back at the speaker and opens up connections with the language theory distinction between the *sujet de l'énonciation* and the *sujet de l'énoncé*, which reaches back from Lacan (*Écrits*, 664, 800), via Jakobson (1974b, 35 ff.), to Husserl's doctrine of occasional expressions. Cf. also below, On 4:8: hybrid forms of discourse. Here possibilities are available for thinking the dialogical occurrence further, which I hope to return to elsewhere.

Lateral Universality. Merleau-Ponty speaks of a "lateral universal" (*universel latéral*) in his ethnologically oriented reflections on Mauss and Lévi-Strauss (cf. Merleau-Ponty in Métraux/Waldenfels 1986, 20; Eng.: 120). In his last work *The Visible and the Invisible,* under headings like intertwining, radiation, overlapping, or transgression, he seeks *horizontal* forms of connection that solidify into meshes and webs, constellations and configurations. In the framework of epistemological considerations, Castoriadis counters the vertical organization of the traditional theory of science with a "fanned-out organization"—a formation of strata that run unlimitedly into the depth, always organized, but never completely so, always interconnected but never completely bound (*Durchs Labyrinth,* 149).

Instead of lateral and horizontal universality one could also speak of a *consonantal* one, namely, a universality that re-sounds without ever *vocalically* giving the tone.

It seems obvious to me that bridges can be built from here to Walter Benjamin's "constellations" and to a universal that "dwells in the center of the individual thing" (T. W. Adorno, *Negative Dialektik,* 162; Eng.: 162). Actually nothing leading any further can be expected from an "anti-universal affect," but there are different forms of universal.

On 1: 9

Action as Open Encounter (offene Auseinandersetzung). This conception is found in Kurt Goldstein's biologically grounded theory of behavior: *Der Aufbau des Organismus* (1934; Eng.: *The Organism: A Holistic Approach to Biology,* 1939), on which Merleau-Ponty expressly bases himself in his early work *The Structure of Behavior* (cf. the foreword to the German translation of this work).

Demand Characters and Requirements (Gefordertheiten). Gestalt theory, which in its theory of perception so decisively rejected the duality of crude *matter* and *form* imprinted from the outside, likewise, where it expanded into a theory of behavior, had to undermine the duality of what *is* and *what is supposed to be* or *is required.*

Thus Kurt Lewin (1926, 317) says that the perception of a structure or event can:

1. Cause the *emergence* of a certain tense mental system that formerly did not exist, at least not in this form. Such a lived experience, for instance, is the direct occasion for a resolve, or else a longing is awakened that was not present until then.
2. An intrinsically already existing *state of tension* harking back, say, to a resolve, a need, or a half-performed action reacts to a determinate object or event experienced as an enticement, for example, in such a way that precisely this tensed system gains dominance over the motor system. Of such objects we want to say that they have a "demand character."

3. Such demand characters (like certain other events) at the same time act as field forces in the sense that they *influence* the psychic processes, especially the *motor system,* in the sense of a *guidance.*
4. Certain operations partly occasioned by the inviting characters lead to *satiation processes,* or respectively to the carrying out of the intentions and hence to relaxation of the tensions of the underlying system at a state of equilibrium on a lower level of the tension.

Examples: "The beautiful weather, a certain landscape invites one to go for a walk. A staircase entices the two-year old child to climb up and jump down; doors entice one to open and shut them, little crumbs to pick them up, a dog to pet it; the sandbox to play in it; chocolate or a piece of cake want to be eaten, etc." (Lewin 1926, 350).

Or in Wolfgang Köhler (1968, 242 f.; Eng.: 336 f.):

A datum, an entity or an act is required *within a context* of other data, entities or acts. This holds both for negative and for positive requiredness. . . . Within the context in question requiredness is a *dependent* characteristic that has no existence of its own, apart from the entities that fit or do not fit each other in these contexts. . . . All requiredness *transcends* from certain parts of a context to others of the same context. Like all other kinds of reference, it is in this sense a directed translocal trait, a vector, that cannot be split into bits which have a merely local existence. . . . Requiredness differs strikingly from other forms of reference by its *demanding* character. It involves acceptance or rejection of the present status of the context in question, often more particularly, acceptance or rejection of some part by the remainder of the context. This demanding character has degrees of intensity.

Finally, the educator M. J. Langeveld (1968, 146 f.), writes "We know the peculiar appeal of things, which is also especially important for children. Some quality of things appeals to us, and the object appeals to us, so to speak, *in the gerundive:* the object invites us to have something to do with it."

Parallel to this, Scheler, Heidegger, and hesitantly also Husserl (cf., for instance, Husserl, IV) have initiated a revision of the traditional concept of sensation (cf. on this topic, my *SV,* chap. 4). In Merleau-Ponty's theory of perception, which starts from a symbiosis of organism and world, the appeal, *invitation,* claim, and *challenge* of things play a completely central and increasing role. Cf. on this entire theme-complex Käte Meyer-Drawe's thorough discussion (1984, 166 ff.).

Crude Sensation. The young Marx suggested that the crudity and lack of expressiveness of sensation also has something to do with socially conditioned crudeness and scantiness of the look (*MEW,* supplementary volume I, 542): ". . . the dealer in minerals sees only the mercantile value but not the beauty and peculiar nature of the mineral; he has no minerological sense. . . ."

If this could also be read in Novalis and elsewhere, so much the better. At any rate, there is also an economy of the look.

Collaboration of things. Similarly to the way semiotics accepts communications without an addressee (Jakobson 1974b, 168 f.), in pragmatics one could speak of a collaboration without actors, without thereby adopting the fragmentation of communication in one's information theory.

Invitation versus Challenge. Have we not exaggerated with action-theory's *"sententia communis"*? Let us take an example that seems to show otherwise: Dieter Böhler's broad-scoped *reconstructive pragmatics,* where besides direction of the goal and the normative claims, a central role is assigned to the situational reference, namely, in determining action as the *response to a challenge* by the situation. But immediately reservations begin. (1) Challenge is not invitation, for the situation contains only the fact of a responsive behavior, not its content (Böhler 1985, 260). (Counterquestion: would such a nondirectional challenge be more than a mere shock?) (2) This question-answer relation is only *quasi-dialogical,* because reciprocity is lacking (Böhler 1985, 257). (Counterquestion: can one respond to something that challenges to nothing?) (3) This "deficiency model" (Böhler 1985, 329) requires fully valid dialogue that confronts us with another's and our own challenges and thus also with validity claims that elevate dialogue to "unrestricted dialogue" in the familiar way. For "situational justice" all that remains is the success that allows a response to appear suitable and appropriate to the situation, and finally right, as in a mere poll (Böhler 1985, 333–38). That one cannot simply read off and gather from the situation what must be done is gladly conceded, but is the only alternative the strange construction of a *self-challenge that intervenes between situation and action* (Böhler 1985, 319)? What if what is encountered in the situation is also supposed to have a say?

On 1: 10

Act and Event. If, like Georg Henrik von Wright and many others, one distinguishes *act* as an "effecting ('at will') of a change" from the *event* as a "change in the world," then there is from the outset a distinction between what comes from an actor and what things and fellow actors contribute, indeed expressly on the pattern of activity and passivity, which in the case of "collective" action allows only for individual acts bound together by "joint efforts" (*Norm and Action,* 35–38). One cannot avoid speaking of ontological pre-decisions concealed behind the otherwise thoroughly helpful work of making distinctions. Even the logic of action requires a genealogy.

Responsivity and Dialogicity. Kurt Goldstein, in reference to a patient, speaks of a "lack of responsiveness" (1934, 270; cf. *The Organism,* 433). Cf., on this topic, Bakhtin and Voloshinov's dialogue theory of language:

> In dialogue the word is born as a living reply; it attains its form in the object in dialogical interaction with another's word. The designing of the object by the word is dialogical. But this by no means exhausts the inner dialogicity of the word. Every word is directed toward an answer. . . . (Voloshinov 1975, 129)

For corresponding possibilities of a pragmatic dialogistics, cf. Jacques's work, which is mentioned under 2:7.

Acting and Forbearance. A responsive theory of action also casts some light on the problem of the forbearance of actions. The distinction between forebearance and mere inaction is matter-of-course to every lawyer, but it presents particular difficulties for the logic of action and norms. Thus the formula $[\sim p] \times \to \sim [p] \times$ (to be read: "If someone forbears to do the action designated by p, then this person does not perform this action") cannot be reversed. An illiterate person does not leave reading undone (cf. von Wright 1974, 14f., and in more detail von Wright 1963, chap. 3). In order to articulate the difference, G. H. von Wright here has recourse, among other things, to an *ability.* I would add a *demand* that calls for a response, namely, in such a way that the refusal to respond would itself be a response ("We cannot not communicate," Watzlawick); this response would still lie before the threshold of universal commands and prohibitions, and it would also not let itself be captured normatively by reinterpreting requests such as "N.N., open the window right now" into particular prescriptions (as does von Wright 1963, 81). Such forbearances cut across the distinction between speech and action; remaining silent cannot be true or false, but overcautious or—in the case of the receiver of stolen goods—contrary to the law. A responsive theory of speech and action would thus go beyond a mere theory of the sentence as well as beyond a mere theory of the deed. Once again saying and doing would be more than what is said and done. For further consequences of this, see On 6:3, below.

CHAPTER 2: ORDER AS SELECTION AND EXCLUSION

In this chapter the attempt is made to bring into fruitful interchange the familiar phenomenological, Gestalt-theoretical, and pragmatic field theories with theories of a social setting such as those of G. Politzer, E.

Goffman, or P. Bourdieu, with narrative theories of action, and finally with Foucault's discourse theory. For further details I refer to my Foucault essay "Verstreute Vernunft" and the above-mentioned essay "Dialog und Diskurse" (both 1986), where I study the fanning out of the great dialogue into regional and specific discourses. On shifting the norms-problematic back into fields of experience, speech, and action, I mention my programmatic sketch "Die Herkunft der Normen aus der Lebenswelt," in the book *In den Netzen der Lebenswelt* (1985, abbreviated *NL,* chap. 7), which discussion I continue at this point.

On 2: 1

Moral Action in Context.

Like money, the moral dimension can be a universal form for which almost anything can be done. . . . The moral act, the move in human relationships, is therefore more than the activities of making, servicing, exchanging, and simple doing, but it is . . . more without being separate, without being radically other. . . . A move in the web of human relationships is never an act just by itself; it needs to be embodied. . . .

So writes Robert Sokolowski in his study *Moral Action* (1985, 47f.), which is obligated equally to Aristotle and to Husserl, and which extracts from the ethics of antiquity what can be extracted from there, including precisely the definition of moral acts as "being-at-work of human nature" (Sokolowski 1985, 51), which evades the selection and exclusion pressure of concrete orders of action and restricts conflicts to casuistry, where they are mastered by recourse to unwanted side effects, legal commands, and considerations of property damage (Sokolowski 1985, 106ff.). Cf. on this point, our critical analysis 3:2–4.

On 2: 2

Plots. Ricocur uses the term "plot" (*intrigue*) in his theory of narrativity to translate the *mythos* of Aristotelian *mimēsis* doctrine (*Temps et récit,* I, 57ff.). Paul Veyne had already used this expression to designate a "very human and not very 'scientific' mixture of material causes, aims, and chances" (*Comment on écrit l'histoire,* 46; Eng.: 32f.).

On 2: 3

The Concept of Field. On the meaning potential of the term "field," which was developed in physics, see Maxwell, *A Treatise on Electricity and Magnetism,* II, 176f.:

We are accustomed to consider the universe as made up of parts, and mathematicians begin by considering a single particle, and then conceiving its relation to another particle, and so on. This has generally been supposed the most natural method. To conceive of a particle, however, requires a process of abstraction, since all our perceptions are related to extended bodies, so that the idea of the *all* that is in our consciousness at a given instant is perhaps as primitive an idea as that of any individual thing. Hence there may be a mathematical method in which we proceed from the whole to the parts instead of from the parts to the whole. For example, Euclid, in his first book, conceives a line as traced out by a point, a surface as swept out by a line, and a solid as generated by a surface. But he also defines a surface as the boundary of a solid, a line as the edge of a surface, and a point as the extremity of a line. . . .

He (Faraday) never considers bodies as existing with nothing between them but their distance, and acting on one another according to some function of that distance. He conceives all space as a field of force, the lines of force being in general curved, and those due to any body extending from it on all sides, their directions being modified by the presence of other bodies.

On reworking the concept of field based on the theory of action, cf. Kurt Lewin, *Feldtheorie in den Sozialwissenschaften.*

In phenomenologists—starting with Husserl, who in the *Ideen* speaks of a "field of freedom" (Husserl, III, 195; *Ideas,* 233) and a "field of practice" (Husserl, IV, 261 n), down to Merleau-Ponty's phenomenal field (*champ phénoménal*) (*PhP,* 52 ff.) and Aron Gurwitsch's "field of consciousness"—the concept of field becomes a central component of a theory of open-finite experience.

Meaning and Force. This is not a pair of concepts that stems from pure phenomenology. Thus Husserl, for instance, in a passage of the *Nachlass* (C 16 III, 1932, 9–10), sounding much like Max Weber, speaks of a "reciprocal accomplishment of interests," only then to conjure up the "harmony of directed life in the unity of a total interest." The situation changes when Marx, Nietzsche, and Freud enter the field of view. For Scheler, in history ideal factors accompany real factors, which still makes possible the drawing of a clear boundary. To cite more recent texts: Ricoeur, in his Freud book, in the chapter on the archaeology of the subject, discusses the connection between *intention* and *tension,* reaching back to the *conatus* and *appetitus* of Spinoza and Leibniz respectively, and the early Derrida, in an essay on literary theory, expressly links together "force and meaning" (see *Writing and Difference*).

On 2: 4–6

Theme, Interest, Relevance. Theme and interest are concepts that show up early in Husserl (cf. Husserl, III, § 122; *Ideas,* 59; IV, § 5; additional references in my *ZD,* 88 ff.). Closely related is the careful distinction between active attention (quest) and passive attention (obtrusion), and the noticeability of the object, direction of interests, and framework, as we find them in Scheler in *Formalismus in der Ethik* (158 f.). Another seminal author is William James with his distinction between *object* and *topic*—the latter a word that points back to the rhetorical "topics"—and with his emphasis on the *selectivity* of consciousness (*Principles of Psychology,* I, 275 ff. and 284 ff.), which finds its corollary in Bergson's selective "attention to life."

The preeminence of certain forms of perception, proclaimed in the well-known gestalt laws, was broadened by Kurt Goldstein to the preeminence of distinctive ways of movement and behavior (1934, 219 ff.; *The Organism,* 447 ff.).

These philosophical and Gestalt-theoretical initiatives have all entered into Gurwitsch's theory of the field of consciousness and into Schutz's theory of circumscribed provinces of meaning, multifarious realities, and type formation. On more recent research, cf. Grathoff/ Waldenfels 1983.

Theme in the Language Theory Sense. Voloshinov (1975, 163 ff.) tries to grasp the realization of a linguistic meaning (*Sinn*) from two boundary concepts. The upper boundary of a linguistic meaning is the unitary, concrete, contextual theme that remains bound to the historical situation, the lower boundary is the detached, isolated *meaning* (*Bedeutung*). If one of these two boundaries were reached, then we would attain either the pure *difference* of singular uniqueness or else the pure *identity* of mere repetition. Pure production would, in the extreme case, stand opposite pure reproduction, which is rightly criticized by the editor S. Weber (Foreword, 29 ff.). On this topic, see On 5:3, below.

Cur potius quam. That the question of the organization of the world first assumes a radical form only when the Leibnizian formula of "rather than" (*potius quam*) is constantly implied by thought can be learned, now as always, from Heidegger's essay *Vom Wesen des Grundes* [On the Essence of the Ground], even if abysmality cannot simply be translated into freedom. On the historical surrounding field of the principle of sufficient reason, see Lovejoy 1985, chap. 5.

Ontological Interpretation of Gestalt. It is important that the occurrence of "something" or "someone" not be understood as mere phenomenal gestalt-formation, which then is necessarily doubled by a real substratum, but that it rather is understood as the emergence of an *ontological relief,* down to the "solid wall" of a *milieu* (Scheler 1966): something or someone is, insofar as such a something or someone stands out. On the "something" or "someone" this side of essence and fact, cf. Merleau-Ponty, *V&I,* 105–29; the ontological interpretation of gestalt and what is formed (*Gestalthaftem*) may be traced by consulting the index to my German translation (or see under "Gestalt" in *V&I*).

On 2: 6

Typology and Repetition. "The calculability of an event . . . lies in the recurrence of 'identical cases,'" which do not get quotations marks for no reason (Nietzsche, III, 768, *Nachlass*).

On 2: 7

Deictic field. On the anchoring of speech and action in a deictic field, see Karl Bühler, *Sprachtheorie,* Part II.

Logical Space of Conversation. On the formation of a "logical space of interlocution," which sets certain restrictive conditions for beginning, course, and conclusion, we refer to the very thorough and wide-ranging dialogical investigations of Francis Jacques (*Dialogiques,* 1979; Ger.: 1986), which concentrate on dialogical-linguistic work on the referent. What is traditionally called "object," "subject," and "fellow subject" is obtained anew from the conversational exchange in the form of *co-reference* and *retro-reference*. In this speech pragmatics, the limitation of the thematic field runs via the presuppositions that are contained in every initial question and that channel the further course of the conversation in certain directions (Jacques 1986, 168 ff.). Within the model of dialogue that operates with idealizing presuppositions, however, the conversational barriers lose importance, which they do not regain in the closing perspective of an "ideal and unrestricted communication community." The bracketed-out institutional intermediary stages would, in my opinion, necessarily damage the cautiously sought final stage.

Topology and Chronology. Important initiatives toward a political topology of speech and action are found in Hannah Arendt, *The Human Condition,* chap. 5. The "referential fabric" of human speech and action decides on what someone is; in the background stands the public *agora* of the Greeks, the *forum* of the Romans, which admittedly are used altogether too directly as standard. The spatial and temporal structure of action also plays a notable role in Bourdieu's ethnologically corroborated reflections on a theory of praxis (1976), which has meanwhile not only condensed but also congealed into a theory of social space (1985). A balancing act between subjectivism and objectivism ends up in a double game if the antithetical movable pieces are not melted down again.

Selection and Exclusion of Social Discourses. Foucault writes in *Die Ordnung des Diskurses,* 7:

> I presuppose that in every society the production of discourse is simultaneously controlled, selected, organized, and channeled—namely,

by certain procedures whose task it is to restrain the forces and the dangers of discourse, to stem its unpredictable eventfulness, and to avoid its heavy and threatening materiality.

Decisive is the insight that selection and exclusion are built into "production" itself—a viewpoint that is further strengthened in Foucault's later writings, but runs the danger of consigning discourse to a mere play of power (see On 3:9, below). It is clear that the "spatial metaphor of inclusive and exclusive reason . . . remains stuck to the presuppositions of subject philosophy" (J. Habermas, *Der philosophische Diskurs der Moderne,* 360); this is clear, however, only if one first personifies all "key power" oneself as if there were not at least such a thing as the principle of the "excluded" middle. Foucault's attempt at a "thinking from and of the outside" (*penser du dehors*) is then changed into a simple thinking of what is outside. If thinking were not itself "outside," if reason did not have its own otherness, then there would in fact remain only "*the* Other of *the* Reason" (*Das Andere der Vernunft*), a title that— taken literally—runs onto a treadmill through the doubly placed definite article. Who could resist *the* Reason with impunity?

Some Assistance from Scientific Theory. According to Paul Feyerabend, *Wider den Methodenzwang* (1976) 368, the following is true: "Principles cause a certain self-containedness: there are things that cannot be said or 'discovered' without violating principles (and that does *not* mean: without contradicting them)."

A suggestion that should not be taken just tactically: "It is the paradox of modern irrationalism that its proponents implicitly equate rationalism with order and well-composed discourse instead of with *a certain kind* of order or discourse and thus are compelled to propagate stammering and absurdity . . ." (Feyerabend 1976, 307).

On 2: 9

Normalization. Important in this connection are all attempts in more recent psychiatry and psychopathology that aim at overcoming the purely negative and fixed determination of pathologies and anomalies by going back to normalization processes that leave room for an otherness and a becoming-other of norms. Cf., on this topic, G. Canguilhem, *The Normal and the Pathological,* a copiously documented work that appeared at the same time as Merleau-Ponty's *The Structure of Behavior;* both authors owe decisive insights to K. Goldstein's *The Organism: A Holistic Approach to Biology.* Also belonging to this same context are older works by L. Binswanger and E. Minkowski, as well as more recent works by Foucault on medicine and legal history, which are partly based on Canguilhem. From a German perspective, cf. the informative article by the medical doctor W. Blankenburg in Grathoff/

Waldenfels (1983) or an exemplary study based on narrative interviews like C. Hoffmann-Riem's *Das adoptierte Kind* (1984), where normalization processes are amalgamated with the question of identity formation.

On 2: 10–11

Normativity. On the distinction between different forms of normativity, see Max Weber, *Soziologische Grundbegriffe*, §§ 4 ff. The typological distinctions are characterized by a wealth of nuances and a sense for transitions that are in complete accord with our genealogically oriented investigation. Obviously, moreover, our reflections have in mind a conception of order that is neither restricted to purposive rational order, nor stresses the question of the legitimacy of order to the extent that Max Weber does in the wake of neo-Kantianism. Let it be noted, however, that Weber considers a "clear type of rightness" for investigating the "rightness rationality of action" to be unrealizable (1968b, 438).

On 2: 12

Habit. This concept, which Bourdieu (1974, chap. 4; also 1976, 164 ff.; Eng.: *Outline of a Theory of Practice,* chaps. 2, 4, etc.) obtains from quite far afield in Panofsky, has, of course, since Aristotle (*Nic. Eth.* II, 1) had its appointed place in tradition, including in the phenomenological tradition (see Husserl, IV; Merleau-Ponty, *PhP,* 142 ff., 152; Merleau-Ponty 1976, 109 ff.; Eng.: 120 ff.); similarly, it played a role in the early debates of the social sciences (cf., e.g., Mauss 1978, II, 202). The clue to its rediscovery resides in the upgrading of this concept with regard to the carryover of normative or, conversely, behavioristic theories of speech and action. Significantly, even so inflexible a theorist of action as G. H. von Wright does not go beyond mixed and negative determinations in the case of "customs," which he interprets as "social habits"; customs resemble in part the regularities of natural events, in part the regularity of norms, but in the latter regard they are *merely* anonymous and implicit as they exercise a "normative pressure" (von Wright 1963, 8 f.).

Embodiment. In France, mundane-socially dimensioned corporeality, which only a theorist much influenced by Kant can accommodate directly with the subject or even with the philosophy of the subject, benefits from a fruitful tension between the philosophy (Bergson, Sartre, Merleau-Ponty), the sociology (Mauss, Lévi-Strauss), and the paleontology (Leroi-Gourhan) of corporeality, a field of tension that extends from the zone of desire to the intricate ceremonies based on a tradition that tends to embody language rather than to "language-ify" the body. Analyses like Foucault's or Bourdieu's would be unthinkable otherwise. From the vantage point of corporeality, the late Merleau-Ponty developed a theory of institutions that are located in a symbolic intermediary world (*intermonde*) (*V&I,* 48, 84; 1973, 74–77) and that can help one arrive at the idea of a "political body" (*corpus politicum*), as in John O'Neill (1985). This corporeality has a great deal to do with the order of things and not merely with expressive behavior, movements, and preoccupations of a freewheeling subject. For the attempt to make the phenomenological theory of the body fruitful in the field of society and socialization, I refer to the recent monographs of Käte Meyer-Drawe (1984) and Herman Coenen (1985).

CHAPTER 3: GROUNDED OR ARBITRARY ORDER?

On 3: 4

Cosmos as the "Great Chain of Beings." Arthur O. Lovejoy, in his monograph on this theme (1960; Ger.: 1985), shows how under Pope's much-cited motto of a "chain of being" the Platonic-Aristotelian vision of an abundance of order, interconnected without any gap and hierarchically articulated, developing all possibilities out of itself and stemming from a profuse goodness without envy, held thought, research, and politics breathless for centuries, until Romanticism. This vision of a global rational order was interrupted only by increasing lightning bolts of an autarchic, indolent counter-god, who gives his will free rein in his creation and, in secular terms, leaves room for chance, so that more open forms of order gain ground.

On 3: 5

Order and Chaos. For a warning against practical chaos, see Hobbes, *Leviathan* III, 36: "Rebellion . . . reduces all order, government, and society, to the first Chaos of violence and civil war."

In view of the increasing danger of undermining the comprehensive world order, the rationalist supporters of order push the idea of order so far as to eliminate all chance. Thus in Leibniz's *Theodizee* (Gerhardt, VI, 386; Ger.: *Phil. Schriften,* II/2, Darmstadt, 1985, 31), we read:

If the will of God did not have the principle of the best as its guideline, then it would either be directed toward the evil that would be worst, or it would in a certain way be indifferent to good and evil and guided by chance; but a will that always left itself to chance would be hardly better for world governance than the chance interaction of atoms without there being any Godhead. And even if God abandoned himself to chance only in some cases and in a certain way . . . he would be just as imperfect as the object of his choice; he would then not deserve perfect trust; he would in such a case act without reason, and world governance would resemble certain card games in which reason partly decides and luck partly.

On 3: 7–8

Universalization. On the various universal-pragmatic, transcendental-pragmatic, constructivist, and utilitarian variants of universalization, we refer to R. Wimmer, *Universalisierung in der Ethik* (1980). In the introduction it is stated tersely that only with the concept "of general or universal validity . . . is the proper field of ethics entered." And since in this field actually not much can be produced, it is not surprising that in the end nothing is left for the "proper field" but the critical judgment of norms, which ultimately depends "on the principle of argumentation and transsubjectivity" (Wimmer 1980, 360). Elsewhere (*SV,* chap. 11; *NL,* chaps. 5, 6) I have expressed myself at length on Apel's and Habermas's theories, which occupy an important place in this phalanx.

On 3: 8

Hiatus between Desire and Action. Can this hiatus be bridged by *mere* feelings, appeals, values, and so on? As long as something is *"mere,"* it is still waiting to be clothed in ideas and norms. Pity (*Mitleid*) yes, but is there not such a thing as false pity, and is mere suffering (*Leid*) not too little?

Let us take an example. Wilhelm Kamlah—not a normativist, but an ethician who founds his ethics anthropologically and seeks an "art of life" (*ars vitae*)—starts from such a hiatus in his *Philosophische Anthropologie* (1972, 102–8) and seeks to bridge it by a leap into the universal by an *attentiveness* (a remarkable thought!) that is supposed to be universal and unrestricted and is already based on a comparison: "Notice that the others are people in need like yourself and act accordingly!"

To demonstrate that no challenge and *a fortiori* no commandment is required to give this sentence validity but that one's own insight suffices, he offers an indicative substitute formula: "Everyone is always commanded to pay attention that one's fellow humans are needy like oneself and to act accordingly." The vanished exclamation mark [of the German imperative] sneaks in by the back door when an appeal is made in opposition to the "malicious" Callicles to living practice: "Whoever has never at some time in his life seen that he must be attentive to the needs of others and take them into consideration in his actions . . ."— such a person is incapable of learning the basic norm (cf. Wimmer 1980, 55ff.). Is not the genealogy of morals here replaced by a genealogy of moral philosophy? Callicles, of course, is thus simply left sitting as morally deaf, or rather deaf and dumb.

Hence a more decisive ethics from below? It will fall short of the mark as long as one settles for merely reversing the scale from top to bottom instead of tilting it sideways. In this context we refer to Werner Marx, who in his more recent efforts has made human mortality and vulnerability to injury the starting point, and especially to Levinas, who operates with terms like "face," "longing," "hospitality," or "warranty," on a level that could be called "pre-normative," borrowing a term from Husserl.

On 3: 9

Arbitrariness. Castoriadis repeatedly points out that the variability of the world order by no means conjures up pure arbitrariness and an amorphous chaos, since every organization of the world, including the linguistic one, presupposes its organizability—Kant's "happy chance"—indeed, presupposes an initial organizedness (1984 [Ger.], 562; 1983, 111 f., 150). To be sure, one should not then flirt with a *creatio ex nihilo* (see On 6:3, below). If in scholastic diction one speaks of something "orderable" (*ordinabile*) that must be presupposed (Krings, in Kuhn/ Wiedmann 1962, 125), then everything depends on how the possibility indicated in the suffix is understood—as something to be merely unfolded or to be shaped selectively.

On the historical dimensions of a great alternative of groundedness and arbitrariness, cf. the critical summary in Lovejoy (chap. 10); furthermore, relative to representative systems of thought, see J. Vuillemin, *Nécessité ou contingence,* chap. 11, where, however, a dubious schematization is indulged in.

Language fibers: "Be-*lieben*," "Will-*kür*" i.e., the German words for "arbitrariness"—contain an allusion to "loving" and "choosing"; the latter applies also to "*arbitrarité*" (cf. Saussure), which maintains the reference to *arbitrium.* Even the "*Gerate-wohl*" (haphazard) depends on a wish.

CHAPTER 4: ORDER WITH OR WITHOUT AN ORDERER?

On 4: 4

Doing and Suffering. Nietzsche, III, 489, *Nachlass:* "The interpretation of an event as *either* doing or suffering (that is, every doing and suffering) says: every change, every becoming-different presupposes an originator and one *on whom* the 'change' is being made."

Husserl incessantly struggled with this pair of concepts (cf. Yamaguchi 1982), "perhaps the darkest heirloom of occidental philosophy" (Derrida 1987, 133; cf. Eng.. 100 n, 107).

On 4: 5

Ownness and Alienness (Eigenheit und Fremdheit). On the historical dimension of this problematic, the seminal Stoic doctrine of *oikeiosis,* an appropriation of the world by domestication, should be considered (cf. Forschner 1981, chap. 9). Modern outriders of this problematic are discussed in my essay "Heimat in der Fremde" (*NL,* chap. 10), where I used the idea of "interregionality" to oppose the centering on an (ersatz)-cosmos.

On 4: 8

Dosaged Collaboration. Bakhtin speaks of a "differing degree of the author's presence and his ultimate meaningful authority in the various moments of a language" (1979, 205), and he went on the track of this "hybridization, mixing of accents, blurring of the boundary between auctorial discourse and others' discourse" (Bakhtin 1979, 209) in his analyses of novels, noting, for instance, a multiple interference of direct and indirect discourse. Yet Bakhtin does not by any means restrict this movement "on the boundary between one's own and someone else's" to the art of literary language. "The word of language is a semi-foreign word. . . . Language is not a neuter that enters the speaker's intentional property quickly and unimpededly; it is charged, indeed supercharged with others' intentions" (Bakhtin 1979, 185).

Not to be overlooked is the correspondence with the theory of language and conversation elaborated by Merleau-Ponty with growing radicality in his *Prose of the World* and *The Visible and the Invisible*. Shouldn't what is right for language also be right for action? And isn't such walking-along-the-border more adequate to the thing than a turn that amounts to a reversal of roles?

Otherness of the Self/of the Others. This section seeks to make it clear that a bodily oriented and radicalized phenomenology à la Plessner or Merleau-Ponty is perfectly capable of breaking through the pseudo-centering of a "subject- or consciousness-philosophy." But it turns out that the fissure in the self that the reflexive doubling produces does not itself stem from any original sin of reflection, but from a self-withdrawal that brackets together the otherness of the self with that of the other and thus cannot be matched by any "paradigm of communication." A communication that is itself selective and exclusive because no participants in it appear fully as themselves (see above, 1:8–10; 2:4–7) necessitates orders of discourse through which "communicative reason" too is pushed into the twilight. For further treatment I refer to my essay "Dialog und Diskurse" (1986), where I seek to demonstrate the intermeshing of *intra*-subjective and *inter*subjective otherness by references to the human, social, and literary-theoretical research of G. H. Mead, L. S. Wygotski, D. Lagache, R. Spitz, D. Winnicott, J. Lacan, and M. Bakhtin.

CHAPTER 5: EMERGENT AND EXISTING ORDER

On 5: 4

Tracery (Masswerk). To designate what is envisaged here with a term from the history of architecture, the late Merleau-Ponty repeatedly speaks of axes, hinges, dimensions, vectors of force, structures, articulations or also—following Heidegger—of "being in a verbal sense" (*V&I*, 115), that is, of a *generality* that, like the element, lies midway between individuality and ideality (*V&I* 139), that encroaches generatively on other things as radiation, vibration, luxuriance, promiscuity (*V&I*, 153), and that has its "metaphysical" corollary in the "uniqueness of the world" that cannot be subsumed under any law (cf. Kanitscheider 1984, 396 ff.). Everything that occurs is bound historically and geographically to the flesh (*chair*) of the world and the body, which latter itself becomes a worldly standard. So Merleau-Ponty says, based on Proust's thoughts on the "little passage" of the Vinteuil Sonata (Proust, I, 530 f.; Eng.: I, 571 f.):

The invisible and, as it were, weak being is alone capable of having this close texture. There is a strict ideality in experiences that are experiences of the flesh: the moments of the sonata, the fragments of the luminous field, adhere to one another with a cohesion without concept, which is of the same type as the cohesion of the parts of my body, or the cohesion of my body with the world. Is my body a thing, is it an idea? It is neither, being the measurant of the things. We will therefore have to recognize an ideality that is not alien to the flesh, that gives it its axes, its depth, its dimensions" (*V&I*, 151–52).

Castoriadis seizes on the idea of a thus incarnated, materialized meaning when he entrusts to the productive imagination the creation of an eidos that is designated, with Platonic-Husserlian undertones, as the "unlimitedly replicable type of its exemplars," whether it be a tool or a word (1984 [Ger.], 307; cf. also 1983, 203). For our own use of "type" and "eidos," cf. 2:6, above. Derrida, with Husserl in mind, already distinguishes carefully between *idealization* and *ideation* and calls the idealizing procedure of geometry likewise "creation of an eidetics" (1987, 179; Eng.: 135).

The radicality of this framing of the question is not rendered moot by justified objections to an overlaid creationism. A critique of a "paradigm of production" that stems from a two-stage model of creation of meaning and empirical verification, of opening a horizon and filling the horizon (Habermas 1985, 372 f.), misses the decisive point—namely, that the creation of a new typical gestalt produces a specific prototype that "*from then on* 'is' independent of its empirical exemplars" (Castoriadis 1983, 302, italics added), hence not already beforehand. A sensory idea need fear no "profanization"; its "verification" has already begun when it occurs.

On 5: 5

Key Events. An event that is more than an empirical event, than a spatiotemporal happening leading over from one inner-worldly state to another, would have to be thought completely from its key aspect. In a similar sense Foucault, in his work *Die Ordnung der Dinge* (1971, 273), speaks, concerning the transition from one *epistēmē* to the other, of a "fundamental event" (*événement fondamental*) that does not find an adequate place in any existing discourses and to that extent means neither a general law nor an individual fact. Later in *Ordnung des Diskurses* (1974, 40) he calls for a "philosophy of the event" that aims for a "materialism of the incorporeal." Echoes of Heidegger's onto-historical event can be heard unmistakably, except that the whole scale of ownness (*Eigenheit*), appropriation (*Aneignung*), and dedication (*Zueignung*) is missing (Heidegger, *Identität und Differenz*, 24 ff.).

Key Words. Merleau-Ponty, *The Prose of the World*, 41: the power of creative language "lies entirely in its present, insofar as it succeeds in ordering the would-be key words (*mots clefs*) to make them say more than they have ever said . . ."—*would-be* key words because they do not *possess* their key power like "first words whose function would be to designate the elements of being." On determining the meaning of "key words" in cultural anthropological fieldwork, see E. E. Evans-Pritchard, *Social Anthropology*, 80.

On 5: 6

Alienation, Deformation, Deviation. On the origins of concepts in literary and artistic theory that point back to the Aristotelian category of the strange, unusual (*xenikon*) (*Rhetoric*, III, 2–3) cf. A. A. Hansen-Löve, *Der russische Formalismus*, or, especially on the category of deviation, Fricke 1981. Ricoeur too reaches back to Aristotelian poetics and rhetoric when he discusses the innovative power of the metaphor (*Die lebendige Metapher*).

Merleau-Ponty stands in the tradition of the Russian Formalists when he speaks, with Malraux, of a *déformation cohérente* (*The Prose of the World*, 69, 91, 104; *V&I,* 262), and he follows Saussure's doctrine of the differential character of signs when he repeatedly speaks of *écart* (deviation, distance). But he also retains proximity to a Gestalt-theoretical theory of experience (transformation, deviating from a level, standing out from a background). Likewise, there are similarities to the alienatory art of the Surrealists (1976, 192).

On the biological origin of the category of anomaly as deviation, on the ambivalence of abnormal phenomena, and on the normal as a polemical concept, see G. Canguilhem, *The Normal and the Pathological,* esp. 69 ff. and 146 ff.

On 5: 7

Old and New. Kant distinguishes between *amazement* as an "affect in the presentation of novelty that exceeds expectation," and *admiration* as an "amazement that does not cease after the loss of novelty" and that occurs "when ideas in their portrayal unintentionally and without artistry accord with aesthetic pleasure" (*KU* B, 122). Even if we distrust the pure counterposing of temporary deviation and ideal correctness, the question remains as to what makes amazement more than a transitory affect that is worn out like a newspaper item.

Maximal Information and Redundancy. As is known, there is an aesthetics that tries to approach artistic productions by means of information theory. The contrast of new and old would thus approach the contrast between maximal information and redundancy. A Mozart string quartet, compared with the musical repertoire customary at the time, will display highly improbable structural traits and sequences of events, but its rank would be proven only if one performed an information theory *petitio principii* and defined intellectual flashes by bit-quantities. What is significant may be improbable, but not everything that is improbable is significant. Cf. on this Monroe C. Beardsley, "Order and Disorder in Art," in Kuntz 1968.

Pre-beginnings. If the beginning has already been made and always made again and again for the individual and for us all, before we gather our thoughts and know what to make of it, then something of the "work at myth" also goes into work on tradition. However, what is leaped over in the question of a de- or re-mythization or also of the aesthetic saving of the mythical potential of meaning is the question why one thing is useable for a myth and the other not; to that extent myth is a second-order concept (Merleau-Ponty, *V&I*, 188).

On 5: 8

Selfhood and Constancy. As opposed to harping on *sameness* that looks now one way, now another, let us remind the reader of Gestalt theory's critique of the assumption of constancy (Gurwitsch, *The Field of Consciousness;* Merleau-Ponty, *Phenomenology of Perception*), which poses for us the task, here too, of investigating the process of "constantization" (cf. H. Hörmann, *Psychologie der Sprache,* 297 ff.). That this does not occur completely arbitrarily can be expected and is documentable.

Incommensurability. I have dealt elsewhere with the objective relationship of Kuhn's and Feyerabend's theories with phenomenological and Gestalt-theoretical modes of procedure ("Wider eine reine Erkenntnis-und Wissenschaftstheorie," in *Phänomenologie und Marxismus,* vol. 4). The decisive question seems to me to be on what level one is operating. That it cannot be a matter of all or nothing, of a simple contrasting of relativity and universality, is shown, for example, by psycho- and socio-linguistic findings, presented in impressive abundance by Hörmann (1970, chap. 15).

Meaning and Validity. The "Janus face" that Habermas ascribes to validity claims (1985, 375) characterizes only the scale between ideal-universal and factual-local validity; thus it actually looks in only one direction. "Meaning must not consume validity" (Habermas 1985, 372). How can one avoid having validity consume meaning, letting it cause the silencing of claims that are neither universal nor merely local or provincial?

On 5: 9

Poetics and Techniques of Cognition and Action. The wide meaning of the word *"poiēsis"* can be found in Plato's *Symposium* (204b–c), where one reads: ". . . whatever the cause is for anything to go from non-being to being is altogether poetry (*poiēsis*)." Characteristically, Aristotle does not classify lawgiving, which in an eminent sense creates, within political activity, but within production; the lawmaker resembles the architect (*Nic. Ethics,* VI, 8, 1141b, 25; on this, H. Arendt, 1981, 187f.; Eng.: 194f.). The establishment of order is, as it were, transposed from the ordering-oriented and law-applying action (and cognition) and entrusted to a political (and cosmic) demiurge. The failure to recognize the ordering achievement is facilitated by the meaning of *heuriskein* in Greek, and *invenire* in Latin, which glimmers between "finding" and "inventing."

Variants of the Art of Landscape Gardening. On the variable formation of nature in the form of the English, French, and Japanese garden, cf. Rudolf Arnheim, "Order and Complexity in Landscape Design," in Kuntz 1968. A significant trait is provided by the varying placement of the human dwellings: in the English garden the house remains hidden; the Japanese garden leads to the house; the French garden is dominated by the house. Landscape style and living style intermesh, and both manifest a particular style of order. For the present, the author predicts that hybrid media such as gardening art, ballet, photography and cinema will have their most felicitous results "when they frankly admit the contribution of the natural raw material by keeping the imposed order loose, open, partial" (Arnheim, in Kuntz 1968, 157).

Tychistic Art. On the paradox of an art that only remains art when it does not itself become chance, but utilizes chance, cf. Monroe C. Beardsley, in Kuntz 1968. The author refers to modern artists such as J. Pollock, G. Matthieu, and J. Cage and to the techniques of Surrealism.

CHAPTER 6: THE ORDINARY AND THE EXTRAORDINARY

On 6: 2

The Third Party. Merleau-Ponty breaks through the fixation on "*the* other" by pointing out that "the relation with someone is always mediated by the relationship with third parties," all the way to the Oedipal situation (*V&I*, 81 n). This must not be understood as a mere multiplication of the relation-structure, but as an alteration of each relation, which leads to none being self-containable.

On 6: 4

Sound Contacts. How very much near and far are interpenetrated is shown by an impressive essay of Sapir's. He had five hundred test-persons assign the syllables "mal" and "mil" selectively to a large and a small table; 80% decided for one of the two possibilities—the reader may guess which (cf. Hörmann 1970, chap. 12: "Lautnachahmung und Lautsymbolik," 235 f.).

On 6: 8

The Exalted and the Sublime. Isn't Kant drawn overhastily into modern art, especially abstract expressionism and minimal art, when he is attested to have an "incommensurability of thought and the real world"? That the idea cannot be made visible does not preclude its being thought, which leads to the conclusion that reason need not fear any deregulation by the sublime (cf., on this topic, Lyotard, "Das Erhabene und die Avantgarde," 1984, 154–58, also *Le différand,* Kant 4). What Lyotard has in mind presupposes that the invisible is present in the visible, the immeasurable in the measurable, as is imagelessness in the image. Would this then still be an "infinitely mere" event, a pure "it happens"?

Simultaneity of the Incompossible. Merleau-Ponty, in his late hyper-ontology, operates with this idea, which shatters the Leibnizan world-system. Cf., on this theme, my essay "Das Zerspringen des Seins," in Métraux/Waldenfels 1986.

Excess. The term "excess," whose economic connotation cannot be ignored (cf. Fr.: *excès, excédent,* but also *surplus*), can be found in various contexts, but with a common feature: what shoots beyond a boundary keeps movement going. A few examples of this. Husserl, in his early theory of meaning, speaks of an "excess in the meaning" of a word compared with what appears to the senses (Husserl, XIX/2, 660), and Jacques Taminiaux draws a line from there to Heidegger's critique of the sovereignty of a look that planes down everything excessive (*Le regard et l'excédent,* x, 166 ff.). Plessner sees the "backbone of reality" in a "surplus factor of substantial being-for-itself," which cannot be exhausted by the course of perceptions (*Gesammelte Schriften,* IX, 36). Merleau-Ponty conceives the dynamics of discourse as a mutual excess of what is to be said and what is said (1984, 28; *Prose,* chap. 2); I myself referred to that in my theory of open structures of behavior (*SV* 69, 90 94, 157f.). In Lévi-Strauss's linguistic approach this becomes a mutual surplus of signifier and signified; it is a part of the human intellectual condition that "the universe is never charged with enough meaning and . . . the mind always has more meanings available than there are objects to which to relate them" (*Strukturale Anthropologie,* I, 202; Eng.: 184). Adorno counters the omnipotence of a thinking of identity with a "surplus of nonidentity" (*Negative Dialektik,* 182; Eng.: 183), which also appears as an "surplus over the subject" (*ibid.,* 366; Eng.: 375). In Levinas, finally, it is the face of the Other who exceeds the range of intentionality, "exceeding the *here* as place and the *now* as time, exceeding contemporaneity and consciousness, who leaves a trace" (*Autrement qu'être* . . . , 115; cf. Eng.: 89ff.).

Excess as Surplus and Extravagance. For Bataille, openly turning against classical economics, the surplus becomes a *surplus of energy* that crosses beyond the realm of production and consumption and thus cannot be used as *surplus value,* but can only be wasted in *superfluity* (Bataille 1975; cf., in the same volume, G. Bergfleth, 323–25). The countermove, still obligated to Hegel and Kojève, to a self-rounding *whole* that by all means counts on a finally rounded action (Bataille 1975, 171), has the consequence that this *surplus* can only be wasted in immoderate *extravagance.* For a self-consciousness that in the end denies itself every something (Bataille 1975, 233), it becomes indifferent where the excess leads to (6:9, below). This is no reason to defame the idea of surplus and extravagance—but instead of abolishing the economy, a perforation is recommendable, in which giving and spending cross the threshold of the *oikos* in many ways and repeatedly without leaving it behind once and for all. What a rich variety of semantic and pragmatic potential is contained to this day in "gift"—incidentally gliding all the way to the German "*Gift*" (poison)—can be read in the basic text of Marcel Mauss himself (cf. Mauss 1978, Vol. II).

On 6: 9

Excessive Mastering of Suffering. Elsewhere I have discussed the effects of an overprotection against everything *pathic,* and the ambivalence of healing as assuagement of suffering and creation of suffering, under the title "Das überwältigte Leiden" (1986).

On 6: 11

Order of All Orders. On this see J. K. Feibleman, "Disorder":

Chaos is the sum of all orders, the *matrix* from which particular orders are derived. That it must remain a chaos and not become itself a kind of superorder is required by Gödel's theorem. Chaos cannot therefore be defined as order in the sense of 'all orders,' for if it contains all orders it cannot itself be an order. But it can be chaos, or disorder in the positive sense defined. (In Kuntz 1968, 10.)

Similarly, P Weiss, "Some Paradoxes relating to Order":

Disorder is an excess of order; it occurs when there are too many orders imposed upon a set of entities. Like the contradiction, something is both a cat and not a cat, it faces us not with nothing, but with too much. (In Kuntz 1968, 16 f.).

BIBLIOGRAPHY

Older classics such as Plato, Aristotle, St. Augustine, Hobbes, or Hume are cited according to the customary page or line markings and chapter divisions.

Kant quotations are cited according to the six-volume editon by W. Weischedel (Darmstadt, 1963–64), while the standard Kant page numbers are used: A = the first "Original Edition," B = Kant's own revised "Second Edition." Abbreviations: *GMS = Grundlage der Metaphysik der Sitten; MS = Metaphysik der Sitten; KrV = Kritik der reinen Vernunft; KU = Kritik der Urteilskraft.*

Nietzsche is cited based on the three-volume edition by K. Schlechta (Munich, 1973), Husserl according to the *Husserliana* (The Hague: Martinus Nijhoff/Dordrecht: Kluwer Academic Publishers, 1950–). Occasionally quoted works of older authors are identified in the text as they occur.

The following bibliography is limited to titles expressly cited or referred to in the text. Works of newer writers are identified in the text by date of publication, title, or designated abbreviation. Some available English translations of newer and older authors are also listed.

Adorno, Theodor W. *Negative Dialektik*. Frankfurt am Main: Suhrkamp, 1966. Eng.: *Negative Dialectics*. Trans. E. B. Ashton, New York: Continuum, 1984.

Arendt, Hannah. *Vita activa oder Vom tätigen Leben*. Munich: Piper 1981. Eng.: The Human Condition. Chicago: University of Chicago Press, 1958.

Bakhtin, Michail M. *Rabelais and His World*. Trans. H. Iswolsky. Cambridge, MA, 1968.

————. *Probleme der Poetik Dostoevskijs*. Trans. A. Schramm. Munich, 1971. Eng.: *Problems of Dostoevski's Poetics*. Trans. R. W. Rotsel. Ann Arbor, MI: Ardis, 1973.

————. *Die Aesthetik des Wortes*. Ed. R. Grübel. Trans. R. Grübel and S. Reese. Frankfurt am Main: Suhrkamp, 1979.

Barthes, Roland. *Über mich selbst*. Trans. J. Hoch. Munich: Mathes & Seitz, 1978.

Bataille, Georges. *Das theoretische Werk*. Bd. I, *Die Aufhebung der Oekonomie*, mit einer Studie von G. Bergleth. Trans. T. König and H. Abosch. Munich: Rogner & Bernhard, 1975.

Benjamin, Walter. *Das Passagen-Werk*. 2 vols. Frankfurt am Main: Suhrkamp, 1983.

Berger, Peter L. "Das Problem der mannigfaltigen Wirklichkeiten: Alfred Schütz und Robert Musil." In Grathoff/Waldenfels, 1983, 87–120.

Blankenberg, Wolfgang. "Phänomenologie der Lebenswelt-Bezogenheit des Menschen und Psychopathologie." In Grathoff/Waldenfels, 1983, 182–207.

Blumenberg, Hans. *Säkularisierung und Selbstbehauptung*. Frankfurt am Main: Suhrkamp, 1974.

———. *Wirklichkeiten in denen wir Leben*. Stuttgart: Reclam, 1981.

Böhler, Dieter. *Rekonstruktive Pragmatik*. Frankfurt am Main: Suhrkamp, 1985.

Borges, Jorge Luis. *Sämtliche Erzählungen*. Trans. K. A. Horst. Munich: Hanser, 1970.

Bourdieu, Pierre. *Zur Soziologie der symbolischen Formen*. Trans. K. A. Horst. Frankfurt am Main: Suhrkamp, 1974.

———. *Entwurf einer Theorie der Praxis*. Trans. C. Pialoux and B. Schwibs. Frankfurt am Main: Suhrkamp, 1976. Eng.: *Outline of a Theory of Practice*. Trans. Richard Nice. New York: Cambridge University Press, 1977.

———. "Ökonomisches Kapital, kulturelles Kapital, soziales Kapital." In R. Kreckel (ed.). *Soziale Ungleichheiten, Soziale Welt*. Sonderband 2. Göttingen, 1983.

———. *Sozialer Raum und "Klassen." Leçon sur la leçon*. Trans. B. Schwibs. Frankfurt am Main: Suhrkamp, 1985.

Bremer, D. *Licht und Dunkel in der frühgeschichtlichen Dichtung. Interpretationen zur Vorgeschichte der Lichtmetaphysik*. Bonn: Bouvier, 1976.

Bühler, Karl. *Sprachtheorie*. Stuttgart: Fischer 1965. Eng.: *Theory of Language*. Trans. D. F. Goodwin. Amsterdam and Philadelphia, 1990.

Calvino, Italo. *Die unsichtbaren Städte*. Trans. H. Riedt. Munich, 1977. Eng.: *Invisible Cities*. Trans. W. Weaver. New York: Harcourt Brace Jovanovich, 1972.

Canguilhem, Georges. *Das Normale und das Pathologische*. Trans. M. Noll und R. Schubert. Munich, 1977. Eng.: *On the Normal and the Pathological*. Trans. Carolyn R. Fawcett. Dordrecht: D. Reidel, 1978.

Cassirer, Ernst. *Substanzbegriff und Funktionsbegriff.* Berlin: Cassirer, 1910. Eng.: *Substance and Function and Einstein's Theory of Relativity.* New York, 1953.

Castoriadis, Cornelius. *Durchs Labyrinth. Seele—Vernunft—Gesellschaft.* Trans. H. Brühmann. Frankfurt am Main: Suhrkamp, 1983. Eng.: *Crossroads in the Labyrinth.* Trans. K. Soper and M. H. Ryle. Cambridge, MA: MIT, 1984.

————. *Gesellschaft als imaginäre Institution.* Trans. H. Brühmann. Frankfurt am Main: Suhrkamp, 1984. Eng.: *The Imaginary Institution of Society.* Trans. K. Blamey. Cambridge: Polity, 1987.

Cavaillès, J. *Sur la logique et la théorie de la science.* Paris, 1947.

Coenen, Herman. *Diesseits von subjektivem Sinn und kollektivem Zwang.* Munich: Fink, 1985.

Derrida, Jacques. *Die Schrift und die Differenz.* Trans. R. Gasché and U. Köppen. Frankfurt am Main: Suhrkamp, 1972. Eng.: *Writing and Difference.* Trans. Alan Bass. Chicago: University of Chicago Press, 1978.

————. *Husserls Weg in die Geschichte am Leitfaden der Geometrie.* Trans. R. Hentschel and A. Knop. Munich: Fink, 1987. Eng.: *Edmund Husserl's Origin of Geometry: An Introduction.* Trans. John P. Leavey, Jr. Stony Brook, NY: N. Hays, 1978.

Deutsch, W., and Jarvella, R. J. "Asymmetrien zwischen Sprachproduktion und Sprachverstehen." In C. F. Graumann and T. Hermann (eds.). *Karl Bühler's Axiomatik.* Frankfurt am Main: Aula, 1984.

Ebbinghaus, Julius. *Gesammelte Aufsätze, Vorträge und Reden.* Darmstadt: Olms, 1968.

Ellul, Jacques. *La technique ou l'enjeu du siècle.* Paris, 1954. Eng.: The Technological Society. Trans. R. K. Merton. New York: Knopf, 1964.

Evans-Pritchard, Edward E. *Social Anthropology.* London, 1959.

Feyerabend, Paul. *Wider den Methodenzwang.* Frankfurt am Main: Suhrkamp, 1976. Eng.: *Against Method: Outline of an Anarchistic Theory of Knowledge.* Atlantic Highlands, NJ: Humanities Press, 1975.

Forschner, Maximilian. *Die stoische Ethik.* Stuttgart: Klett-Cotta, 1981.

Foucault, Michel. *Die Ordnung der Dinge.* Trans. U. Köppen. Frankfurt am Main: Suhrkamp, 1971. Eng.: *The Order of Things.* New York: Vintage Books, 1973.

————. *Die Ordnung des Diskurses.* Trans. W. Seitter, Munich: Ullstein, 1974.

————. *Sexualität und Wahrheit.* Vols. 2 and 3. Trans. U. Raulff and W. Seitter. Frankfurt am Main: Suhrkamp, 1986.

Freud, Sigmund. *Traumdeutung,* II/III. Frankfurt am Main: Fischer,

1948. Eng.: *The Interpretation of Dreams,* Vol. II. Trans. J. Strachey, London: Hogarth, 1953.

Fricke, Herald. *Norm und Abweichung. Eine Philosophie der Literatur,* Munich: Beck, 1981.

Goffman, Erving. *Stigma.* Trans. F. Haug. Frankfurt am Main: Suhrkamp, 1967. Eng.: *Stigma: Notes on the Management of Spoiled Identity.* Englewood Cliffs, NJ: Prentice Hall, 1963 (= *Stigma*).

———. *Das Individuum im öffentlichen Austausch.* Trans. R. and R. Wiggershaus. Frankfurt am Main, 1974. Eng.: *Relations in Public.* New York: Basic Books, 1971.

———. *Rahmen-Analyse.* Trans. H. Vetter. Frankfurt am Main, 1977. Eng.: *Frame Analysis: An Essay on the Organization of Experience.* Cambridge: Harvard University Press, 1974.

Goldstein, Kurt. *Der Aufbau des Organismus.* The Hague: Martinus Nijhoff, 1934. Eng.: *The Organism, a Holistic Approach to Biology,* New York and Cincinnati: American Book Company, 1939.

Grathoff, R./Waldenfels, B. (eds.). *Sozialität und Intersubjektivität.* Munich: Fink, 1983.

Gurwitsch, Aron. *Studies in Phenomenology and Psychology.* Evanston, IL: Northwestern University Press, 1966.

———. *Das Bewusstseinsfeld.* Berlin-New York: de Gruyter, 1975. Eng.: *Field of Consciousness.* Pittsburgh: Duquesne University Press, 1964.

Habermas, Jürgen. *Der philosophische Diskurs der Moderne.* Frankfurt am Main: Suhrkamp, 1985. Eng.: *The Philosophical Discourse of Modernity.* Trans. F. T. Laurence. Cambridge, MA: MIT, 1987.

Hansen-Löve, A. A. *Der russische Formalismus.* Vienna: Austrian Academy of Sciences, 1978.

Heidegger, Martin. *Identität und Differenz.* Pfullingen: Neske, 1957. Eng.: *Identity and Difference.* Trans. Joan Stambaugh. New York: Harper & Row, 1969.

———. *Vom Wesen des Grundes. Gesamtausgabe,* Vol. 9: *Wegmarken (1919-1961).* Ed. Friedrich-Wilhelm von Hermann. Frankfurt am Main: Klostermann, 1976. Eng.: *The Essence of Reasons.* Trans. T. Malick. Evanston, II.: Northwestern University Press, 1969.

Heringer, H. J. (ed.), *Der Regelbegriff in der praktischen Semantik.* Frankfurt am Main: Suhrkamp, 1974.

Hörmann, Hans. *Psychologie der Sprache.* Berlin: Springer, 1970. Eng.: *Meaning and Content: An Introduction to the Psychology of Language,* New York: Plenum, 1986.

Hoffmann-Riem, Christa. *Das adoptierte Kind.* Munich: Fink, 1984.

Husserl, Edmund. *The Crisis of European Sciences and Transcendental Phenomenology.* Trans. David Carr. Evanston, IL: Northwestern University Press, 1970 (= *Crisis*).

———. *Ideas for a Pure Phenomenology and Phenomenological Philosophy.* Trans. W. R. Boyce Gibson. New York: Collier, 1962.

Jacques, Francis. *Über den Dialog.* Trans. S. M. Kledzik. Berlin: de Gruyter, 1986. Fr.: *Dialogiques: Recherches Logiques sur le Dialogue.* Paris: Presses Universitaires, 1979.

Jakobson, Roman. *Kindersprache, Aphasie und allgemeine Lautgesètze.* Frankfurt am Main: Suhrkamp, 1972. Eng.: *Child Language: Aphasia and Phonological Universals.* The Hague: Mouton, 1968.

———. *Aufsätze zur Linguistik und Poetik.* Ed. W. Raible, Munich: Nymphenberger, 1974 (= 1974a).

———. *Form und Sinn.* Munich: Fink, 1974 (= 1974b).

James, William. *The Principles of Psychology.* Vols. I and II, New York, 1960.

Kamlah, Wilhelm. *Philosophische Anthropologie.* Mannheim: Bibliogr. Institut, 1972.

Kanitscheider, Bernulf. *Kosmologie.* Stuttgart: Reclam, 1984.

Kant, Immanuel. *Critique of Pure Reason.* Trans. J. M. D. Meiklejohn. Buffalo, NY: Prometheus, 1990 (= *CPR*). *Critique of Pure Reason.* Trans. N. K. Smith, New York: Modern Library, 1958 (= *CPRb*).

Kiwitz, Peter. *Lebenswelt und Lebenskunst.* Munich: Fink, 1986.

Köhler, Wolfgang. *Werte und Tatsachen.* Berlin, 1968. Eng.: *The Place of Value in the World of Facts.* New York: Liveright, 1938.

Krings, H. Ordo. *Philosophisch-historische Grundlegung einer abendländischen Idee.* Hamburg: Meiner, 1982.

Kuhn, Helmut. *Das Sein und das Gute.* Munich: Kosel, 1962.

———, und Wiedmann, F. (eds.). *Das Problem der Ordnung.* Meisenheim/Glan, 1962.

Kuntz, Paul G. (ed.). *The Concept of Order.* Seattle and London: University of Washington, 1968.

Lacan, Jacques. *Écrits.* Paris, 1966. Ger.: *Schriften.* Bd. II. Trans. C. Creusot and W. Fierkau. Olten-Freiburg: Walter, 1978.

———. *Die vier Grundbegriffe der Psychoanalyse.* Das Seminar, Buch XI. Trans. N. Haas. Olten-Freiburg: Walter, 1978.

Landsberg, Paul-Louis. *Die Erfahrung des Todes.* Frankfurt am Main: Suhrkamp, 1973. Eng.: *The Experience of Death.* New York: Arno, 1977.

Langeveld, M. J. *Studien zur Anthropologie des Kindes.* Tübingen: Niemeyer, 1968.

Leroi-Gourhan, André. *Gesture and Speech.* Trans. Anna Bostock Berger. Cambridge, MA: MIT, 1993 (= *G&S*). Fr.: *Le geste et la parole*. Vols. I and II. Paris: Albin Michel, 1964.

Levinas, Emmanuel. *Totalité et Infini*. The Hague: Martinus Niijhof, 1971. Eng.: *Totality and Infinity: An Essay on Exteriority*. Trans. A. Lingis. Pittsburgh: Duquesne University Press, 1969.

_____. *Autrement qu'être ou au-delà de l'essence*. The Hague: Martinus Nijhoff, 1974. Eng.: *Otherwise than Being: or, Beyond Essence*. The Hague: Martinus Nijhoff, 1981.

_____. *Die Zeit und der Andere*. Trans. L. Wenzler. Hamburg: Meiner, 1984. Eng.: *Time and the Other*. Trans. R. A. Cohen. Pittsburgh: Duquesne University Press, 1987.

Lévi-Strauss, Claude. *Strukturale Anthropologie*. Vol. I. Trans. H. Naumann. Frankfurt am Main: Suhrkamp, 1968. Fr.: *Anthropologie structurale*. Paris: Plon, 1958. Eng.: *Structural Anthropology*. Trans. C. Jacobson and B. G. Schoepf. New York: Basic Books, 1953.

_____. *Das wilde Denken*. Trans. H. Naumann. Frankfurt am Main: Suhrkamp, 1968. Eng.: *The Savage Mind*. Chicago: University of Chicago Press, 1966.

Lewin, Kurt. "Untersuchungen zur Handlungs- und Affektpsychologie." In *Psychologische Forschung* 7 (1926), 294–385.

_____. *Feldtheorie in den Sozialwissenschaften*. Bern and Stuttgart, 1963. Eng.: *Field Theory as Human Science*. New York: Gardner, 1976.

Lovejoy, Arthur O. *Die große Kette der Wesen*. Trans. D. Turck, Frankfurt am Main: Suhrkamp, 1985. Eng.: *The Great Chain of Being,* New York: Harper, 1960.

Lyotard, Jean-François. "Das Erhabene und die Avantgarde." *Merkur* 38 (1984), 151–64.

_____. *Der Widerstreit*. Trans. J. Vogl. Munich: Fink, 1987. Eng.: *The Differend. Phrases in Dispute*. Trans. G. Abbeele. Minneapolis: University of Minnesota Press, 1987.

Mauss, Marcel. *Soziologie und Anthropologie*. 2 vols. Trans. H. Ritter, E. Moldenhauer, and A. Schmalfuss. Frankfurt am Main: Hauser, 1978. Eng.: selections in *Sociology and Psychology: Essays*. Trans. Ben Brewster. Boston and London: Routledge, 1979.

Maxwell, James Clerk. *A Treatise on Electricity and Magnetism*. Vols. I and II. New York, 1954.

Mead, George H. *Geist, Identität und Gesellschaft*. Trans. U. Pacher, Frankfurt am Main: Suhrkamp, 1973. Eng.: *Mind, Self and Society*. Chicago: University of Chicago Press, 1934.

Merleau-Ponty, Maurice. *Phänomenologie der Wahrnehmung*. Trans. R. Boehm, Berlin: de Gruyter, 1966. Eng.: *Phenomenology of*

Perception. Trans. Colin Smith. London: Routledge & Kegen Paul, 1962 (= *PhP*).

———. *Die Abenteuer der Dialektik.* Trans. A. Schmidt and H. Schmitt. Frankfurt am Main: Suhrkamp, 1968. Eng.: *Adventures of the Dialectic.* Trans. J. Bien. Evanston, IL: Northwestern University Press, 1973.

———. *Vorlesungen* I. Trans. A. Métraux. Berlin: de Gruyter, 1973.

———. *Die Struktur des Verhaltens.* Trans. B. Waldenfels. Berlin: de Gruyter, 1976. Eng.: *The Structure of Behavior.* Trans. by A. L. Fisher. Boston: Beacon, 1963 (= *SB*).

———. *Die Prosa der Welt.* Trans. R. Giuliani. Munich: Fink, 1984. Eng.: *The Prose of the World.* Trans. John O'Neill, Evanston, IL: Northwestern University Press, 1973 (= *Prose*).

———. *Das Sichtbare und das Unsichtbare.* Trans. R. Giuliani and B. Waldenfels. Munich: Fink, 1968. Eng.: *The Visible and the Invisible.* Trans. A. Lingis. Evanston, IL: Northwestern University Press, 1968 (= *V&I*).

———. "Von Mauss zu Claude Lévi-Strauss." Trans. B. Waldenfels. In Métraux/Waldenfels, 1986, 13–28. Eng.: "From Mauss to Claude Lévi-Strauss." In *Signs.* Trans. Richard C. McCleary. Evanston, IL: Northwestern University Press, 1964, 114–25.

Métraux, A./Waldenfels, B. (eds.). *Leibhaftige Vernunft. Spuren von Merleau-Pontys Denken.* Munich: Fink, 1986.

Meyer-Drawe, Käte. *Leiblichkeit und Sozialität.* Munich: Fink, 1984.

O'Neill, John. *Five Bodies.* Ithaca, NY: Cornell University Press, 1985.

Plessner, Helmut. *Gesammelte Schriften.* Vol. 9: *Schriften zur Philosophie.* Frankfurt am Main: Suhrkamp, 1985.

Politzer, G. *Kritik der Grundlagen der Psychologie. Psychologie und Psychoanalyse.* Trans. H. Füchter, Frankfurt am Main: Suhrkamp, 1978. Eng. *Critique of the Foundations of Psychology. The Psychology of Psychoanalysis.* Trans. M. Apprey, Pittsburgh: Duquesne University Press, 1994.

Proust, Marcel. *À la recherche du temps perdu.* Paris, 1954. Eng.: *Remembrance of Things Past.* Trans. C. K. Scott Moncrieff and Terence Kilmartin. New York: Random House, 1981.

Ricoeur, Paul. *Die Interpretationen.* Trans. E. Moldenhauer. Frankfurt am Main: Suhrkamp, 1969.

———. *Temps et récit.* Vol. I. Paris, 1983. Ger.: *Zeit und Erzählung.* Vol I. Trans. R. Rochlitz. Munich: Fink, 1987. Eng.: *Time and Narrative.* Trans. K. McLaughlin and D. Pellauer. Chicago: University of Chicago Press, 1984.

———. *Die lebendige Metapher.* Trans. R. Rochlitz. Munich: Fink, 1986. Eng.: *The Rule of Metaphor.* Trans. R. Czerny with K. McLaughlin and J. Costello. Toronto: University of Toronto Press, 1977.

Sartre, Jean-Paul. *Das Sein und das Nichts*. Trans. J. Streller, K. A. Ott, and A. Wagner. Hamburg: Rowohlt, 1962. Fr.: *L'être et le néant*, Paris: Gallimard, 1943. Eng.: *Being and Nothingness*. Trans. H. Barnes, New York: Citadel, 1969.

Scheler, Max. *Der Formalismus in der Ethik und die materiale Werte-thik*. Gesammelte Werke, Vol. 2. Bern: Franke, 1966. Eng.: *Formalism in Ethics and Non-Formal Ethics of Values*. Trans. by M. S. Frings. Evanston, IL. Northwestern University Press, 1973.

Schutz, Alfred. *Das Problem der Relevanz*. Frankfurt am Main: Suhrkamp, 1971. Eng.: *Reflections on the Problem of Relevance*. New Haven, CT: Yale University Press, 1970.

―――. *Gesammelte Aufsätze* I-III. The Hague: Martinus Nijhoff, 1971-72. Eng.: *Collected Papers* I-III. The Hague: Martinus Nijhoff, 1962.

Searle, J. R. *Intentionality*. New York: Cambridge University Press, 1983.

Sokolowski, Robert. *Moral Action*. Bloomington, IN: Indiana University Press, 1985.

Taminiaux, Jacques. *Le regard et l'excédent*. The Hague: Martinus Nijhoff, 1977.

Theunissen, Michael. *Der Andere*. Berlin: de Gruyter, 1965.

Tinland, Frank. *La différence anthropologique*. Paris: Aubier Montaigne, 1977.

Tricaud, F. "'Homo homini Deus,' 'Homo homini Lupus': Recherche des Sources des deux Formules de Hobbes." In R. Koselleck and R. Schur (eds.). *Hobbes Forschungen*. Berlin, 1969.

Veyne, Paul. *Comment on écrit l'histoire, augmenté de "Foucault révolutionne l'histoire."* Paris: Editions du Seuil, 1971. Eng: *Writing History: Essay on Epistemology*. Trans. M. Moore-Rinvolucri. Middleton, CT: Wesleyan University Press, 1984.

Voloshinov, V. N. *Marxismus und Sprachphilosophie*. Trans. R. Horlemann. Frankfurt: Ullstein, 1975. Eng.: *Marxism and the Philosophy of Language*. Trans. L. Matejka and I. R. Titunik. New York: Seminar, 1973.

Vuillemin, Jules. *Nécessité ou contingence*. Paris: Minuit, 1984.

Waldenfels, Bernhard. *Das Zwischenreich des Dialogs*. The Hague: Martinus Nijhoff, 1971 (= *ZD*).

―――. "Wider eine reine Erkenntnis- und Wissenschafttheorie." In B. Waldenfels, J. M. Broekman, and A. Pazanin (eds.), *Phänomenologie und Marxismus*. Vol. 4. Frankfurt am Main: Suhrkamp, 1979.

―――. *Der Spielraum des Verhaltens*. Frankfurt am Main: Suhrkamp 1980 (= *SV*). Eng.: Atlantic Highlands, NJ: Humanities Press, forthcoming.

————. "Das umstrittene Ich. Ichloses und ichhaftes Bewuβtsein bei A. Gurwitsch und A. Schutz." In Grathoff/Waldenfels 1983, 15–30.

————. *In den Netzen der Lebenswelt*. Frankfurt am Main: Suhrkamp, 1985 (= *NL*).

————. "Das überwältigte Leiden." In W. Oelmüller (ed.). *Religion und Philosophie*. Vol. 3: *Leiden*. Paderborn: Schöningh, 1986. Reprinted in: *Der Stachel des Fremden*. Frankfurt am Main: Suhrkamp, 1990, 120–34.

————. "Das Zerspringen des Seins." In Métraux/Waldenfels 1986, 144–61, Reprinted in: *Deutsch-Französische Gedangengänge*. Frankfurt am Main: Suhrkamp, 1995.

————. "Dialog und Diskurse." In *Intersoggettività Socialità Religione, Archivio di Filosofia*. LIV (1986), nrs. 1–3. Reprinted in: *Der Stachel des Fremden*. Frankfurt am Main: Suhrkamp, 1990, 43–56. Eng.: "Dialogue and Discourses." In Hugh J. Silverman (ed.). *Writing the Politics of Difference*. Albany, NY: State University of New York Press, 1991, 165–75, 33–32.

————. "Verstreute Vernunft. Zur Philosophie von Michel Foucault." In *Studien zur neueren französischen Philosophie. Phänomenologische Forschungen 18,* Freiburg and Munich, 1986. Reprinted in: *Deutsch-Französische Gedankengänge*. Frankfurt am Main: Suhrkamp, 1995.

Weber, Max. *Wirtschaft und Gesellschaft*. 2 vols. Tübingen: Siebeck, 1976. Eng.: *Economy and Society*. Trans. E. Fischoff et al. New York: Bedminster, 1968 (= 1968a)

————. *Gesammelte Aufsätze zur Wissenschaftslehre*. Tübingen: Mohr, 1968 (= 1968b).

Wimmer, R. *Universalisierung in der Ethik*. Frankfurt am Main: Suhrkamp, 1980.

Wittgenstein, L. *Philosophische Untersuchungen*. In *Schriften*. Vol. 1. Frankfurt am Main: Suhrkamp, 1960. Eng.: *Philosophical Investigations,* Trans. G. E. M. Anscombe. Oxford: Blackwell, 1968.

————, *Bemerkungen über die Philosophie der Psychologie. Schriften*. Vol. 8. Frankfurt am Main: Suhrkamp, 1982.

Wolf, Christa. *Kein Ort. Nirgends*. Darmstadt and Neuwied: Luchterhand, 1985.

Wright, G. H. von. *Norm and Action*. London: Routledge & Kegan Paul, 1963.

————, "Handlungslogik." In H. Lenk (ed). *Normenlogik*. Pullach: Suhrkamp, 1974.

Yamaguchi, I. *Passive Synthesis und Intersubjektivität bei Edmund Husserl*. The Hague: Martinus Nijhoff 1982.

ARTICLES BY BERNHARD WALDENFELS
IN ENGLISH

"Perception and Structure in Merleau-Ponty." Trans. J. Claude Evans. *Research in Phenomenology* 10 (1980), 21-38. Reprinted in: John Sallis (ed.). *Merleau-Ponty: Perception, Structure, Language.* Atlantic Highlands, NJ: Humanities Press, 1981, 21-38.

"The Despised Doxa: Husserl and the Continuing Crisis of Western Reason." Trans. J. Claude Evans. *Research in Phenomenology* 12 (1982), 21-38. Reprinted in: John Sallis (ed.). *Husserl and Contemporary Thought.* Atlantic Highlands, NJ: Humanities Press, 1983, 21-38.

"The Ruled and the Unruly: Functions and Limits of Institutional Regulations." *Graduate Faculty Philosophy Journal* (New School for Social Research, New York) 9 (1982), 125-34. Reprinted in: Reiner Schürmann (ed.). *The Public Realm: Essays on Discursive Types in Political Philosophy.* Albany, NY: State University of New York Press, 1989, 183-92.

"Towards an open dialectic." In Bernhard Waldenfels, Jan M. Broekman and Ante Pažanin (eds.). *Phenomenology of Marxism.* Trans. J. Claude Evans, Jr. London: Routledge & Kegan Paul, 1984, 102-16.

"Behavioural norm and behavioural context." In Bernhard Waldenfels, Jan M. Broekman, and Ante Pažanin (eds.). *Phenomenology of Marxism.* Trans. J. Claude Evans, Jr. London: Routledge & Kegan Paul, 1984, 237-57.

"Rethinking Technology." Trans. Evaline Lang. *Quarterly Journal of Ideology* 12 (1988), 47-59.

"Experience of the Other: Between Appropriation and Disappropriation." Trans. Bernahrd Waldenfels with Fred Dallmayr and Stephen White. In Stephen K. White (ed.). *Life-World and Politics: Between Modernity and Postmodernity. Essays in Honor of Fred R. Dallmayr.* Notre Dame, IN: University of Notre Dame Press, 1989, 66-77.

"Experience of the Alien in Husserl's Phenomenology." Trans. Anthony J. Steinbock. *Research in Phenomenology* 20 (1990), 19–33.

"Between Necessity and Superabundance: Meta-economic Reflections on Marxism." *Graduate Faculty Philosophy Journal* (New School of Social Research, New York) 14 (1991), 23–33.

"Dialogue and Discourses." In Hugh J. Silverman (ed.). *Writing the Politics of Difference.* Albany, NY: State University of New York Press, 1991, 165–75, 330–32.

"Limits of Legitimation and the Question of Violence." In James B. Brady and Newton Garver (eds.). *Justice, Law, and Violence.* Philadelphia: Temple University Press, 1991, 99–111.

"Vérité à Faire: Merleau-Ponty's Question Concerning Truth." Trans. Mark Basil Tanzer. *Philosophy Today* 35 (1991), 185–94.

"Meaning without Ground: A Critique of Husserl's Idea of Foundation." Trans. Katharina Mai and Thomas R. Thorp. *Encyclopaedia Moderna* (Zagreb) 13 (1932), 375–83.

"Interrogative Thinking: Reflections on Merleau-Ponty's Later Philosophy." In Patrick Burke and Jan van der Veken (eds.). *Merleau-Ponty in Contemporary Perspectives.* Dordrecht: Kluwer Academic Publishers, 1993, 3–12.

"Hearing Oneself Speak: Derrida's Recording of the Phenomenological Voice." *Southern Journal of Philosophy* 32, Supplement (1993), 65–77.

"The other and the foreign." Trans. James Swindal. *Philosophy and Social Criticism* 21 (1995), 111–24.

"Response to the Other." In Gisela Brinker-Gabler (ed.). *Encountering the Other(s): Studies in Literature, History, and Culture.* Albany, N.Y: State University of New York Press, 1995, 35–44.

"Response and Responsibility in Lebinas." In Adriaan T. Peperzak (ed.). *Ethics as First Philosophy.* New York: Routledge 1995, 39–52.

INDEX OF PERSONS

INDEX OF TOPICS

A NOTE ABOUT THE AUTHOR

Bernhard Waldenfels is Professor of Philosophy at the Ruhr University, in Bochum, Germany. He has written books about phenomenology, dialogue theory, the "life world," structures of behavior, and order and normativity.

A NOTE ABOUT THE TRANSLATOR

David J. Parent, Professor of German at Illinois State University, has translated books on philosophical anthropology, phenomenology, and Friedrich Nietzsche.

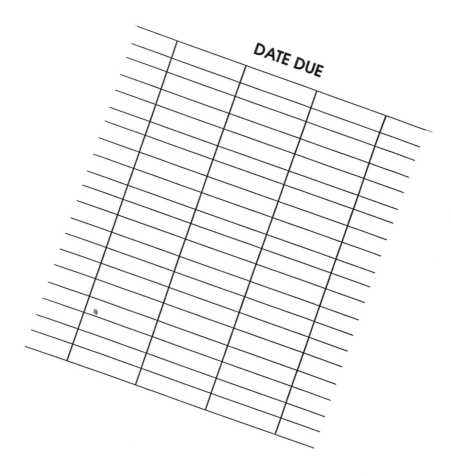